THE SCOTTISH JACOBITES
OF 1715
AND THE JACOBITE DIASPORA

I0042267

By David Dobson

CLEARFIELD

Copyright © 2017
by David Dobson
All Rights Reserved

Printed for Clearfield Company by
Genealogical Publishing Company
Baltimore, Maryland
2017

ISBN 978-0-8063-5856-7

INTRODUCTION

In 1689, James Stuart, King of Scotland, England, and Ireland, abandoned his thrones, went into exile in France, to be replaced by William and Mary as sovereigns. Thereafter, there were several attempts by supporters of the House of Stuart to replace the new House of Hanover and restore the former royal family. One of these was the Great Rising, alias "the '15".

The Jacobites were the supporters of the House of Stuart between 1688 and 1746. On several occasions, during the period, followers of the Stuarts, with continental support, rose unsuccessfully in armed rebellion to overthrow the House of Hanover and restore the Stuart monarchy. Support for the Stuarts existed throughout Great Britain and Ireland but was particularly strong in Scotland where it identified with nationalism and especially with Episcopalianism and Roman Catholicism. It is true to say that as a rough rule of thumb Scotland north of Stirling was pro-Jacobite while south of Stirling it was pro-Hanoverian. Practical military support for the Stuarts came mainly from the conservative north-east of Scotland, the Grampian Highlands, and Inverness-shire. There were also pockets of Jacobitism in the Scottish Lowlands, Northumberland, Lancashire and south-western England. Campaigns were mounted in Scotland and in northern England in 1715. The Scottish campaign culminated in the indecisive Battle of Sheriffmuir on 13 November 1715, which coincided with the Jacobite surrender after the Siege of Preston in Lancashire which marked the end of the English campaign. The Jacobite army which fought at Preston had a substantial Scottish element as well as men from northern England. This Scottish element was largely formed by the McIntosh Regiment which had been raised in Inverness-shire, as well as Catholic gentry from the Borders with their followers. It should be noted that in the aftermath of the Rebellion or Rising many prisoners were marched south to England where more severe punishments were being meted out, including execution and transportation. Most of the nobility who supported the Jacobites had their lands forfeited to the Crown, some were executed, while others fled to continental Europe, especially to France, Italy, and Spain.

While the leaders of the '15 – Mar, Derwentwater, Forster, and McIntosh of Borlum – are well known, little survives to identify the rank and file who supported the Stuart Cause. This contrasts with the subsequent uprising, the '45, for which there are a number of books listing or identifying the Jacobite participants. Who were the people who provided the military and civilian support which was so essential and who, in many cases, suffered transportation, exile, banishment, or a loss of social or economic position within their community? It is difficult, in many instances, to positively identify certain individuals or families as sympathetic to the House of Stuar,t as many landed families, as ever, hedged their bets, by providing one son for one side and another for the rival side. Such a policy, generally, enabled families to retain their land and property in the aftermath of hostilities. However, most participants did not have such a problem and either fought voluntarily for the Old Pretender, the exiled King James VIII, or were pressurised by their feudal superiors.

Information on the ordinary Jacobites is generally difficult to find, apart from those who fell into the hands of the government. This volume, therefore, provides a partial list of Jacobites of 1715 and is based on manuscript or printed primary sources. This compilation has been accumulated over several years and some of the data has been used in previous books, such as 'Dictionary of Scots Banished to the American Plantations, 1650-1175'. However, there is significant new material in the book resulting from more intensive research, for example by Richard MacGregor, who provided information on those Jacobites held in Lancaster Jail. One of the best sources that I have used lay in the records of the Sheriff Court of Argyll where all adult men living in Mull, Iona, Tiree, and other islands, as well on Morvern, were identified as to name, residence, weapons held, and whether they had fought for the Jacobite Cause in 1715. Burgh records have been scrutinised with some success, as have estate papers of major landowners, such as the Earl of Dalhousie. For those wishing to read a reliable study of the subject probably the best single book on the subject is Daniel Szechi's '1715, the Great Jacobite Rebellion' [Yale, 2006]

David Dobson

Dundee, Scotland, 2017.

THE SCOTTISH JACOBITES OF 1715
AND THE JACOBITE DIASPORA

APB = Aberdeen Proprinquity Books

BL = British Library, London

CAT = Chronicles of Atholl and Tullibardine, [Edinburgh, 1988]

CC = The Caledonian Connection, [Aberdeen, 1996]

CRA = Jacobite Cess Roll for Aberdeen, 1715, [Aberdeen,1932]

CS = Chetham Society

CTB = Calendar of Treasury Books

CTP = Calendar of Treasury Papers

DCA = Dundee City Archives

EF = Episcopacy in Forfar, 1560-1910, [Forfar]

F   = Fasti Ecclesiae Scoticanae, [Edinburgh 1915]

HHA = Hay's History of Arbroath, [Arbroath, 1876]

HM = History of Maryland, [Hatboro, 1879]

HMC = Historical Manuscript Commission, [London]

HS = History Scotland, series

JAB = Jacobites of Aberdeen and Banff, [Aberdeen, 1934]

JCR = Jacobite Court In Rome, 1719, [Edinburgh, 1938]

JP = The Jacobite Peerage, [London, 1904]

JRA = Justiciary Records of Argyll, [Edinburgh, 1969]

JRC = Jacobite Risings, 1715-1745, [Cumberland, 1954]

JU = The Jacobites at Urbino, [Basingstoke, 2009]

LBR = Lancaster Burial Register, ms

LC = Calendar of the Laing Charters, [Edinburgh, 1899]

THE SCOTTISH JACOBITES OF 1715
AND THE JACOBITE DIASPORA

MdArch = Maryland Archives, series

MHP = Military History of Perthshire, [Perth, 1908]

MSA = Maryland State Archives, Annapolis

NLS = National Library of Scotland, Edinburgh

NRAS= National Register of Archives, Edinburgh

NRS = National Records of Scotland, Edinburgh

OG = Oliphants of Gask, [London, 1910]

OR = The Forfarshire Regiment, [Inverness, 194]

OT = Ormistons of Teviotdale, [Exeter, 1951]

SG = Scottish Genealogist, series

SI = The Stuarts in Italy, 1719-1766, [Cambridge, 2011]

SM = Scots Magazine, series

SP = Scots Peerage, [Edinburgh, 1904]

SPC = Calendar of State Papers, America & West Indies

SUL = St Andrews University Library

TBD = The Three Bishops of Dunkeld, [Perth, 1925]

TNA = The National Archives, Kew

UAL = University of Aberdeen Library

VMBH = Virginia Magazine of History & Biography

VSP = Calendar of Virginia State Papers

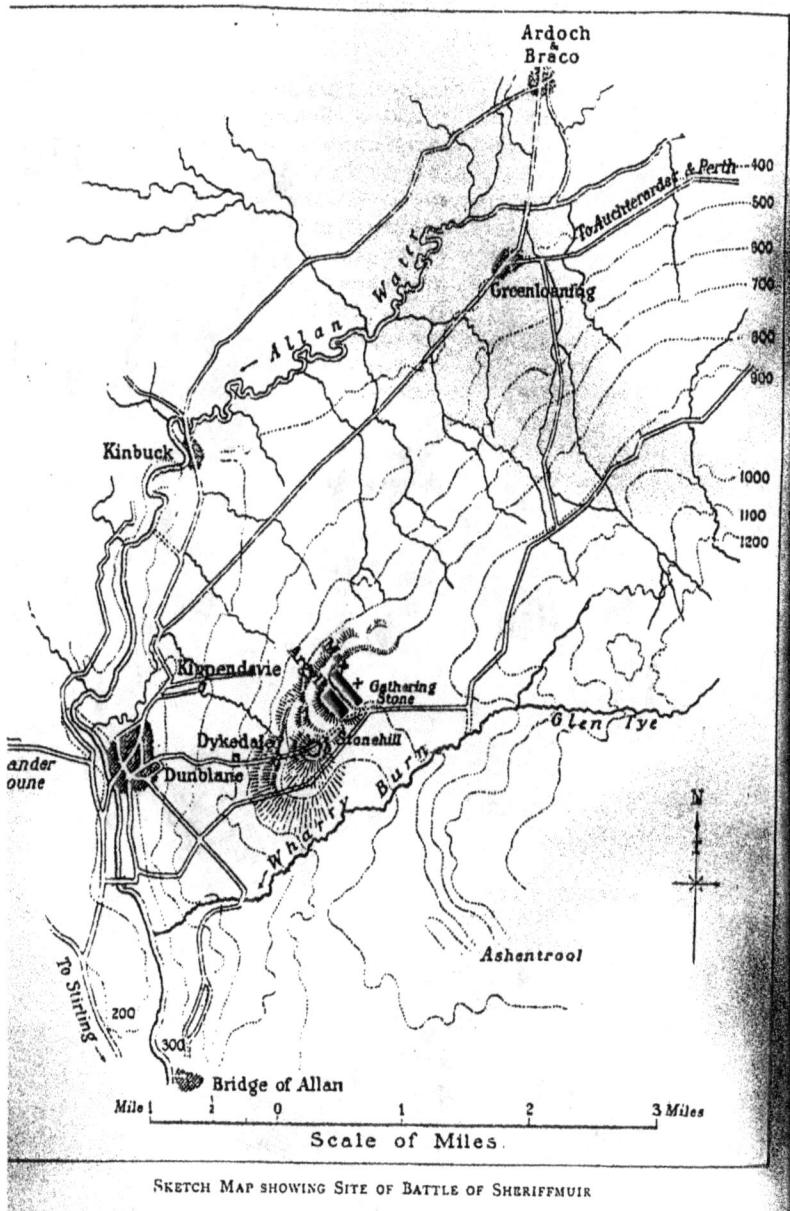

Ardoch
&
Braco

To Auchterarder & Perth ---400

---500

---600

---700

Greenloaning

---800

---900

Kinbuck

---1000

---1100

---1200

Kippendavie

+ Gathering Stone

Dykedale

Stonehill

Glen Tye

ander oune

Dunblane

Whaury Burn

N

Ashentrool

To Stirling

200

300

Bridge of Allan

| Mile 1 | | 0 | 1 | 2 | 3 Miles |

Scale of Miles.

Sketch Map showing Site of Battle of Sheriffmuir

vii

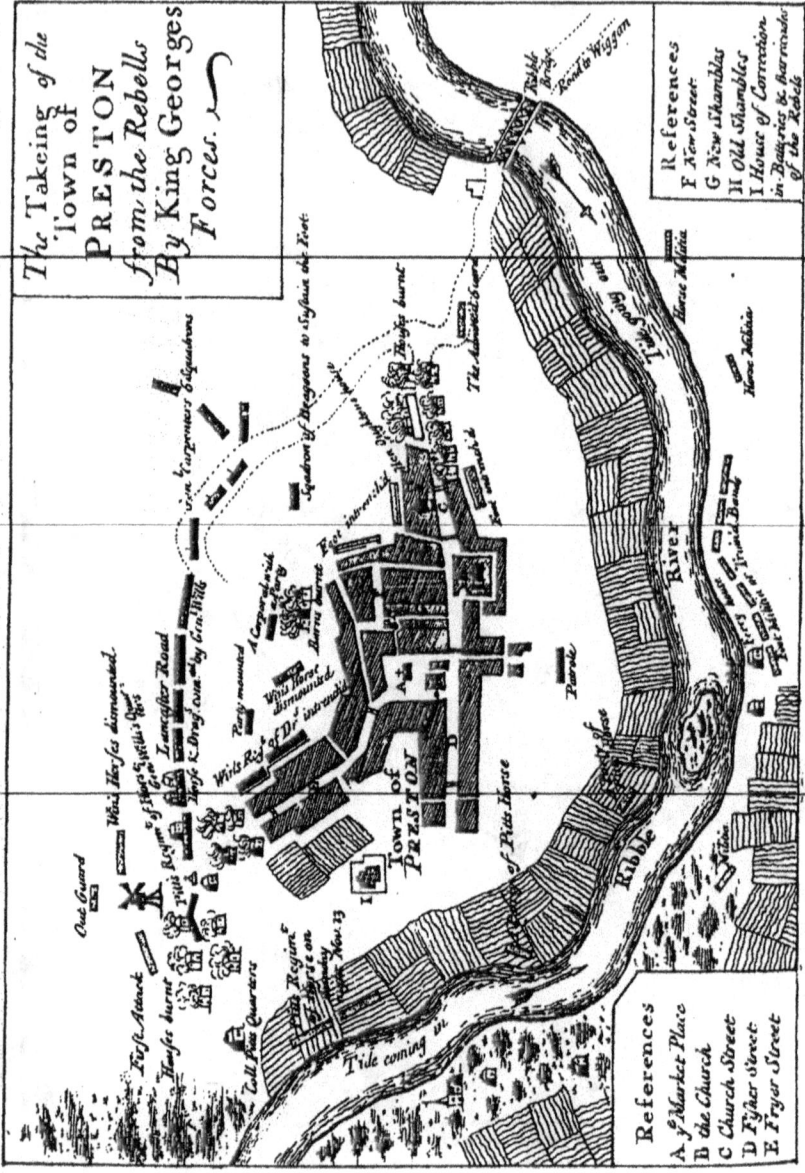

THE SCOTTISH JACOBITES OF 1715 AND THE JACOBITE DIASPORA

ABBOTT, FREDERICK, was captured at Preston, transported from Liverpool to Jamaica or Virginia aboard the Elizabeth and Anne on 29 June 1716. [SPC.1716.310]

ABERCROMBY, ALEXANDER, of Brunstane, a Jacobite in 1715. [JAB.1]

ABERCROMBY, ALEXANDER, of Clothal, the younger, born 1662, son of Thomas Abercromby of Clothal and his wife Isobel Bisset of Lessendrum, Aberdeenshire, educated at Douai, a Jacobite in 1715. [JAB.2]

ABERCROMBY, GEORGE, son of Alexander Abercromby of Nether Skeith, Banffshire, surrendered at Banff in March 1716. [JAB.3]

ABERCROMBY, Sir JAMES, of Birkenbog, born 1669, son of Sir Alexander Abercromby and his wife Elizabeth Baird, surrendered at Banff in March 1716. [JAB.2]

ABERCROMBY, JOHN, of the family of Skeith, Banffshire, was captured at the Siege of Preston, Lancashire, and transported via Liverpool aboard the Elizabeth and Anne bound for Jamaica or Virginia on 29 June 1716. [JAB.3][SPC.1716.310]

ABERCROMBY, JOHN, of Authorsk, born 1655, second son of Alexander Abercromby of Fetternear and his wife Jean Seton, a Lieutenant of Mackintosh of Borlum's Battalion, captured at the Siege of Preston in 1715. [JAB.5][CS.V.162] [NRS.GD1.53.72]

ABERCROMBY, Dr PATRICK, born 1656, son of Alexander Abercromby of Fetternear and his spouse Jean Seton, educated at the universities of Doui and St Andrews, fled to St Germain, France ,in 1716, dead by 18 May 1718. [JAB.6][CRA.92][HMC.Stuart.ii.71]

ABERCROMBY, STEWART, son of an Episcopal clergyman, hanged in Edinburgh in 1718. [JAB.8]

ABERDEEN, ALEXANDER, of Cairnbulg, a merchant in Aberdeen, son of Andrew Aberdeen, a Jacobite in 1715. [JAB.9]

ABERNETHY, JOHN, of Mayen, eldest son of Alexander Abernethy of Mayen and his wife Isobel Hacket, a Jacobite, surrendered in Banff in March 1716, died 2 May 1779. [JAB.10]

ADAMSON, WILLIAM, a Lieutenant in Tullibardine's Regiment at the Battle of Sheriffmuir, 1715, captured, possibly imprisoned at Carlisle in December 1716. [CAT.II.206][SUL.Cheap ms5.537]

ADE, DAVID, son of David Ade of Easter Echt, a merchant in Aberdeen, a Lieutenant of Bannerman's Horse in 1716. [CRA.68][JAB.13]

AINSLIE, WILLIAM, of Blackhill, a prisoner in Carlisle in December 1716. [CS.V.57][SUL.Cheap ms5.537]

AINSLIE, PATRICK, servant to Mary Duncan in the Mains of Kildrummy, Aberdeenshire, was captured at Burntisland, Fife, on 11 January 1716. [JAB.13]

AIR, WILLIAM, transported from Liverpool aboard the Friendship bound for the Chesapeake on 24 May 1716, landed in Maryland in August 1716, sold as an indentured servant to Aaron Rawlings in Maryland on 20 August 1716. [HM.387][SPC.1716.311]

ALEXANDER, ALEXANDER, a writer in Edinburgh, a Jacobite imprisoned in Preston, Lancashire, in 1715. [CS.V.161] [NRS.GD1.53.72]

ALEXANDER, JOHN, born around 1690, son of John Alexander and is wife Marjorie Jamesone, a painter, a Jacobite in 1715. [JAB.14]

ALEXANDER, JOHN, minister of Kildrummy, Aberdeenshire, a Jacobite in 1715, deposed 1716, died in August 1717, testament, 24 July 1738, Comm. Aberdeen, [NRS] [F.6.133][JAB14]

ALISON, CHARLES, a town councillor and Deacon of the Fleshers in Perth, a Jacobite in 1715, carried arms, surrendered. [NRS.B59.30.37/40]

ALISON, DAVID, a flesher and burgess of Perth, a Jacobite in 1715. [NRS.B59.30.37/40]

ALLAN, JAMES, beadle of Arbroath parish, Angus, a Jacobite in 1715, was suspended from duty in 1716. [HHA.170]

ALLARDYCE, JOHN, born 1657, son of John Allardyce and his wife Isobel Walker, a merchant and Provost of Aberdeen, a Jacobite, imprisoned in Edinburgh, died 25 May 1716. [JAB.16]

ALLEN, JAMES, was captured at the Siege of Preston, transported from Liverpool aboard the Friendship bound for the Chesapeake on 24 May 1716, landed in Maryland in August 1716. [SPC.1716.311][HM.387]

ANDERSON, ALEXANDER, son of Captain John Anderson of Bourtree, a Jacobite in 1715, died 1728, testament, 18 May 1728, Comm. Aberdeen. [NRS]

ANDERSON, ALEXANDER, of Arradoull, son of James Anderson of Auchinreath, a Jacobite in 1715, died 1727. [JAB.17]

ANDERSON, THOMAS, of Whitburgh, a Jacobite in 1715, imprisoned in Preston and in London. [CS.V.186]

ANDERSON, WILLIAM, a Jacobite in 1715, imprisoned in Preston and in London. [CS.V.160/186][NRS.GD1.53.72.1]

ARBUTHNOTT, ALEXANDER, of Findowrie, Angus, Captain of the Earl of Panmure's Regiment of Foot in 1715. [NRS.GD45.1.201]

ARBUTHNOTT, ALEXANDER, son of Nathaniel Arbuthnott and his wife Elspet Duncan, a litster in Peterhead, Aberdeenshire, a Jacobite, fled to France in 1716. [JAB.18]

ARBUTHNOTT, THOMAS, of Peterhead and of Rora, born 1681, eldest son of Nathaniel Arbuthnott and his wife Elspet Duncan, a Jacobite in 1715, died 24 March 1762. [JAB.17/217][CRA.149]

ARCHIBALD, ALEXANDER, minister at Barry, Angus, a Jacobite in 1715. [HHA.171]

ARNOTT, DAVID, was captured at the Siege of Preston, transported from Liverpool aboard the Elizabeth and Anne on 29 June 1716, landed in Virginia, 1716. [CTB.31.208][SPC.1716.310] [VSP.1.186]

ARTHUR, THOMAS, a former Ensign of the Scots Guards, plotted to capture Edinburgh Castle in 1715. [TNA.SP54.8.33]

ARTHUR, Dr WILLIAM, plotted to capture Edinburgh Castle in 1715. [TNA.SP54.8.33]

AUCHENLECK, ..., an Episcopal preacher in Arbirlot, Angus, a Jacobite in 1715. [HHA.170]

AUCHINLECK, ANDREW, a Jacobite in 1715, a prisoner in Carlisle in December 1716. [SUL.Cheap ms5.537]

AUCHENLECK, GILBERT, born 1693, son of the laird of Auchenleck, Angus, Ensign of the Earl of Panmure's Regiment of Foot in 1715. [NRS.GD45.1.201]

AUCHINLECK, HARRY, brother to the laird of Auchenleck, Angus, Lieutenant of the Earl of Panmure's Regiment of Foot in 1715. [NRS.GD45.1.201]

AUCHINLECK, HARRY, Quarter-master of the Earl of Panmure's Regiment of Foot in 1715. [NRS.GD45.1.201]

AUCHENLECK, JOSEPH, was transported via Liverpool aboard the Scipio bound for Antigua on 30 March 1716. [SPC.1716.310][CTB.31.204]

AUCHMUTIE, Captain PATRICK, a Jacobite in 1715, imprisoned in Carlisle in December 1716. [SUL.Cheap ms5.537]

BAILLIE, ..., of Dauchfour, the younger, a Jacobite at Sheriffmuir, 1715. [NRS.RH2.4.308/170];

BAINE, JOHN, a Jacobite captured at the Siege of Preston, Lancashire, transported via Liverpool aboard the Wakefield bound for South Carolina on 21 April 1716. [SPC.1716.311]

BAIN, WILLIAM, a Jacobite captured at the Siege of Preston, transported via Liverpool aboard the Friendship bound for the colonies, 24 May 1716. [SPC.1716.311]

BAIRD, WILLIAM, of Auchmeddan, Aberdeenshire, born 16 August 1676, son of James Baird and his wife Lady Katherine Hay, died 22 August 1720 in London. [JAB.18]

BALFOUR, Major HENRY, of Dunbog, Fife, son of John Balfour, Earl of Burleigh, estate forfeited in 1715, imprisoned in Carlisle in December 1716. [SUL.Cheap ms5.537][NRS.E627]

BALFOUR, JAMES, a Captain in Strathmore's Regiment, imprisoned in Preston in 1715. [CS.V.162] [NRS.GD1.53.72]

BALFOUR, Colonel JOHN, of Fernie, Fife, a Jacobite, imprisoned in Carlisle in December 1716; estate forfeited, 1715. [SUL.Cheap ms5.537][NRS.E619]

BALFOUR, MICHAEL, of Forret, parish of Logie, Fife, estate forfeited in 1715. [NRS.E672]

BALFOUR, ROBERT, Lord Balfour of Burleigh, estate forfeited in 1715. [NRS.E619]

BALLINTYNE, WILLIAM, was captured at the Siege of Preston and transported via Liverpool aboard the Scipio bound for Antigua on 30 March 1716. [SPC.1716.310]

BALMAIN, WILLIAM, a meal-man burgess of Perth, carried arms, imprisoned. [NRS.B59.30.36/40]

BANNERMAN, Sir ALEXANDER, of Elsick, eldest son of Sir Alexander Bannerman of Elsick, a merchant in Aberdeen, Quartermaster of Bannerman's Horse in 1716, died 1742. [JAB.19]

BANNERMAN, ALEXANDER, minister at Peterhead, Aberdeenshire, was deposed in 1716. [JAB.222]

BANNERMAN, GEORGE, son of Sir Alexander Bannerman of Elsick and his wife Margaret Scott, surrendered in 1716. [TNA.SP54.11.106][JAB.19]

BANNERMAN, JOHN, son of Alexander Bannerman of Elsick, a Captain of Bannerman's Horse in 1715. [JAB.20]

BANNERMAN, MARK, son of Reverend Robert Bannerman and his wife Margaret Carse, was captured at Preston, and transported v Liverpool aboard the Hockenhill bound for St Kitts, mutinied and took the vessel to Sint Maarten, a Dutch West Indian island in August 1716, from there to Bordeaux, France, in December 1716. [JAB.21][CTB.3][CS.V.160] [NRS.GD1.53.72]

BANNERMAN, Sir PATRICK, son of Sir Alexander Bannerman of Elsick and his wife Margaret Scott, a merchant and Provost of Aberdeen, a Jacobite in 1715, imprisoned in Edinburgh and Carlisle, died 4 June 1733. [JAB.20][SUL.Cheap ms5.537]

BARBOUR, ..., son of ..... Barbour a baillie of Inverness, a Jacobite at Sheriffmuir, 1715. [NRS.RH2.4.308/170];

BARCLAY, Reverend GEORGE, an Episcopalian chaplain at the Jacobite Court in Urbino, Italy, 1717. [JU]; chaplain, 1717-1726. [SI.357]

BARNS, JOHN, a Lieutenant of Strathmore's Regiment, a prisoner at Preston, 1715. [NRS.GD1.53.72]

BARRY, THOMAS, was captured at the Siege of Preston in 1715, was transported via Liverpool aboard the Goodspeed on 21 April 1716, landed in Maryland in October 1716. [HM.389][SPC.1716.310][CTB.31.209]

BAYNE, JOHN, a barber and burgess of Perth, Deacon of the Wrights, carried arms, a Lieutenant of the Perth Company in 1715. [NRS.B59.30.10/17/40]

BEAN, DUNCAN, captured at Preston, transported via Liverpool aboard the Two Brothers bound for Jamaica on 26 April 1716, landed on Montserrat in June 1716. [SPC.1716.33][CTB.31.205][CTP.CC.43]

BEAN, KENNEDY, captured at Preston, transported from Liverpool mutinied and took the vessel to Sint Maarten, Dutch West Indies, in September 1716. [JAB.21][SPC.1716.312][CTB.31.207]

BEATON, ALAN, was captured at the Siege of Preston, transported via Liverpool aboard the Susanna bound for South Carolina on 7 May 1716. [SPC.1716.309][CTB.31.206]

BEATON, JAMES, of Balfour, Fife, a Jacobite in 1715, was imprisoned in Edinburgh and in Carlisle, escaped and fled to France on 31 August 1716. [CRA.226] [TNA.SP54.18.147][JAB.156]

BEATON, JOHN, in Knocknaferaig, Ross of Mull, Argyll, a Jacobite in 1715. [NRS.SC54.22.17.1-2]

BEATON, JOHN, a Jacobite in 1715, in Ardchroisnais, Broloss, son of Ferquhard Beaton, 1716. [NRS.SC54.22.17.2]

BEATON, JOHN, in Beach, Brolas, Mull. Argyll, a Jacobite in 1715. [NRS.SC54.22.17.1-2]

BEATON, MALCOLM, in Pennycross, Brolas, Mull, Argyll, a Jacobite in 1715. [NRS.SC54.22.17.2]

BEATTY, FRANCIS, was captured at the Siege of Preston, transported via Liverpool aboard the Elizabeth and Anne bound for Jamaica or Virginia on 29 June 1716, landed in Virginia. [VSP.1.185][SPC.1716.310][CTB.31.208]

BILL, DAVID, a burgess of Perth, carried arms, imprisoned in 1715. [NRS.B59.30.37/40]

BINNIE, ALEXANDER, a laborer, imprisoned in Preston, condemned to death on 25 January 1716. [CS.V.193]

BIRD, GEORGE, was captured at the Siege of Preston, transported via Liverpool aboard the Scipio bound for Antigua on 30 March 1716. [SPC.1716.310][CTB.31.204]

BISSET, JAMES, of Lessendrum, Aberdeenshire, eldest son of Robert Bisset of Lessendrum and his wife Agnes Abercromby, escaped to Rotterdam in 1716, returned in 1718, died 1747, testament, 18 June 1747, Comm. Aberdeen. [NRS][JAB.22][CRA.196]

BISSETT, ..., of Monbuddo, Kincardineshire, a Jacobite imprisoned in Edinburgh Castle, 1715. [NRS.RH15.123.40]

BLACK, ARCHIBALD, a Jacobite in 1715, on Iona, Argyll, in 1716. [NRS.SC54.22.17.2]

BLACK, GILBERT, son of Gilbert Black, a school-teacher in Aberdeen, a Jacobite in 1715. [JAB.23]

BLACK, MALCOLM, a Jacobite in 1715, on Iona, Argyll, in 1716. [NRS.SC54.22.54]

BLACK, WILLIAM, Regent of King's College, Aberdeen, a Jacobite in 1715. [JAB.23]

BLACK, WILLIAM, a laborer and a Jacobite, was executed at Preston on 9 February 1716. [CS.V.192]

BLAIR, JAMES, a tailor and burgess of Perth, carried arms, imprisoned in 1715. [NRS.B59.36/37/40]

BLAIR, JAMES, was captured at Preston, transported via Liverpool aboard the Scipio bound for Antigua on 30 March 1716. [SPC.1716.310][CTB.31.204]

BLAIR, JOHN, Captain of the Earl of Panmure's Regiment of Foot in 1715. [NRS.GD45.1.201]

BLAIR, JOHN, a malt-man in Perth, carried arms, a Jacobite in 1715, imprisoned. [NRS.B59.30.36]

BLAIR, JOHN, of Glasclune, Kinloch, Perthshire, Major of Nairne's Regiment, imprisoned at Preston in 1715, tried 18 May 1716 – found guilty, estate forfeited in 1716. [NRS.GD1.53.72] [CAT.II.210][CS.V.161][MHP.296/303][NRS.E632]

BLAIR, Dr JOHN, a physician at the Jacobite Court in Urbino, Italy, 1719. [JU][NRS.GD45.26.74]

BLAIR, PATRICK, a surgeon in Nairne's Regiment, imprisoned in Preston in 1715, tried 31 May 1716 – pled guilty. [CAT.II.210][CS.V.161][MHP.303] [NRS.GD1.53.72]

BLAIR, Dr ROBERT, physician to Lord Panmure, fought at the Battle of Sheriffmuir in 1715, escaped via Arbroath to France. [JAB.24]

BLAIR, WILLIAM, a minister in Aberdeen, a Jacobite, died 1716. [JAB.222]

BOW, JAMES, a laborer, a Jacobite in 1715, was captured at Siege of Preston, transported via Liverpool aboard the Godspeed bound [CS.V.194][SPC.1716.310][CTB.31.209][HM.388]

BOWIE, THOMAS, son of Baillie Bowie in Falkirk, Stirlingshire, a Jacobite imprisoned at Preston in 1715. [CS.V.161] [NRS.GD1.53.72]

BOWMAN, JOHN CAMERON, in Polloch, Sunart, Mull, Argyll, a Jacobite in 1715. [NRS.SC54.22.17.1-2]S

BOWMAN, JAMES, a farmer from Aberdeenshire, a Jacobite captured in Burntisland, Fife, on 11 January 1716. [JAB.13]

BREBNER, JAMES, son of John Bremner in Cottown of Overcorskie, Kinerney, a merchant in Aberdeen, a Jacobite in 1715. [JAB.24]

BROCAS, GEORGE, school-master of St Vigeans, Angus, a Jacobite in 1715, was suspended from duty in 1716. [HHA.170]

BROCKIE, JAMES, a shipmaster in Aberdeen, a Jacobite in 1715. [JAB.213]

BRODIE, GEORGE, a servant to Sir James Gordon of Park, a Jacobite in 1715, imprisoned in Stirling. [JAB.110]

BRODY, JOHN, a slater and burgess of Perth, carried arms, fought at Sheriffmuir, imprisoned in 1715, declaration made in Perth on 21 February 1717. [NRS.GD241.380.23; B59.30.10/36/37/40]

BROWN, ANDREW, a merchant in Fraserburgh, Aberdeenshire, a Jacobite in 1715. [JAB.217]

BROWN, JOHN, captured at Preston, transported via Liverpool aboard the Elizabeth and Anne bound for Jamaica or Virginia on 29 June 1716, landed in Virginia. [VSP.1.186][SPC.1716.310][CTB.31.208]

BROWNE, JOHN, was captured at the Siege of Preston, transported via Liverpool aboard the Anne bound for Virginia on 31 July 1716. [SPC.1716.310][CTB.31.209]

BROWNE, MARK, was captured at the Siege of Preston, transported via Liverpool aboard the Anne bound for Virginia on 31 July 1716. [SPC.1716.310][CTB.31.209]

BROWN, NINIAN, from Coldstream, Berwickshire, captured at the Siege of Preston, transported via Liverpool aboard the Godspeed bound for Maryland, on 28 July 1716, landed in Maryland in October 1716. [HM.389][SPC.1716.310][CTB.31.209][CS.V.160] [NRS.GD1.53.72.1]

BRUCE ALEXANDER, was captured at the Siege of Preston, transported via Liverpool aboard the Elizabeth and Anne bound for Jamaica or Virginia on 29 June 1716, landed in Virginia. [VSP.1.185][SPC.1716.310][CTB.31.208]

BRUCE, ALEXANDER, late of Comrie, Perthshire, then in Clackmannanshire, once a Lieutenant in Grant's Regiment, a Jacobite in 1715, Captain of Clova's company in Drummond's Regiment, declaration made in Perth on 21 February 1717. [NRS.GD241.380.23]

BRUCE, DAVID, of Kinnaird, a Jacobite in 1715, a prisoner in Preston and London. [CS.V.160/186] [NRS.GD1.53.72]

BRUCE, JAMES, captured at the Siege of Preston, transported via Liverpool aboard the Susannah bound for South Carolina on 7 May 1716. [SPC.1716.309][CTB.31.206]

BRUCE, Captain JOHN, a Jacobite, was executed in Lancaster on 2 October 1716. [CS.V.241]

BRUCE, ROBERT, from Edinburgh, captured at the Siege of Preston, transported via Liverpool aboard the Elizabeth and Anne bound for Jamaica or Virginia on 29 June 1716, landed in Virginia. [CS.V.161][VSP.1.185][SPC.1716.310][CTB.31.208]

BRUCE, ROBERT, from Edinburgh, was captured at the Siege of Preston, transported via Liverpool aboard the Anne bound for Virginia on 31 July 1716. [SPC.1716.310][CTB.31.209] [NRS.GD1.53.72]

BRUCE, THOMAS, the 7th Earl of Kincardine, in Brussels, a letter, 1715. [NRS.GD160.549]

BRUCE, Sir THOMAS, of Hope, a Jacobite imprisoned in Edinburgh Castle, 1715. [NRS.RH15.123.40; GD220.5.458.43]

BRUCE, WILLIAM, a Jacobite from Perthshire in 1715. [NRS.B59.20.1]

BRYSON, JOHN, a soldier of the Perth company in 1715. [NRS.B59.30.17]

BRYSON, PATRICK, carried arms, surrendered, 1715. [NRS.B59.30.36]

BRYSON, WILLIAM, carried arms, surrendered, 1715. [NRS.B59.30.36]

BUCHAN, THOMAS, born 1641, third son of James Buchan of Auchamoy and his wife Margaret Seton, a professional soldier, a Major-General, died 1721 in Fyvie, Aberdeenshire; testaments, 2 September 1728 and 25 June 1741, Comm. Aberdeen. [NRS]. [JAB.26][NRAS.2232]

BULLOCH, JOHN, a soldier of the Perth company in 1715.
[NRS.B59.30.17]

BURGESS, THOMAS, servant to James Graham of Braco,
Perthshire, a Jacobite in 1715. [NRS.B59.20.1]

BURNES, JOHN, a Lieutenant of Strathmore's Regiment
imprisoned at Preston in 1715. [CS.V.162]

BURNETT, ANDREW, son of Robert Burnett of Elrick and his wife
Bessie Burnett, Newmachar, Aberdeenshire, a Jacobite in 1715,
died in 1720. [JAB.29][CRA.237]

BURNETT, ANDREW, son of James Burnett a burgess of Aberdeen,
minister in Aberdeen, a Jacobite, died 24 October 1716. [JAB.222]

BURNETT, ARCHIBALD, of Carlops, imprisoned at Preston, was
executed in Liverpool on 25 February 1716, his estates in
Midlothian and Tweedale were forfeited in 1715. [CS.V.161/195]
[NRS.E668] [NRS.GD1.53.72]

BURNETT, GEORGE, an apothecary in Aberdeen, a Jacobite in
1715. [JAB.213]

BURNETT, JAMES, of Monbuddo, Kincardineshire, born 1688, son
of Alexander Burnett of Monbuddo and his wife Margaret
Burnett, captured at the Battle of Sheriffmuir, imprisoned in
Stirling and in Carlisle. [JAB.30][SUL.Cheap ms5.537]

BURNETT, JOHN, son of John Burnett of Daladies and his wife
Agnes Turnbull, a merchant in Aberdeen, a Jacobite in 1715.
[JAB.30]

BURNETT, THOMAS, of Kirkhill, son of Alexander Burnett of
Kirkhill, [JAB.31]; probably transported via Liverpool aboard the
Wakefield to South Carolina on 21 April 1716.
[SPC.1716.310][CTB.31.205]

BURNETT, Baillie, a prisoner at Carlisle in December 1716. [SUL.Cheap ms5.537]

BUTLER, ARCHIBALD, Captain of Nairne's Regiment, a prisoner at Preston in 1715, died in prison. [CS.V.161]

BUTTER, ARCHIBALD, of Pitlochry, Perthshire, a Captain of Nairne's Regiment, captured at Preston in 1715, tried 29 June 1716, imprisoned in London, pardoned. [CAT.II.209/210][MHP.296] [NRS.GD1.53.72]

BUTTER, THOMAS, captured at Preston, transported via Liverpool aboard the Friendship bound for Maryland on 24 May 1716, landed in Maryland in August 1716. [HM.387][SPC.1716.311]

CADDELL, PATRICK, a corporal of the Perth company, in 1715. [NRS.B59.30.17]

CALDER, ALEXANDER, the younger of Aswanley, born 1681, son of George Calder, a Jacobite in 1715, a merchant and coppersmith burgess of Aberdeen, died in Old Aberdeen on 6 February 1768. [JAB.31]

CALDER, Sir THOMAS, of Moretoun, a prisoner in Carlisle, in December 1716. [SUL.Cheap ms5.537]

CALDERWOOD, ..., from Dalkeith, Midlothian, a prisoner at Preston, 1715. [CS.V.160] [NRS.GD1.53.72]

CALDERWOOD, WILLIAM, formerly in Dutch service, a quartermaster, a prisoner at Preston in 1715. [CS.V.41/160] [NRS.GD1.53.72]

CAMERON, ALEXANDER, a slater from Perth, carried arms, imprisoned, 1715. [NRS.B59.30.10.36]

CAMERON, ALEXANDER, a Jacobite in 1715, in Ardtorinish, Morvern, 1716. [NRS.SC54.22.17.2]

CAMERON, ALEXANDER, a Jacobite in 1715, in Glenbeg, Ardnamurchan, 1716. [NRS.SC54.22.17.1]

CAMERON, ALEXANDER, a Jacobite in 1715, in Glensanda, Kingerloch, 1716. [NRS.SC54.22.17.2]

CAMERON, ALLAN, a Jacobite in 1715, in Drumnine, Morvern, 1716. [NRS.SC54.22.17.2]

CAMERON, ALLAN, a groom at the Jacobite Court in Urbino, Italy, 1717. [JU]; died in November 1730. [SI.356]

CAMERON, ALLAN, of Lochaber, Inverness-shire, brother of Donald Cameron of Lochaber, landed at Peterhead, with King James VIII, on 22 December 1715, at the Jacobite Court in Urbino, Italy, 1719. [JU][JCR.19][CAT.II.219][NRS.GD27.6.14]

CAMERON, ANGUS, a Jacobite in 1715, in Arle, Aros, Mull, in 1716. [NRS.SC54.22.17.2.]

CAMERON, ARCHIBAL, a Jacobite in 1715, in Drumchragaig and Polcovian, Morvern, 1716. [NRS.SC54.22.17.2]

CAMERON, DONALD, a Jacobite in 1715, in Kinlohteacus, Morvern, 1716. [NRS.SC54.22.17.2]

CAMERON, DONALD, a burgess of Perth, a councillor and Commissary Depute, a Jacobite in 1715. [NRS.B59.30.36/37/40]

CAMERON, DONALD, servant to Alexander Robertson of Struan, Perthshire, a Jacobite in 1715. [NRS.B59.20.1]

CAMERON, DONALD, a Jacobite in 1715, in Sallachan, Morvern, 1716. [NRS.SC54.22.17.2]

CAMERON, DONALD, was transported via Liverpool aboard the Susannah bound for South Carolina on 7 May 1716. [SPC.1716.309][CTB.31.206]

CAMERON, DONALD, in Ardnacross, Mull, Argyll, a Jacobite in 1715. [NRS.SC54.22.17.1-2]

CAMERON, DONALD, in Achatashenaig, Aross, Mull, Argyll, a Jacobite in 1715. [NRS.SC54.22.17.1-2]

CAMERON, DONALD, in Sallachan, Morvern, Inverness-shire, 1716, a Jacobite in 1715. [NRS.SC54.22.17.2]

CAMERON, alias MCALLAN, VCDHOIL, DONALD, a Jacobite in 1715, in Achanalia, Sunart, 1716. [NRS.SC54.22.17.1]

CAMERON, DONALD, a Jacobite in 1715, in Glenbeg, Ardnamurchan, 1716. [NRS.SC54.22.17.1]

CAMERON, DONALD, a Jacobite in 1715, in Achatashenaig, Aros, 1716. [NRS.SC54.22.17.2.]

CAMERON, DONALD, the bard, a Jacobite in 1715, in Strone, Morvern, 1716. [NRS.SC54.22.17.2]

CAMERON, DONALD, a Jacobite in 1715, in Aulastine, Morvern, 1716. [NRS.SC54.22.17.2]

CAMERON, DONALD, a Jacobite in 1715, in Achaforses, Morvern, 1716. [NRS.SC54.22.17.2]

CAMERON, DUGALD, a Jacobite in 1715, in Lettermore, Aros, Mull, 1716. [NRS.SC54.22.17.2.]

CAMERON, DUNCAN, a Jacobite in 1715, in Achalinan, Morvern, 1716. [NRS.SC54.22.17.2]

CAMERON, DUNCAN, was transported via Liverpool aboard the Hockenhill bound for St Kitts, mutinied and landed on Sint Maartens in September 1716. [CTB.31.207][JAB.21]

CAMERON, alias MCEWAN, DUNCAN, a Jacobite in 1715, in Strontian, Sunart, 1716. [NRS.SC54.22.17.1]

CAMERON, DUNCAN DONALD, was transported via Liverpool aboard the Hockenhill bound for St Kitts, mutinied and landed on Sint Marteens in September 1716. [CTB.31.207][JAB.21]

CAMERON, EOWN, in Lochnameall, Aross, Mull, Argyll, a Jacobite in 1715. [NRS.SC54.22.17.1-2]

CAMERON, EWAN, a Jacobite in 1715, in Glenbeg, Ardnamurchan, in 1716. [NRS.SC54.22.17.1]

CAMERON, EWAN, a Jacobite in 1715, in Ardnastaink, Sunart, 1716. [NRS.SC54.22.17.1]

CAMERON, EWAN, a Jacobite in 1715, in Drumnine, Morvern, 1716. [NRS.SC54.22.17.2]

CAMERON, EWAN, a Jacobite in 1715, in Strone, Morvern, 1716. [NRS.SC54.22.17.2]

CAMERON, EWAN, a Jacobite in 1715, in Kinlochteacus, Morvern, 1716. [NRS.SC54.22.17.2]

CAMERON, EWAN, a Jacobite in 1715, in Kinlochaline , Morvern, 1716. [NRS.SC54.22.17.2]

CAMERON, EWAN, a Jacobite in 1715, in Glenleid, Morvern, 1716. [NRS.SC54.22.17.2]

CAMERON, EWAN, a Jacobite in 1715, in Achanaha, Morvern, 1716. [NRS.SC54.22.17.2]

CAMERON, FINLAY, a Jacobite in 1715, in Ternait, Morvern, 1716. [NRS.SC54.22.17.2]

CAMERON, FINLAY, was transported via Liverpool aboard the

Friendship bound for Virginia on 24 May 1716, landed in Maryland in August 1716. [HM.387][SPC.1716.311]

CAMERON, JOHN, in Kilmallie, Inverness-shire, son of Sir Ewen Cameron of Lochiel and his wife Isobel McLean, a Jacobite in 1715, estate forfeited in 1715, escaped to Bordeaux, France, at the Jacobite Court in Urbino, Italy, 1717; participated in the 1719 Rising, died in Flanders in 1748. [JP.77][JU][NRS.E682]

CAMERON JOHN, a slater and burgess of Perth, carried arms, imprisoned in 1715. [NRS.B59.30.10/36/37/40]

CAMERON, JOHN MCDHOIL, a Jacobite in 1715, in Drumnine, Morvern, 1716. [NRS.SC54.22.17.2]

CAMERON, JOHN, a Jacobite in 1715, in Aulasine , Morvern, 1716. [NRS.SC54.22.17.2]

CAMERON, JOHN MCINNISH VCEWAN, a Jacobite in 1715, in Glencremisdale, Morvern, 1716. [NRS.SC54.22.17.2]

CAMERON, JOHN, a Jacobite in 1715, in Acharanich, Morvern, 1716. [NRS.SC54.22.17.2]

CAMERON, JOHN, was transported via Liverpool aboard the Godspeed bound for Virginia on 28 July 1716, landed in Maryland in October 1716. [HM.388][SPC.1716.310]

CAMERON, JOHN, a Jacobite in 1715, a bowman in Polloch, Sunart, 1716. [NRS.SC54.22.17.1]

CAMERON, JOHN, a Jacobite in 1715, in Resopole, Sunart, 1716. [NRS.SC54.22.17.1]

CAMERON, JOHN MCEAN VCDONACHIE, a Jacobite in 1715, in Drumchragaig and Polcovian, Morvern, 1716. [NRS.SC54.22.17.2]

CAMERON, JOHN, was transported via Liverpool aboard the

Susannah bound for South Carolina on 7 May 1716.
[SPC.1716.309][CTB.31.206]

CAMERON, JOHN, of Dunavourd, a Subaltern in Murray's
Regiment, a prisoner at Preston in 1715. [CAT.II.211][CS.V.161]
[NRS.GD1.53.72]

CAMERON, JOHN, a Subaltern in Murray's Regiment, a prisoner at
Preston in 1715. [CAT.II.211][CS.V.161]

CAMERON, JOHN, a Jacobite in 1715, in Tarbert, Ardnamurchan,
1716. [NRS.SC54.22.17.1]

CAMERON, JOHN, a Jacobite in 1715, tenant in Ranochanmore,
Sunart, 1716. [NRS.SC54.22.17.1]

CAMERON, JOHN, a Jacobite in 1715, in Achatasashenaig, Aros,
1716. [NRS.SC54.22.17.2.]

CAMERON, JOHN, a Jacobite in 1715, in Sallachan, Morvern,
1716. [NRS.SC54.22.17.2]

CAMERON, JOHN, a Jacobite in 1715, in Penguila , Morvern, 1716.
[NRS.SC54.22.17.2]

CAMERON, ..., of Lochiel, the younger, a Jacobite at Sheriffmuir,
1715. [NRS.RH2.4.308/170];

CAMPBELL, COLIN, of Ormadale, a Jacobite in Italy, 1717.
[JCR.186]

CAMPBELL, COLIN, of Glendaruel, parish of Kilmodan, Argyll, a
conspirator in 1715, [NRS.GD27.3.17]; estate forfeited in 1715,
[NRS.676]; from Le Havre to participate in the 1719 Rising, a
Jacobite in Rome, 1720. [JCR.192]; a Jacobite at Sheriffmuir,
1715. [NRS.RH2.4.308/170];

CAMPBELL, DUNCAN, a Subaltern of Murray's Regiment, a prisoner at Preston in 1715. [CAT.II.211] [NRS.GD1.53.72]

CAMPBELL, GEORGE, minster at Alvah, Turriff, Aberdeenshire, deposed in 1717. [F.6.247][JAB.223]

CAMPBELL, JAMES, was transported via Liverpool aboard the Scipio bound for Antigua on 30 March 1716. [CTB.31.204]

CAMPBELL, JOHN, Earl of Breadalbane, at the Jacobite Court in Urbino, Italy, 1717. [JU]

CAMPBELL, JOHN, of Glen Lyon in Perthshire, a Jacobite in 1715. [MHP.374]

CAMPBELL, JOHN, was transported via Liverpool aboard the Susannah bound for South Carolina on 7 May 1716. [SPC.1716.309][CTB.31.206]

CAMPBELL, MALCOLM, a Jacobite in 1715, in Brechachie, Coll, Argyll, in 1716. [NRS.SC54.22.54; NRS.SC54.22.17.1]

CAMPBELL, MALCOLM, a Jacobite in 1715, in Cragart, Treshnish, 1716. [NRS.SC54.22.17.2.]

CAMPBELL, PATRICK, in Tullibardine's Regiment at the Battle of Sheriffmuir, taken prisoner in 1715. [CAT.II.206]

CAMPBELL, Brigadier, imprisoned at Carlisle in December 1716. [SUL.Cheap ms5.537]

CAMPBELL, ..., of Keithock, captured at Sheriffmuir, was transported aboard the pink Marlborough of Leith master John Hutton, from Leith to London in December 1715. [NRS.RH2.4.308]

CAMPSIE, GEORGE, a soldier of the Perth company in 1715. [NRS.B59.30.36]

CANE, HUGH, was transported via Liverpool aboard the Elizabeth and Anne bound for Jamaica or Virginia on 29 June 1716, landed in Virginia. [SPC.1716.310][CTB.31.208][VSP.1.186]

CANNON, JOHN, was transported via Liverpool aboard the Two Brothers bound for Jamaica on 26 April 1716, landed on Montserrat in June 1716. [SPC.1716.313][CTP.CC43]

CANT, JOHN, was transported via Liverpool aboard the Scipio bound for Antigua on 30 March 1716. [CTB.31.204]

CANTRIE, ROBERT, a prisoner at Preston in 1715. [CS.V.160] [NRS.GD1.53.72]

CARDEN, ROBERT, a Lieutenant of Mar's Regiment, a prisoner at Preston 1715. [NRS.GD1.53.72]

CARGILL, THOMAS, in Auchtydonald, a Jacobite in 1715. [JAB.32][CRA.149]

CARGILL, WILLIAM, sr., a hammerman burgess and baillie of Perth, carried arms, surrendered in 1715. [NRS.B59.36/37/40]

CARGILL, WILLIAM, jr., carried arms, surrendered in 1715. [NRS.B59.36/37/40]

CARNEGIE, ALEXANDER, of Balnamoon, Menmuir, Angus, a prisoner at Carlisle in December 1716, estate forfeited, 1715. [SUL.Cheap ms5.537][NRS.E615]

CARNEGIE, CHARLES, son of the late Sheriff Depute, a Lieutenant of the Earl of Panmure's Regiment of Foot in 1715, escaped to Lille, France, in 1716. [NRS.GD45.1.201]

CARNEGIE, JAMES, Earl of Southesk, born 4 April 1692, son of Charles Carnegie and his wife Mary Maitland, fought at the Battle of Sheriffmuir, escaped to France in 1716, his estate was forfeited in 1715, at the Jacobite Court in Urbino, Italy, by 1717. [JAB.189][JU][SI.366][NRS.E657]

CARNEGIE, JAMES, a surgeon, at the Battle of Sheriffmuir, a prisoner possibly in Carlisle in December 1716. [CAT.II.205][SUL.Cheap ms5.537]

CARNEGIE, JAMES, of Finavon, Angus, Captain of the Earl of Panmure's Regiment of Foot in 1715. [NRS.GD45.1.201]; was imprisoned at Carlisle in December 1716. [SUL.Cheap ms5.537]; letters from prison in Carlisle. [NRS.GD205.33.3]

CARNEGIE, JAMES, of Boysack, a Jacobite in 1715, was appointed Envoy to the States of Switzerland on 6 November 1716. [JP.232]

CARNEGIE, JOHN, born 1666, son of James Carnegie and his wife Jean Ferguson, a litster in Aberdeen, tax-collector of Aberdeen from 1715 to 1716, died 6 October 1726, testament, 28 August 1735, Comm. Aberdeen. [NRS] [JAB.33]

CARNEGIE, JOHN, a Captain of Logie's Regiment, a prisoner at Preston in 1715. [CS.V.161] [NRS.GD1.53.72]

CARNEGIE, JOHN, a Lieutenant, escaped to Lille, France, by 1716, a letter. [NRS.GD45.14.219.5/1]

CARNEGIE, JOHN, of Boysack, Angus, escaped to Italy in 1716, at the Jacobite Court in Urbino in 1718. [JCR.18]

CARR, ALEXANDER, was transported via Liverpool aboard the Elizabeth and Anne bound for Jamaica or Virginia on 29 June 1716, landed in Virginia, [SPC.1716.310][CTB.31.208][VSP.1.186]

CARRICK, GEORGE, an inn-keeper from Dumfries, a prisoner at Preston in 1715. [CS.V.160] [NRS.GD1.53.72]

CARRUTHERS, ROBERT, of Rammerscales, imprisoned at Preston and in London in 1716. [CS.V.160/186] [NRS.GD1.53.72]

CARSE, MARK, of Cockpen, imprisoned at Preston and in London. [CS.V.160/186] [NRS.GD1.53.72]

CARSTAIRS, JOHN, of Kinneuchar, Fife, imprisoned at Preston, in December 1716; estate forfeited in 1715. [SUL.Cheap.ms5.537] [NRS.E639]

CASSIE, ANDREW, of Kirkhouse, Traquair, Peebles-shire, a prisoner at Preston and in London 1716, estate forfeited in 1715. [CS.V.160/186][NRS.E641] [NRS.GD1.53.72]

CATMOST, JOHN, a Lieutenant in Mar's Regiment, a prisoner at Prston, 1715. [NRS.GD1.53.72]

CATTENACH, GEORGE, from Aberdeen, a Jacobite in 1715. [JAB.213]

CATTENACH, JAMES, a baillie of Aberdeen a Jacobite in 1715. [JAB.33]

CATTENACH, JOHN or GEORGE, of Bellastraid, a Jacobite in 1715. [JAB.33]

CATTENACH, JOHN, a Lieutenant of Mar's Battalion, a prisoner at Preston in 1715. [CS.V.161]

CATTENACH, PATRICK, in Mickle Mill, Ellon, Aberdeenshire, a Jacobite in 1715. [JAB.33]

CATTO, JAMES, a shipmaster in Fraserburgh, Aberdeenshire, a Jacobite in 1715. [JAB.217]

CHALMERS, CHARLES, a writer in Portlethan, Aberdeenshire, son of Professor James Chalmers, was killed at the Battle of Sheriffmuir in 1715. [JAB.34]

CHALMERS, CHARLES, a Major of Mar's Regiment, fought at the Battle of Sheriffmuir in 1715, a prisoner. [CAT.II.205]

CHALMERS, GEORGE, born 1654, minister at Botriphnie, Banffshire, a Jacobite in 1715, died on 24 February 1727. [JAB.224]

CHALMERS, Dr PATRICK, eldest son of Reverend William Chalmers in Skene, Aberdeenshire, Professor of Medicine at Marischal College, Aberdeen, a Jacobite in 1715, died 1727. [JAB.34]

CHALMERS, PATRICK/PETER, a merchant in Edinburgh, a prisoner at Preston, was transported via Liverpool aboard the Anne bound for Virginia on 31 July 1716. [NRS.GD1.53.72] [CS.V.161][SPC.1716.310][CTB.31.209]

CHAMBERS, JOHN, was transported via Liverpool aboard the Goodspeed bound for Virginia on 28 July 1716, landed in Maryland in October 1716. [HM.388][SPC.1716.310][CTB.31.209] [MdArch.25.347]

CHAMBERS, JOSEPH, was transported via Liverpool aboard the Susannah bound for South Carolina on 7 May 1716. [SPC.1716.309][CTB.31.206]

CHAPMAN, LAURENCE, a writer and burgess of Perth, carried arms, a Jacobite in 1715, surrendered. [NRS.B59.30/36/40]

CHARLES, ALEXANDER, born 1672, Advocate and Procurator of Aberdeen, a prisoner in Edinburgh and in Carlisle, a Jacobite in 1715, died 25 March 1754, testament, 20 October 1755, Comm. Aberdeen. [NRS][JAB.35][SUL.Cheap.ms5.537]

CHARTERIS, LAWRENCE, was transported via Liverpool aboard the Hockenhill bound for St Kitts on 25 June 1716, mutinied and landed on Sint Maartens in September 1716; in Rotterdam by 1718. [JAB.21][SPC.1716.312][CTB.31.207][HMC.Stuart.vii.274]

CHEAP, JAMES, a saddler and burgess of Perth, carried arms, a Jacobite in 1715, a prisoner. [NRS.B59.30.36/37/40]

CHISHOLM, ADAM, was transported via Liverpool aboard the Elizabeth and Anne bound for Jamaica or Virginia on 29 June 1716, landed in Virginia. [SPC.1716.310][CTB.31.208][VSP.1.186]

CHISHOLM, RODERICK MACIAIN, of Comar or Strathglass, Inverness-shire, a Jacobite in 1715, fought at Sheriffmuir, estate forfeited in 1715. [NRS.621]; a Jacobite at Sheriffmuir, 1715. [NRS.RH2.4.308/170]

CHISHOLM, ..., of Knockfin, a Jacobite at Sheriffmuir, 1715. [NRS.RH2.4.308/170];

CHRISTIE, ARCHIBALD, was transported via Liverpool aboard the Hockenhill bound for St Kitts on 25 June 1716, mutinied and landed on Sint Maarten in September 1716. [JAB.21][SPC.1716.312][CTB.31.207]

CHRISTIE, WILLIAM, a burgess of Perth, a Jacobite in 1715. [NRS.B59.30.37/40]

CLARK, Captain, a shipmaster in Portsoy, Banffshire, a Jacobite in 1745, testament, 8 April 1742, Comm. Aberdeen. [NRS] [JAB.36]

CLARK, ALEXANDER, a shipmaster in Banff, a Jacobite in 1745, imprisoned in Newgate, died 8 October 1732. [JAB.37]

CLERK, ANDREW, a baker and burgess of Perth, carried arms, a prisoner in 1715. [NRS.B59.30.36/40]

CLARK, DONALD, from Dors, Inverness-shire, died in Lancaster Prison, on 30 May 1716. [LBR]

CLARK, DUNCAN, was transported via Liverpool aboard the Elizabeth and Anne bound for Jamaica or Virginia on 29 June

1716, landed at York, Virginia.
[SPC.1716.310][CTB.31.208][VSP.1.185]

CLARK, HUGH, was transported via Liverpool aboard the
Susannah bound for South Carolina on 7 May 1716.
[SPC.1716.309][CTB.31.206]

CLARK, JAMES, was transported via Liverpool aboard the
Wakefield bound for South Carolina on 21 April 1716.
[SPC.1716.309][CTB.31.205]

CLARK, JOHN, a merchant in Aberdeen, a Jacobite in 1715, dead
by 1736, testament, 12 October 1736, Comm. Aberdeen.
[NRS][JAB.38]

CLARK, THOMAS, was transported via Liverpool aboard the
Wakefield bound for South Carolina on 21 April 1716.
[SPC.1716.309][CTB.31.205]

CLEPHANE, Colonel WILLIAM, formerly an officer of Quuen
Anne's army, a Jacobite in 1715, fought at Sheriffmuir, escaped to
Rome, Adjutant General, in Urbino and in Rome, 1717; a
gentleman at the Jacobite court, 1716-1729.
[JU][JCR.46/51][SI.366][NRS.RH2.4.308/170][TNA.SP54.8.127]
[HMC.Stuart.ii.175]

COCK, PATRICK, a soldier of the Perth company in 1715.
[NRS.B59.30.36]

COCKBURN, Major JOHN, in Urbino, Italy, by 1717; a gentleman
at the Jacobite court, 1716-1726. [JU][SI.366]

COCKBURN, Sir WILLIAM, of Cockburn, Berwickshire, was
imprisoned at Preston and in London in 1716. [CS.V.161/186]
[NRS.GD1.53.72]

COLLIER, Captain, in Urbino, Italy, by 1717; a gentleman at the
Jacobite court 1716-1726. [JU][SI.366]

COLLISON, CHARLES, son of Thomas Collison of Auchlunies and his wife Jean Menzies, a Jacobite in 1715, died 1749. [JAB.38]

COLVILL, WILLIAM, son of the laird of Kincardine, an Ensign of the Earl of Panmure's Regiment of Foot in 1715. [NRS.GD45.1.201]

COMRIE, ALEXANDER, son of Patrick Comrie of Ross and his wife Anna Murray, minister at Kenmore, Perthshire, a Jacobite in 1715, deposed in 1716. [F.4.182]

CONAHER, JOHN, was transported via Liverpool aboard the Friendship bound for Virginia on 24 May 1716, landed in Maryland in August 1716. [HM.387][SPC.1716.311]

CONGLETON, ALEXANDER, a merchant in Edinburgh, imprisoned in Preston and in London in 1716. [CS.V.161/168] [NRS.GD1.53.72]

CONGLETON, FRANCIS, a surgeon in Edinburgh, a prisoner at Preston in 1715. [CS.V.161] [NRS.GD1.53.72]

CONGLETON, JAMES, was transported via Liverpool aboard the Hockenhill on 25 June 1716 bound for St Kitts, mutinied and landed on Sint Maarten in June 1716. [JAB.21][SPC.1716.312][CTB.31.207]

COOK, JAMES, a farmer from Aberdeenshire, a Jacobite in 1715, was captured at Burntisland, Fife, on 11 January 1716, and transported via Liverpool to Virginia in 1716. [JAB.13/150]

COOPER, ALEXANDER, music-master in Aberdeen, a Jacobite in 1715, died 1722. [JAB.39]

COOPER, PATRICK, was transported via Liverpool aboard the Friendship bound for Virginia on 24 May 1716, landed in Maryland in August 1716. [HM.386][SPC.1716.311]

COPLAND, ROBERT, was transported via Liverpool aboard the

Elizabeth and Anne bound for Jamaica or Virginia on 29 June 1716, landed in Virginia. [SPC.1716.310][VSP.1.185]

CORNWALL, JAMES, of Bonhard, a prisoner at Preston and in London in 1716. [CS.V.161/186]

CORNWALL, JAMES, of Banton, Kilsyth, Stirlingshire, estate forfeited, 1715. [NRS.E617] [NRS.GD1.53.72]

COUSINS, JOHN, was transported via Liverpool aboard the Susannah bound for South Carolina on 7 May 1716. [SPC.1716.309][CTB.31.206]

COUTE, JOHN, was transported via Liverpool aboard the Scipio bound for Antigua on 7 May 1716. [SPC.1716.310]

COW, JOHN, in Aberdeenshire or Banffshire, a Jacobite in 1715. [JAB.39]

COWPER, GILBERT, a Lieutenant of the Earl of Panmure's Regiment of Foot in 1715. [NRS.GD45.1.201]

COWTIE, DAVID, was transported via Liverpool aboard the Scipio bound for Antigua 30 March 1716. [SPC.1716.310][CAT.31.204]

CRANSTOUN, THOMAS, clerk of Jedburgh, Roxburghshire, a Jacobite in 1715, a prisoner at Carlisle. [SUL.Cheap.ms5.537]

CRANSTON, ..., a Jacobite, 1716. [NRS.GD1.616.28]

CRAW, ROBERT, of East Renton, Coldingham, Berwickshire, estate forfeited in 1715. [NRS.E628]

CRAWFORD, HARRY, of Crail, Fife, 1716.

CREAGH, MATTHEW, a cook at the Jacobite Court in Urbino, Italy, 1717. [JU]

CREAGH, ROBERT, a secretary at the Jacobite Court in Urbino, Italy, 1717. [JU]

CREIGHTON, JAMES, a maltman and a burgess of Perth, carried arms, a prisoner in 1715. [NRS.B59.30.36/37/40]

CREIGHTON, JAMES, was transported via Liverpool aboard the Susanna bound for South Carolina on 7 May 1716. [SPC.1716.309][CTB.31.207]

CRICHTON, DAVID, in the Mains of Rattray in Perthshire, a Jacobite in 1715. [NRS.B59.20.1]

CRICHTON, JAMES, son of George Crichton of Auchengoul and his wife Jean Irvine, a Jacobite in 1715, possibly fled to Avignon, France, dead by November 1744. [JAB.40]

CRICHTON, WILLIAM, Captain of the Earl of Panmure's Regiment of Foot in 1715, fought at the Battle of Sheriffmuir in 1715, a prisoner, in Brussels in 1718. [CAT.II.205][NRS.GD45.1.201][NRS.GD45.14.219.12]

CROCKAT, JOHN, a maltman and burgess of Perth, a Jacobite in 1715. [NRS.B59.59.30.37]

CROCKETT, JOHN, was transported via Liverpool aboard the Susannah bound for South Carolina on 7 May 1716, Possibly a merchant in Charleston, probate 1759 S.C. [SPC.1716.309] [CTB.31.205]

CROW, ALEXANDER, of Heughhead, a prisoner at Preston and in London in 1716. [CS.V.160/186][NRS.GD1.53.72.1]

CROW, JOHN, a gentleman in Aberdeen, a prisoner in Preston, condemned on 3 February 1716, possibly executed in Lancaster on 18 February 1716. [CS.V.160/194][NRS.GD1.53.72.1]

CROW, ROBERT, a Jacobite, captured at Preston in 1715. [NRS.GD1.53.72.1]

CRUICKSHANK, GEORGE, son of George Cruickshank of Berriehillock, a merchant and baillie of Aberdeen, and his wife Anna Gordon, a tax collector in Aberdeen 1715-1716, died 1737, Testament, 8 April 1737, Comm. Aberdeen. [NRS][JAB.40/217]

CUMINE, GEORGE, of Pitullie, born 1695, son of William Cumine and his wife Christian Gordon, Aide de Camp to Lord Marischal, a Jacobite in 1715, fled to Norway, died in Pittendrum on 12 December 1767. [JAB.41][CRA.168]

CUMMIN, ALEXANDER, was transported via Liverpool aboard the Anne bound for Virginia on 31 July 1716. [JAB.41][CRA.168]

CUMMING, JOHN, a merchant in Aberdeen, a Jacobite tax collector in 1715. [JAB.209]

CUMMIN, PATRICK, was transported via Liverpool aboard the Scipio bound for Antigua on 30 March 1716. [CTB.31.204]

CUMMIN, PETER, was transported via Liverpool aboard the Scipio bound for Antigua on 30 March 1716. [CTB.31.204]

CUMMING, ROBERT, born 1664, minister of Urquhart and Glen Moriston from 1686, a Jacobite and an Episcopalian, dead by 1730. [F.6.482]

CUMMINS, WILLIAM, born 1690, son of David Cummins in Forres, Morayshire, was transported via Liverpool aboard the Friendship bound for Virginia on 24 May 1716, landed in Maryland in August 1716. [HM.386][SPC.1716.311]; [later a Member of the Maryland House of Assembly. [HM.385]

CUNNINGHAM, GEORGE, was transported via Liverpool aboard the Wakefield on 21 April 1716. [SPC.1716.309][CTB.31.205]

CUNNINGHAM, JOHN, of Bogendgreen, a prisoner at Preston and in London in 1716. [CS.V.186]

CUNNINGHAM, JOHN, of Woodhall, a prisoner at Preston in 1715. [CS.V.160][NRS.GD1.53.72.1]

CUNNINGHAM, ..., of Barns, a prisoner at Preston in 1715. [CS.V.160][NRS.GD1.53.72.1]

CUNNISON, JOHN, of Balnacree, a Subaltern in Murray's Regiment, a prisoner at Preston in 1715. [CS.V.161][CAT.II.211] [NRS.GD1.53.72]

CURRIE, JAMES, was transported via Liverpool aboard the Hockenhill bound for St Kitts on 25 June 1716, mutinied and landed on Sint Maarten in September 1716. [JAB.21][SPC.1716.312][CTB.31.207]

CUSSERSON, JOHN, a Captain of Macintosh's Regiment, a prisoner at Preston, 1715. [NRS.GD1.53.72]

CUTHBERT, PATRICK, a barber and burgess of Perth, carried arms, a prisoner in 1715. [NRS.B59.30.10/36/37/40]

CUTHBERT, ..., a Deacon of Perth, carried arms, a prisoner in 1715, [NRS.B59.30.36]

DALGARNO, JAMES, son of Reverend William Dalgarno and his wife Anna Keith, chamberlain to the Earl Marischal, a Jacobite in 1715. [JAB.217]

DALGETTY, ALEXANDER, was transported via Liverpool aboard the Susannah bound for South Carolina on 7 May 1716. [SPC.1716.309][CTB.31.206]

DALGETTY, JOHN, was transported via Liverpool aboard the Friendship bound for Maryland on 24 May 1716. [SPC.1716.311]

DALL, ROBERT, a Lieutenant of the Earl of Panmure's Regiment of Foot in 1715. [NRS.GD45.1.201]

DALMAHOY, ALEXANDER, son of Dalmahoy of that Ilk, a prisoner at Preston and in London in 1715. [CS.V.160] [NRS.GD1.53.72]

DALMAHOY, THOMAS, a gentleman, a prisoner at Preston, was transported via Liverpool aboard the Hockenhill bound for St Kitts on 25 June 1716, mutinied and landed on Sint Maarten in September 1716. [CTB.31.207][CS.V.161] [NRS.GD1.53.72]

DALMAHOY, WILLIAM, son of Dalmahoy of that Ilk, a prisoner at Preston and in London in 1716. [CS.V.186] [NRS.GD1.53.72]

DALZIEL, JAMES, a Captain, uncle of the Earl of Carnwath, a prisoner at Preston and in London in 1716. [CS.V.160/186][NRS.GD1.53.72.1]

DALZIEL, JOHN, a Captain, brother of the Earl of Carnwath, a prisoner at Preston, was transported to Virginia or Carolina. [CS.V.161][SPC.1716.128][CAT.II.217] [NRS.GD1.53.72]

DALZIEL, Sir ROBERT, Earl of Carnwath, Sanquhar, Dumfries-shire, a prisoner at Preston in 1715, estate forfeited in 1715, reprieved, died at Kirkmichael on 9 July 1737. [CS.V.160/212][SP.II.415][NRS.E620][NRS.GD1.53.72

DALZEL, WILLIAM, was transported via Liverpool aboard the Susannah bound for South Carolina on 7 May 1716. [CTB.31.206][SPC.1716.309]

DAVIDSON, ALEXANDER, of Newton, son of Alexander Davidson and his wife Jean Burnett, a Jacobite in 1715, died 1732. [JAB.42]

DAVIDSON, ANDREW, a laborer, a prisoner at Preston, condemned on 25 January 1716. [CS.V.193]

DAVIDSON, ANDREW, was transported via Liverpool aboard the

Friendship bound for Virginia, on 24 May 1716, landed in Maryland in August 1716. [HM.387][SPC.1716.311]

DAVIDSON, DAVID, a soldier of the Perth company in 1715. [NRS.B59.30.17]

DAVIDSON, DONALD, was transported via Liverpool aboard the Susannah bound for South Carolina on 7 May 1716. [SPC.1716.309][CTB.31.206]

DAVIDSON, JAMES, of Tillymorgan, son of James Davidson, a guilds brother and burgess of Aberdeen, a Jacobite in 1715, died 17 September 1720. [JAB.43][CRA.78]

DAVIDSON, PATRICK, a burgess and Provost of Perth, Jacobite Commissioner for Perth in 1715. [NRS.B59.30.36/37/40]

DAVIDSON, PATRICK, in Bordland, a Jacobite in 1715. [JAB.206]

DAVIDSON, WILLIAM, a farmer in Cushnie, Aberdeenshire, was transported via Liverpool aboard the Friendship bound for Virginia on 24 May 1716, landed in Maryland in August 1716. [SPC.1716.311][JAB.151][HM.387]

DAVIE, JOHN, minister at Strathcathro, Angus, 1715, factor for the Earl of Southesk, a Jacobite, deposed 1715. [F.V.418][NRS.CH2.575.1]

DAW, ANDREW, was transported via Liverpool aboard the Friendship bound for Virginia on 24 May 1716, landed in Maryland on 20 August 1716. [HM.387][SPC.1716.311]

DEANS, ALEXANDER, from Edinburgh, a prisoner at Preston and in London in 1716. [CS.V.161/186] [NRS.GD1.53.72]

DENHAM, JAMES, was transported via Liverpool aboard the Friendship bound for Virginia on 24 May 1716, landed in Maryland in August 1716. [HM.387][SPC.1716.311]

DEUCHAR, ALEXANDER, a merchant in Aberdeen, a Jacobite in 1715. [JAB.43]

DHOILE, JOHN, a Jacobite in 1715, a workman in Achinellan, Sunart, 1716. [NRS.SC54.22.17.1]

DICKSON, JAMES, a prisoner at Preston, was transported via Liverpool aboard the Goodspeed, bound for Virginia on 28 July 1716, landed in Maryland in August 1716. [NRS.GD1.53.72.1] [HM.387][CS.V.160][SPC.1716.310][CTB.31.209]

DOCTOR, DAVID, was transported via Liverpool aboard the Susannah on 7 May 1716 bound for South Carolina. [SPC.1716.309][CTB.31.206]

DONALD, JAMES, in Banchory-Ternan, Aberdeenshire, a Jacobite in 1715. [JAB.43]

DONALDSON, CHARLES, was transported via Liverpool aboard the Goodspeed bound for Virginia on 24 May 1716, landed in Maryland in August 1716. [HM.387][SPC.1716.311]

DONALDSON, JOHN, a vintner and a councillor of Perth, a Jacobite in 1715. [NRS.B59.30.36]

DONALDSON, JOHN, a writer in Turriff, Aberdeenshire, and in Banff, a Jacobite in 1715. [JAB.44]

DONALDSON, JOHN, was transported via Liverpool aboard the Elizabeth and Anne bound for Jamaica or Virginia on 29 June 1716, landed in Virginia in August 1716. [SPC.1716.310][CTB.31.208][VSP.I.186]

DONALDSON, NICOL, an Ensign, fought at the Battle of Sheriffmuir, a prisoner in 1715. [CAT.II.205]

DONALDSON, THOMAS, was transported via Liverpool aboard the

Friendship bound for Virginia on 24 May 1716, landed in Maryland in August 1716. [HM.387][SPC.1716.311]

DONALDSON, WILLIAM, a prisoner at Preston, was transported via Liverpool aboard the Elizabeth and Anne bound for Jamaica or Virginia on 29 June 1716, landed in Virginia in August 1716. [SPC.1716.310][CTB.31.208][VSP.I.185][CS.V.160] [NRS.GD1.53.72]

DORIE, DANIEL, was transported via Liverpool aboard the Scipio bound for Antigua on 30 March 1716. [CTB.31.204]

DOUGAL, ANDREW, a labourer, a prisoner at Preston, condemned on 25 January 1716. [CS.V.193]

DOUGLAS, GEORGE, born 1681, a Roman Catholic priest, son of Colin Douglas and his wife Elizabeth Irvine, a Jacobite in 1715, died in Morar, Inverness-shire, on 29 April 1748. [JAB.215]

DOUGLAS, JOHN, son of Sylvester Douglas, a merchant in Aberdeen, a Jacobite in 1715, testament, 5 January 1723, Comm. Aberdeen, [NRS] [JAB.45]

DOUGLAS, PATRICK, Ensign of the Earl of Strathmore's Battalion, a prisoner at Preston in 1715. [CS.V.162] [NRS.GD1.53.72]

DOUGLAS, PATRICK, born 1700, son of John Douglas, a Jacobite in 1715, imprisoned at Marshalsea, London, released. [JAB.46][TNA.SP54.12.61]

DOUGLAS, Reverend ROBERT, minister at Bothwell, Lanarkshire, son of Robert Douglas the Episcopal Bishop of Dunblane, a Jacobite in 1715. [JAB.45][TNA.SP35.6.77]

DOUGLAS, ROBERT, a burgess of Perth, a Jacobite in 1715. [NRS.B59.30.37/40]

DOUGLAS, ROBERT, brother to the laird of Fingland, a Jacobite in 1715. [CS.V.47]

DOUGLAS, ROBERT, brother to .... Douglas of Glenbervie, was captured at Sheriffmuir, was transported aboard the pink Marlborough of Leith master John Hutton, from Leith to London in December 1715. [NRS.RH2.4.308]

DOUGLAS, SYLVESTER, of Whiteriggs, Kincardineshire, eldest son of Robert Douglas the Episcopal Bishop of Dunblane, a prisoner at Carlisle in 1715, estate forfeited in 1716. [JAB.45][TNA.SP35.6.77][SUL.Cheap ms5.537][NRS.E687]

DOUGLAS, WILLIAM, son of John Douglas, a Jacobite in 1715, imprisoned at Marshalsea, London, released. [JAB.46][TNA.SP54.12.61]

DOUGLAS, WILLIAM, of Glenbervie, Kincardineshire, a Captain of Strathmore's Battalion, a prisoner at Preston in 1715, possibly escaped at Liverpool or Chester, his estate in the parish of Leuchars, Fife, was forfeited in 1715. [CS.V.162/166][NRS.674][NRS.GD1.53.72]

DRUMMOND, ALEXANDER, a Captain of Logie's Regiment, a prisoner at Preston in 1715. [CS.V.161][MHP.303]

DRUMMOND, ALEXANDER, a gentleman, a prisoner at Preston, executed at Liverpool on 25 February 1716. [CS.V.194]

DRUMMOND, CHARLES, brother of Strathallan, a prisoner at Carlisle in December 1716. [SUL.Cheap ms5.537]

DRUMMOND, DAVID, a Captain of Logie's Regiment, a prisoner at Preston in 1715. [CS.V.161] [NRS.GD1.53.72]

DRUMMOND, GEORGE, of Callendar, his estates in the parishes of Crieff and Blackford in Perthshire, were forfeited in 1715. [NRS.E667]

DRUMMOND, Lord EDWARD, at the Jacobite Court in Urbino, Italy, 1717. [JU]

DRUMMOND, JAMES, brother of Sir James Drummond of Invermay, was executed in Preston on 9 February 1716. [CS.V.192]

DRUMMOND, JAMES, 2nd Duke of Perth, born 1674, son of James Drummond the 1st Duke of Perth, and his wife Jane Douglas, a Jacobite in 1715, his estate would have been forfeited however he had disposed of it to his son, aged two, on 28 August 1715, he escaped to France in February 1716, at the Jacobite Court in Urbino, Italy, 1717, he died in Paris on 17 April 1720. [JP.146][SP.VII. 54][JU]

DRUMMOND, JAMES, a Captain of Logie's Regiment, a prisoner at Preston in 1715. [CS.V.161] [NRS.GD1.53.72]

DRUMMOND, JOHN, Viscount Forth, born 26 May 1682, son of the Earl of Melfort, a Major General, a Jacobite in 1715, escaped to France, died in Paris on 29 January 1754. [SP.VI.70]

DRUMMOND, THOMAS, of Logie Almond, Perthshire, a Colonel, fought at the Battle of Sheriffmuir, a prisoner in Edinburgh Castle, pardoned on 25 October 1716 and released from prison in Carlisle on 29 October 1716. [CAT.II.205][MHP.298/303][Laing Charters#3080] [MHP.298][NRS.RH15.123.40]

DRUMMOND, WILLIAM, a weaver and a burgess of Perth, a soldier in the Perth company, a prisoner, 1715. [NRS.B59.30.37/40]

DRUMMOND, WILLIAM, of Machan, fought at the Battle of Sheriffmuir in 1715, a prisoner there and in Carlisle, died at Culloden in 1746. [SP.VIII.228]

DRUMMOND, WILLIAM, at the Jacobite Court in Urbino, Italy, 1717. [JU]

DRUMMOND, WILLIAM, Viscount Strathallan, captured at Sheriffmuir, a prisoner in Edinburgh Castle 1715, released in 1717. [MHP.298][CAT.II.205][NRS.RH15.123.40]

DRUMMOND, ..., of Drumquharry, fought at Sheriffmuir in 1715, a prisoner. [CAT.II.205]; was transported aboard the pink Marlborough of Leith master John Hutton, from Leith to London in December 1715. [NRS.RH2.4.308]

DUFF, ALEXANDER, of Drummuir, born 1657, son of Provost William Duff of Inverness and his wife Christina Duff, a Jacobite in 1715, died 1726. [JAB.50]

DUFF, ALEXANDER, was transported via Liverpool aboard the Scipio bound for Antigua on 30 March 1716. [SPC.1716.310] [CTB.31.206]

DUFF, DONALD, was transported via Liverpool aboard the Susannah bound for South Carolina on 7 May 1716. [SPC.1716.309][CTB.31.206]

DUFF, JOHN, son of John Duff and his wife Margaret Johnstone, a messenger and burgess of Aberdeen, a Jacobite in 1715, escaped via Banff to the Netherlands in April 1716, died in Rotterdam in 1718; testament, 30 July 1724, Comm. Aberdeen, NRS. [JAB.48][CRA.28]

DUFF, THOMAS, was transported via Liverpool aboard the Susannah bound for South Carolina on 7 May 1716. [SPC.1716.309][CTB.31.206]

DUFFUS, DANIEL, was transported via Liverpool aboard the Scipio bound for Antigua on 30 March 1716. [SPC.1716.310]

DUFFUS, KENNETH, Lord Duffus, his estate in the parish of Dornoch, Sutherland, was forfeited in 1715. [NRS.E670]

DUGUID, ALEXANDER, in Auchenhove, Aberdeenshire, son of Francis Duguid and his wife Marie Abercromby, a Lieutenant in Glenbucket's Regiment, fought at the Battle of Sheriffmuir in 1715, escaped to France. [JAB.54]

DUGUID, PATRICK ROBERT, born 1700, son of Robert Duguid of Auchinhove, Aberdeenshire, and his wife Teresa Leslie, a Lieutenant of Lord Huntly's Squadron at the Battle of Sheriffmuir in 1715, died 11 April 1777. [JAB.48][CRA.46]

DUGUID, ROBERT, of Auchinhove, Aberdeenshire, son of Francis Duguid and his wife Marie Abercromby, a Jacobite in 1715, died 1731, testament, 13 December 1739, Comm. Aberdeen. [NRS][JAB.53]

DUNBAR, Sir JAMES, of Durn, born 1665, son of Sir William Dunbar and his wife Janet Brodie, surrendered in Banff on 24 November 1715, died in 1737, Testament, 23 December 1737, Comm. Aberdeen, [NRS][JAB.55]

DUNBAR, JEREMY, a farmer in Cushnie, Aberdeenshire, was transported via Liverpool aboard the Friendship bound for Virginia on 24 May 1716, landed in Maryland in August 1716, returned to Scotland in 1722. [HM.386][SPC.1716.311][JAB.151/153]

DUNBAR, JOHN, a merchant, an Ensign in Macintosh's Regiment, a prisoner at Preston, was transported via Liverpool aboard the Elizabeth and Anne bound for Jamaica or Virginia on 29 June 1716, landed at Sandy Point on the James River, Virginia, in

August 1716, moved to Newport, Rhode Island, in 1720.
[CS.V.162][SPC.1716.310][CTB.31.208][VSP.I.185] [NRS.GD.298;
GD.103] [NRS.GD1.53.72]

DUNBAR, WILLIAM, born 1661, minister at Cruden,
Aberdeenshire, a Jacobite in 1715, deposed in 1716, died 1745.
[F.6.188][JAB.225]

DUNBAR, WILLIAM, an Episcopalian preacher in Montrose, Angus,
a Jacobite in 1715, deposed in 1716. [NRS.CH2.575.1]

DUNBRECK, PATRICK, chaplain to the Earl Marischal, a Jacobite in
1715. [JAB.225]

DUNCAN, ALEXANDER, of Ardownie, Captain of the Earl of
Panmure's Regiment of Foot in 1715. [NRS.GD45.1.201]

DUNCAN, ALEXANDER, was transported via Liverpool aboard the
Two Brothers bound for Jamaica on 26 April 1716, landed on
Montserrat in June 1716. [SPC.1716.313][CTB.31.205][CTP.CC.43]

DUNCAN, JAMES, brother to Duncan of Ardownie, Angus, a
Lieutenant of the Earl of Panmure's Regiment of Foot in 1715.
[NRS.GD45.1.201]

DUNCAN, JOHN, was transported via Liverpool aboard the Two
Brothers bound for Jamaica on 26 April 1716, landed on
Montserrat in June 1716. [SPC.1716.313][CTB.31.205][CTP.CC.43]

DUNCAN, JOHN, was transported via Liverpool aboard the Two
Brothers bound for Jamaica on 28 April 1716, landed on
Montserrat in June 1716. [SPC.1716,313][CTB.31.205][CTP.CC.43]

DUNCAN, JOHN, was transported aboard the Scipio bound for St
Kitts on 30 March 1716. [SPC.1716.310][CTB.31.204]

DUNCAN, ROBERT, was transported via Liverpool aboard the
Elizabeth and Anne bound for Jamaica or Virginia on 29 June

1716, landed in Virginia in August 1716.
[SPC.1716.310][CTB.31.208][VSP.I.186]

DUNDAS, WILLIAM, of Airth, Stirlingshire, a merchant in
Edinburgh, a prisoner at Preston and in London in 1716; Jacobite
agent in Rotterdam in 1718. [HMC.Stuart pp.V.425-428]

DUNLOP, JAMES, was transported via Liverpool aboard the
Wakefield bound for South Carolina on 21 April 1716.
[SPC.1716.309][CTB.31.204]

DUNN, JAMES, a merchant in Aberdeen, a Jacobite in 1715.
[JAB.55]

DUNN, WILLIAM, was transported via Liverpool aboard the
Elizabeth and Anne bound for Jamaica or Virginia on 29 May
1716, landed in Virginia. [SPC.1716.310][CTB.31.208][VSP.1.185]

DURHAM, HERCULES, a goldsmith, a prisoner at Preston,
executed in Lancaster on 18 February 1716. [CS.V.194]

DYSART, GEORGE, was transported via Liverpool aboard the
Wakefield bound for South Carolina on 21 April 1716.
[SPC.1716.309][CTB.31.205]

ECHLIN, ROBERT, a former Lieutenant General of the British
Army, 1715. [HMC.I.391]

EDGAR, JAMES, secretary at the Jacobite Court in Urbino, Italy,
1717, a gentleman at the Jacobite court, 1716-1725, died in
Rome on 10 October 1762. [JU][SM.24.568][SI.366]

EDGAR, ROBERT, of Keithock, Angus, a merchant in Montrose, a
Jacobite in 1715. [JP.249]

EDMONSTONE, JAMES, of Newton, the Standard-bearer at the
Battle of Sheriffmuir in 1715. [MHP.287]

EGGOE, WILLIAM, was transported via Liverpool aboard the Wakefield bound for South Carolina on 21 April 1716. [SPC.1716.309][CTB.31.206]

ELDER, CHARLES, the Post-master of Perth, carried arms, surrendered, a Jacobite in 1715. [NRS.B59.30.36]

ELPHINSTONE, ARTHUR, Lord Balmerino, born 1688, a Hanoverian officer at Sheriffmuir, defected to the Jacobites, escaped to the continent, executed in London on 1 August 1746. [SP.I.572]

ELPHINSTON, WILLIAM, Episcopalian preacher in Longforgan, Perthshire, from 1715 to 1716. [F.V.353; F.IV.355]

ERSKINE, ALEXANDER, Earl of Mar, a Jacobite in 1715, died at Aix-la-Chapelle, France, in May 1732. [SP.V.630]

ERSKINE, FRANCIS, son of the laird of Kirkbuddo, Angus, a Lieutenant of the Earl of Panmure's Regiment of Foot in 1715. [NRS.GD45.1.201]; possibly court martialled and shot in 1716. [CS.V.175]

ERSKINE, JAMES, son of Thomas Erskine of Pittodrie, Aberdeenshire, and his wife Helen Auchenleck, a prisoner at Carlisle in 1716. [JAB.61][SUL.Cheap.ms5.537]

ERSKINE, JOHN, 11th Earl of Mar, born February 1675, son of Charles Erskine, Earl of Mar, and his wife Mary Maule, a leading Jacobite in 1715, his estates forfeited in 1715, escaped via Montrose, Angus, on 3 February 1716 to St Malo in France, at the Jacobite Court in Urbino, Italy, 1717, died in Aix-la-Chapelle, France, in March 1732. [JU][JP.114][CRA.135][NRS.E646] [SUL.Cheap.5.537]

ERSKINE, Dr JOHN, a Jacobite agent at the Russian Court, 1716. [HS.9.1.23]

ERSKINE, Sir JOHN, of Alva, in France, 1716. [HMC.Stuart.ii.322]

ERSKINE, THOMAS, at the Jacobite Court in Urbino, Italy, 1717. [JU]

ERSKINE, THOMAS, of Pittodrie, Aberdeenshire, son of William Erskine and his wife Mary Grant, a Jacobite in 1715, died 14 October 1761. [JAB.58][CRA.82]

ERSKINE, WILLIAM, at the Jacobite Court in Urbino, Italy, 1717. [JU]

ERSKINE, WILLIAM, born 1688, son of William Erskine of Pittodrie and his wife Mary Grant, a Jacobite in 1715, in Bordeaux, France, by 1719, died in February 1774. [JAB.60][CRA.82]

ERSKINE, ..., an Ensign, a Jacobite in 1715, court-martialled and shot. [CS.V.175][MHP.296][CAT.II.217]

EWAN, GEORGE, son of John Ewan in Greencots, Aboyne, Aberdeenshire, a Jacobite in 1715. [JAB.205]

EWAN, WILLIAM, son of John Ewan in Greencots, Aboyne, Aberdeenshire, a Jacobite in 1715. [JAB.205]

FARQUHARSON, ALEXANDER, the younger, son of Lewis Farquharson of Auchendryne, a Jacobite in 1715, died in 1727, testament, 17 November 1727, Comm. Aberdeen, [NRS][JAB.68]

FARQUHARSON, CHARLES, son of John Farquharson of Inverey Aberdeenshire, and his wife Margaret Gordon, a Writer to the Signet, a Jacobite in 1715, died 1747. [JAB.63]

FARQUHARSON, CHARLES, of Balmoral, Aberdeenshire, son of William Farquharson of Inverey and his wife Agnes Gordon, a Major under Viscount Dundee at the Battle of Killicrankie in 1689, later an agent in France, died 1718. [JAB.66]

FARQUHARSON, CHARLES, son of Harry Farquharson of Whitehouse, a Jacobite in 1715. [JAB.70]

FARQUHARSON, DONALD, of Micras, Glen Muick, Aberdeenhsire, son of Alexander Farquharson of Allanaquaich and his wife Jean Forbes, a Major at Preston, a prisoner there in 1715. [JAB.72][CRA.63]

FARQUHARSON, DONALD, of Coldrach, son of George Farquharson and his wife Margaret Farquharson, a Jacobite in 1715, died after 1733. [JAB.72]

FARQUHARSON, FRANCIS, son of Harry Farquharson of Whitehouse, and his wife Barbara Ross, a Captain in McIntosh's Regiment, imprisoned in Preston and in London in 1716, died 1733. [JAB.70][CRA.43][CS.V.162]

FARQUHARSON, GEORGE, son of Donald Farquharson of Coldrach and his wife Grizell Small, a Jacobite Captain in 1715, died by 1733. [JAB.72]

FARQUHARSON, HARRY, of Whitehouse, son of James Farquharson and his wife Anna Garden, a prisoner in 1715, died before October 1716, testament, 15 May 1724, Comm. Aberdeen, NRS. [JAB.69][CRA.43]

FARQUHARSON, HARRY, son of Arthur Farquharson of Cults, Aberdeenshire, was transported via Liverpool bound for Virginia in 1716. [JAB.72][CRA.58]

FARQUHARSON, JAMES, of Balmoral, Aberdeenshire, son of John Farquharson of Inverey and his wife Marjory Leith, a merchant and burgess of Aberdeen, ADC to the Earl of Mar in 1715, died 1753. [JAB.65][CRA.60]

FARQUHARSON, JOHN, of Kirkton of Aboyne, Aberdeenshire, son of Thomas Farquharson, a Lieutenant of Macintosh's Regiment,

captured at Preston in 1715, a prisoner in London.
[JAB.61][CRA.47][CS.V.162]

FARQUHARSON, JOHN, born 1699, son of Lewis Farquharson of Auchendryne, a Roman Catholic priest, a Jacobite in 1715, died at Balmoral, Aberdeenshire, in 1782. [JAB.69]

FARQUHARSON, JOHN, son of Harry Farquharson of Whitehouse, a Jacobite in 1715, later a surgeon in London. [JAB.70]

FARQUHARSON, JOHN, of Invercauld, Aberdeenshire, born 1674, son of Alexander Farquharson and his wife Isabel Macintosh, a Lieutenant Colonel of Macintosh's Regiment in 1715, a prisoner in Preston and in London, died 1750. [CRA.60][CS.V.161]

FARQUHARSON, LAWRENCE, son of Donald Farquharson and his wife Helen Garden in Cobleton of Tulloch, was transported via Liverpool aboard the Goodspeed bound for Virginia on 28 July 1716, landed in Maryland in October 1716.
[HM.389][SPC.1716.309]JAB.73]

FARQUHARSON, LEWIS, of Auchindryne, son of James Farquharson of Inverey and his wife Agnes Ferris, a Captain under the Earl of Mar in 1715, died by 1729. [JAB.68]

FARQUHARSON, PATRICK, of Inverey, Tullich, and Auchlossin, Aberdeenshire, estate forfeited, 1715. [NRS.E678]

FARQUHARSON, PETER, of Inverey, son of John Farquharson of Inverey and his wife Margaret Gordon, Colonel of Mar's Regiment at the Battle of Sheriffmuir, escaped to France in 1716, died in Scotland in 1737. [JAB.62][CRA.54]

FARQUHARSON, PETER, of Rohalzie, a Captain in the Invercauld Regiment at the Siege of Preston, was killed there on 12 November 1715. [JAB.71][CS.V.131][CAT.II.209]

FARQUHARSON, ROBERT, of Alanaquaich, Aberdeenshire, son of Donald Farquharson and his wife Helen Garden, was transported via Liverpool aboard the Anne bound for Virginia on 31 July 1716, died in Scotland.
[SPC.1716.310][CTB.31.208][JAB.73][TNA.SP.54.26.123][CRA.56]

FARQUHARSON, SHAW, son of Gregor Farquharson of Wester Camdell and his wife Mary Mackenzie, was killed at the Battle of Sheriffmuir in 1715. [JAB.73]

FARQUHARSON, THOMAS, a merchant, the Jacobite collector of taxes in Aberdeen in 1715. [JAB.208]

FARQUHARSON, WILLIAM, of Broughdearg, Glen Shee, Perthshire, a Jacobite in 1715. [OR.86]

FENTON, JAMES, postmaster of Elgin, Morayshire, a Jacobite in 1715. [NRAS.1100.bundle 1517]

FENWICK, JOHN, died in Lancaster Prison, on 1 March 1716. [LBR]

FERGUSON, ALEXANDER, of Balyoukan, a Subaltern in Nairne's Regiment, captured at Preston in 1715. [CAT.II.210][CS.V.161] [NRS.GD1.53.72]

FERGUSON, ALEXANDER, probably from Perthshire, a Jacobite prisoner, petitioned for transportation, was transported via Liverpool aboard the Elizabeth and Ann bound for Jamaica or Virginia on 29 June 1716, landed in Virginia.
[SPC.1716.310][CTB.31.208][VSP.1.186][CAT.II.240]

FERGUSON, DONALD, a Captain in Mar's Battalion, captured at Preston, was transported via Liverpool aboard the Elizabeth and Anne bound for Jamaica or Virginia on 29 June 1716.
[SPC.1716.310][CTB.31.208][CS.V.161] [NRS.GD1.53.72]

FERGUSON, DUNCAN, was transported via Liverpool aboard the

Goodspeed bound for Virginia on 28 July 1716, landed in Maryland in October 1716. [HM.388][SPC.1716.310][CTB.31.209]

FERGUSON, FINLAY, of Baledmond, a Subaltern in Nairn's Regiment in 1715, a prisoner, tried and acquitted on 26 January 1716. [CAT.II.210][CS.V.161] [NRS.GD1.53.72]

FERGUSON, FINLAY, was transported via Liverpool aboard the Wakefield bound for South Carolina on 21 May 1716. [SPC.1716.309][CTB.31.205]

FERGUSON, FRANCIS, a Captain of Macintosh's Regiment, a prisoner at Preston in 1715, a farmer from Cushnie, Aberdeenshire, was transported via Liverpool aboard the Scipio bound for Antigua on 30 March 1716. [SPC.1716.310][CTB.31.204][JAB.151] [NRS.GD1.53.72]

FERGUSON, HENRY, was transported via Liverpool aboard the Friendship bound for Maryland on 24 May 1716, landed there in August 1716. [SPC.1716.311][HM.387]

FERGUSON, JAMES, of Drumfallandie, Perthshire, a Subaltern in Nairne's Regiment, was captured at Preston, petitioned for transportation, was transported via Liverpool aboard the Elizabeth and Anne bound for Jamaica or Virginia on 29 June 1716, landed in Virginia. [CAT.II.210/240] [SPC.1716.310] [CTB.31.208] [VSP.I.186][CS.V.161] [NRS.GD1.53.72]

FERGUSON, JOHN BOUIE, a Jacobite in 1715, in Coulinish, Ulva, 1716. [NRS.SC54.22.17.2]

FERGUSON, LAWRENCE, was transported via Liverpool aboard the Elizabeth and Anne bound for Jamaica or Virginia on 29 June 1716, landed in Virginia. [SPC.1716.310][CTB.31.208][VSP.I.185][CRA.62]

FERGUSON, PATRICK, probably from Perthshire, petitioned for transportation, was transported via Liverpool aboard the Elizabeth and Anne bound for Jamaica or Virginia on 29 June 1716, landed in Virginia.
[CAT.II.240][SPC.1716.310][CTB.31.208][VSP.I.185]

FERGUSON, PETER, was transported via Liverpool aboard the Two Brothers bound for Jamaica on 26 April 1716, landed on Montserrat in June 1716. [SPC.1716.313][CTB.31.206][CTP.CC.43]

FERGUSON, ROBERT, of Middlehaugh, a Subaltern in Nairne's Regiment, captured at Preston, was transported via Liverpool aboard the Anne bound for Virginia on 31 July 1716.
[SPC.1716.310][CAT.II.210][CS.V.161] [NRS.GD1.53.72]

FERGUSON, WILLIAM, a mariner, captured at Preston, condemned on 25 January 1716. [CS.V.193]

FERGUSON, WILLIAM, was transported via Liverpool aboard the Goodspeed bound for Virginia on 28 July 1716, landed in Maryland in October 1716. [SPC.1716.310][CTB.31.209][HM.389]

FERRIES, GEORGE, a farmer in Donside, Aberdeenshire, a Jacobite captured at Burntisland, Fife, on 11 January 1716. [JAB.13]

FIFE, ….., schoolmaster and session-clerk of Arbroath, Angus, a Jacobite, deposed in March 1716. [NRS.CH2.15.3]

FINDLATOR, JAMES, an Excise officer in Peterhead, Aberdeenshire, a Jacobite in 1715. [JAB.218]

FINDLATOR, JOHN, born 1652, son of Alexander Findlator, a master at Aberdeen Grammar School, a Jacobite in 1715, died in Aberdeen on 16 November 1717. [JAB.73]

FINLAY, WILLIAM, was transported via Liverpool aboard the Elizabeth and Anne bound for Jamaica or Virginia on 29 June 1716, landed in Virginia. [SPC.1716.310][CTB.31.208][VSP.I.186]

FINNICK, WILLIAM, a soldier of the Perth company in 1715. [NRS.B59.30.17]

FINNEY, ROBERT, was transported via Liverpool aboard the Elizabeth and Anne bound for Jamaica or Virginia on 29 June 1716, landed in Virginia. [SPC.1716.310][VSP.I.185]

FINNIE, JOHN, a farmer from Cushnie, Aberdeenshire, was transported via Liverpool to Virginia in 1716. [CTB.31.208][JAB.151]

FISHER, JOHN, died in Lancaster Prison, on 1 March 1716.[LBR]

FLEMING, CHARLES, at the Jacobite Court in Urbino, Italy, 1717. [JU]; A gentleman at the Jacobite Court, 1716-1726. [SI.366]

FLEMING, JOHN, Earl of Wigtown, imprisoned as a Jacobite in 1715, died 1749. [SP]

FLIGHT, ALEXANDER, a hammerman in Perth, a soldier of the Perth company, surrendered in 1715. [NRS.B59.30.17/37/40]

FORBES, ALEXANDER, born 1699, son of John Forbes of Balfluig, a Captain who was captured in Dunfermline, Fife, on 4 October 1715, a prisoner at Carlisle. [JAB.74][SUL.Cheap.5.537][CRA.107]

FORBES, ALEXANDER, a Jacobite in 1715. [JAB.217]

FORBES, ALEXANDER, Lord Pitsligo, born 1678, a Jacobite in 1715, fought at Sheriffmuir, escaped to Italy, at Leyden University in 1717, died 1762. [CRA.164][HMC.Stuart.iii.428]

FORBES, ALEXANDER, a Jacobite tax-collector in Aberdeen in 1715. [JAB.208]

FORBES, ALEXANDER, born 1673, son of William Forbes of
Lockermilk, a merchant in Aberdeen, a Jacobite in 1715, died 24
April 1738. [JAB.75]

FORBES, ARCHIBALD, born 3 November 1697, son of William
Forbes, Lord Forbes, and his wife Anne Brodie, a Jacobite in 1715,
escaped to France in 1717. [JAB.75]

FORBES, ARTHUR, a merchant in Echt, Aberdeenshire, a Jacobite
tax-collector in Aberdeen in 1715. [JAB.208]

FORBES, CHARLES, son of Arthur Forbes of Brux, Kildrummy,
Aberdeenshire, and his wife Elizabeth Murray, a Jacobite agent
before 1715, plotted to capture Edinburgh Castle in 1715,
Secretary to the Old Pretender in Rome from 1718 to 1720, died
in St Germain, Paris,
[JR.46/51][JAB.77][CRA.125][SI.366][TNA.SP.54.8.36]

FORBES, CHARLES, a merchant in Aberdeen, a Jacobite in 1715,
escaped via Banff to Norway on 8 April 1716. [JAB.77]

FORBES, GEORGE, was transported via Liverpool aboard the
Susannah bound for South Carolina on 7 May 1716.
[SPC.1716.309][CTB.31.206]

FORBES, GEORGE, son of Arthur Forbes of Culquhanny,
Aberdeenshire, a Jacobite in 1715, dead by 1720. [JAB.78]

FORBES, GEORGE, son of George Forbes of Skellatur, a Jacobite in
1715, died 1730. [JAB.79]

FORBES, JOHN, of Tullibardine's Regiment, a prisoner at
Sheriffmuir in 1715. [CAT.II.206]

FORBES, JAMES, born 1689, son of William Forbes, Lord Forbes, a
Jacobite in 1715, escaped to Rotterdam in the Netherlands in
1716, returned to Scotland, dead by 1761. [JAB.80][CRA.27]

FORBES, JOHN, of Invernan, born 1665, son of William Forbes of Skellatur and his wife Agnes McIntosh, captured at Sheriffmuir, died in Carlisle in 1716. [JAB.21][CRA.55]

FORBES, JOHN, son of William Forbes of Belnabodach and his wife Mary Stewart, a Jacobite in 1715. [JAB.81]

FORBES, JOHN, of Invernetie, son of William Forbes of Edingyglassie, a Jacobite in 1715, was killed in 1716. [JAB.82][CRA.142]

FORBES, JOHN, of Upper Boyndlie, born 1680, son of Sir John Forbes of Monymusk and his wife Barbra Dalmahoy, a Jacobite in 1715, escaped via Banff to Holland in 1716, drowned in Holland in November 1716. [JAB.83][CRA..181]

FORBES, JOHN, son of Thomas Forbes of Waterton and his wife Elizabeth Nicolson, a burgess of Aberdeen, was killed at the Battle of Sheriffmuir in 1715. [JAB.83][CRA.181]

FORBES, JOHN, of Pitfichie, Jacobite tax collector in 1715. [NRAS.1154.104]

FORBES, LACHLAN, of Bellabeg, 1716.

FORBES, NATHANIEL, of Ardgeith, son of George Forbes of Skellatur, a Major of Mar's Battalion, captured at the Siege of Preston on 13 November 1715, imprisoned in London, escaped via Holland to Paris, France in 1718. [JAB.86][CS.V.161] [NRS.GD1.53.72][HMC.II.104/190]

FORBES, THOMAS, a farmer from Cushnie, Aberdeenshire, was transported via Liverpool aboard the Friendship bound for Virginia on 24 May 1716, landed in Maryland in August 1716, returned to Scotland in 1722. [SPC.1716.311][JAB.151/153][HM.387]

FORBES, THOMAS, of Tolquhon, born 1689, son of Thomas Forbes of Little Auchry and his wife Henrietta Erskine, fled via London to France in September 1716, died 1728 in London. [JAB.87/217][CRA.185]

FORBES, WILLIAM, in Ellon, Aberdeenshire, a Jacobite in 1715. [JAB.33]

FORBES, WILLIAM, born 1694, son of John Forbes of Invernettie and his wife Rebecca Forbes, a Jacobite in 1715. [JAB.89]

FORBES, WILLIAM, of Blackton, born 28 November 1689, son of Alexander Forbs and his wife Isabel Hacket, a Lieutenant in Panmure's Regiment, was captured at Sheriffmuir in 1715, a prisoner in Edinburgh and in Carlisle, died 9 October 1771. [JAB.89][CAT.II.205][SUL.Cheap.ms5.557][CRA.203]

FORBES, WILLIAM, from Echt, Aberdeenshire, a merchant in Aberdeen, a Jacobite tax collector in 1715. [JAB.208]

FORBES, WILLIAM, of Tombeg, born 1687, son of John Forbes and his wife Anna Lunan, a Jacobite in 1715. [JAB.89]

FORRESTER, ALEXANDER, of Carsbonny near Edinburgh, a Jacobite in 1715, imprisoned at Preston and in London in 1716. [CS.V.160/161/186] [NRS.GD1.53.72]

FORRESTER, Sir JOHN, a Jacobite agent in Scotland, 1714. [Bodleian ms carte211/320]

FORSYTH, HUGH, was transported via Liverpool aboard the Scipio bound for Antigua on 30 March 1716. [SPC.1716.310][CTB.31 204]

FORTUNE, THOMAS, a soldier in the Perth company in 1715. [NRS.B59.30.17]

FOTHERINGHAM, ARCHIBALD, son of the laird of Powrie, a Lieutenant of the Earl of Panmure's Regiment of Foot, fought at the Battle of Sheriffmuir in 1715, a prisoner at Carlisle. [CAT.II.205][SUL.Cheap.ms5.537][NRS.GD45.1.201]

FOTHERINGHAM, JOHN, was transported via Liverpool aboard the Susannah bound for South Carolina on 7 May 1716. [SPC.1716.309][CTB.31.206]

FOTHERINGHAM, JOHN, of Powrie, Angus, at the Jacobite Court in Urbino, Italy, 1717. [JU]; 1716. [NRS.GD1.616.28]

FOULIS, ALEXANDER, of Ratho, Midlothian, a prisoner at Preston and in London in 1716. [CS.V.160/186] [NRS.GD1.53.72]

FRASER, Lord CHARLES, of Muchals, born 1662, son of Lord Andrew Fraser and his wife Katherine Fraser, a Jacobite in 1715, surrendered on 22 February 1716, died in Banff on 12 October 1716. [JAB.90][CRA.66][SP.IV.119]

FRASER, DUNCAN, was transported via Liverpool aboard the Susannah bound for South Carolina on 7 May 1716. [SPC.1716.309][CTB.31.206]

FRASER, HUGH, an Ensign in Mcintosh's Regiment, a prisoner at Preston in 1715. [CS.V.162] [NRS.GD1.53.72]

FRASER, HUGH, was transported via Liverpool aboard the Susannah bound for South Carolina on 7 May 1716. [SPC.1716.309][CTB.31.206]

FRASER, JAMES, of Lonmay, son of William Fraser, Lord Saltoun, and his wife Margaret Sharpe, a Jacobite in 1715, died on 10 August 1729, testament, 22 July 1730, Comm. Aberdeen. [NRS] [JAB.91]

FRASER, JOHN, brother of Fraser of Culduthill, a Jacobite at Sheriffmuir, 1715. [NRS.RH2.4.308/170]

FRASER, JOHN, was transported via Liverpool aboard the Scipio bound for Antigua on 30 March 1716. [SPC.1716.309][CTB.31.205]

FRASER, JOHN, was transported via Liverpool board the Wakefield bound for South Carolina on 21 May 1716. [SPC.1716.309][CTB.31.205]

FRASER, PATRICK, a Roman Catholic priest, a Jacobite in 1715. [JAB.215]

FRASER, SIMON, a Captain, was captured at Preston in 1715, escaped to France. [JAB.92]

FRASER, SIMON, Lord Lovat, a Jacobite in 1717. [NRS.GD1.616.30]

FRASER, WILLIAM, son of Alexander Fraser of Inveralochy, Aberdeenshire, and his wife Marjorie Erskine, was killed at the Battle of Sheriffmuir in 1715. [JAB.91][CRA.154]

FRASER, WILLIAM, was transported via Liverpool aboard the Susannah bound for South Carolina on 7 May 1716. [SPC.1716.309][CTB.31.206]

FRASER, ..., of Belladrum, a Jacobite at Sheriffmuir, 1715. [NRS.RH2.4.308/170];

FRASER, ..., of Gartmore, a Jacobite at Sheriffmuir, 1715. [NRS.RH2.4.308/170];

FREEBAIRN, JAMES, Jacobite Collector of Taxes in Perth, 1715. [NRS.B59.30.36]; at the Jacobite Court in Urbino, Italy, 171. [JU]

FREEBAIRN ...., 1716. [NRS.GD1.616.28]

FREEBAIRN, ROBERT, a printer in Perth, a Jacobite in 1715, [NRS.GD18.3.62]; at the Jacobite Court in Urbino, Italy, 1717. [JU]

FULLARTON, JAMES, son of Robert Udny of Auchterellon, Aberdeenshire, and Elizabeth Fullarton, an Advocate in Aberdeen and a Jacobite, 1716. [JAB.92]

FULLARTON, JOHN, of Dudwick, son of Robert Udny of Auchterellon, Aberdeenshire, and his wife Elizabeth Fullarton, fought at the Battle of Sheriffmuir in 1715, escaped via Banff, Norway, Hamburg, the Netherlands, to France. [JAB.93][TNA.SP.35.7.75][CRA.91][NRS.GD1.616.28]

FYFE, JAMES, son of John Fyfe and his wife Elizabeth Tulloch, a bailie and merchant of Aberdeen, a Jacobite in 1715, died 13 August 1729. [JAB.94]

FYFFE, NATHANIEL, a burgess and baillie of Perth, a Jacobite in 1715. [NRS.B59.30.36/40]

GAIRN, CHARLES, Adjutant of the Earl of Panmure's Regiment of Foot in 1715. [NRS.GD45.1.201]

GAIRN, DAVID, of Lawtoun, Captain of the Earl of Panmure's Regiment of Foot in 1715, a prisoner at Sheriffmuir. [NRS.GD45.1.201][CAT.II.205]

GALL, PATRICK, a Maltman in Perth, carried arms, a Jacobite in 1715, surrendered. [NRS.B59.30.36/37]

GALLICK, ALEXANDER, a Jacobite in Perthshire, 1715. [NRS.B59.20.1]

GALT, JOHN MCEAN VCEAN, a Jacobite in 1715, in Camiscan, Sunart, 1716. [NRS.SC54.22.17.1]

GARDEN, CHARLES, of Bellastrine, Kinernie, son of James Garden, a prisoner at Sheriffmuir and in Carlisle, 1716. [CRA.65][TNA.SP.35.8.12/35.6.89][JAB.95][CAT.II.205]

GARDEN, DAVID, Captain of Panmure's Regiment, fought at Sheriffmuir in 1715, a prisoner. [CAT.II.205]

GARDEN, GEORGE, born 1648, son of Reverend Alexander Garden, minister of St Nicholas, Aberdeen, a Jacobite in 1715, died 31 January 1733, Testament, 18 February 1733, Comm. Aberdeen, [NRS] [JAB.226]

GARDEN, JAMES, born 1646, son of Reverend Alexander Garden, Professor of Divinity at King's College, Aberdeen, a Jacobite in 1715, died 1726. [JAB.227]

GARDNER, PATRICK, a soldier in the Perth company, was transported via Liverpool aboard the Hockenhill bound for St Kitts on 25 June 1716, mutinied and landed on Sint Maartens in September 1716. [NRS.B59.30.17][SPC.1716.312][CTB.31.207]

GARRIOCH, ALEXANDER, an Ensign, fought at the Battle of Sheriffmuir, a prisoner at Carlisle in December 1716. [CAT.II.205] [SUL.Cheap ms5.537]

GATT, JAMES, born in Cullen, Banffshire, a student at King's College, Aberdeen, a Jacobite in 1715. [JAB.227]

GEDDES, JOHN, a soldier of the Perth company in 1715. [NRS.B59.3.17]

GEDDES, ..., a gentleman servant of the Earl of Southesk, 1715. [TNA.SP54.7.40]

GEDDIE, ANDREW, minister of Farnell, Angus, from 1703, a Jacobite in 1715, deposed in 1716, dead by February 1719. [F.V.393]

GELLIE, JAMES, a merchant in Aberdeen, a Jacobite in 1715, dead by 1744. [JAB.96]

GELLIE, PATRICK, son of Patrick Gellie, merchant in Aberdeen, a Jacobite tax collector in 1715, a merchant and baillie in Aberdeen, testament, 18 July 1743, Comm. Aberdeen. [NRS][JAB.208]

GIBSON, ALEXANDER, a sergeant of the Perth company in 1715. [NRS.B59.30.17]

GIBSON, BARTHOLEMEW, son of Bartholemew Gibson a Quaker, once a volunteer in Orkney's Regiment, now a Customs officer at Leven, a Lieutenant of Drummond's Regiment in 1715, fought at Sheriffmuir, declaration made in Perth on 21 February 1717. [NRS.GD241.380.23]

GILL, HENRY, was transported via Liverpool aboard the Susannah bound for South Carolina on 7 May 1716. [SPC.1716.309][CTB.31.206]

GILMICHAEL, ..., a Jacobite in 1715, in Kilean, Toresay, Mull, 1716. [NRS.SC54.22.17.2]

GLENDINNING, JOHN, was transported via Liverpool aboard the Elizabeth and Anne bound for Jamaica or Virginia on 29 June 1716, landed in Virginia. [SPC.1716.310][VSP.1.185]

GLASS, JOHN, was transported via Liverpool aboard the Scipio bound for Antigua on 30 March 1716. [SPC.1716.310][CTB.31.204]

GOLD, PATRICK, an Ensign of the Earl of Panmure's Regiment of Foot in 1715. [NRS.GD45.1.201]

GORDON, ADAM, of Balgowan, son of William Gordon and his wife Isobel Leith, a Jacobite in 1715, surrendered at Banff on 8 September 1716. [JAB.96][CRA.116]

GORDON, ALEXANDER, a merchant in Aberdeen, a Jacobite in 1715. [JAB.97]

GORDON, ALEXANDER, a farmer in Cushnie, Aberdeenshire, was transported via Liverpool aboard the Friendship bound for Virginia on 24 May 1716, landed in Maryland in August 1716. [SPC.1716.311][JAB.311][HM.386]

GORDON, Dr ALEXANDER, a Roman Catholic priest, a Jacobite in 1715, died in Auchindour in 1763. [JAB.214]

GORDON, ALEXANDER, of Blelack, son of John Gordon, a Jacobite in 1715, died in 1723. [JAB.97]

GORDON, ALEXANDER, of Cairnfield, son of Robert Gordon, a Jacobite in 1715, later a merchant in Amsterdam, Holland. [TNA.SP.54.11.89][JAB.97]

GORDON, ALEXANDER, born 1688, son of John Gordon of Seaton and his wife Elizabeth Irvine, Commissary Clerk Depute in Aberdeen, a Jacobite in 1715, died in 1727. [JAB.98]

GORDON, ALEXANDER, in Comrie, a Jacobite in 1715. [JAB.99]

GORDON, ALEXANDER, son of John Gordon of Knockespock, Glenbucket, mate of the Hope packet, a Jacobite in 1715. [JAB.100][CRA.129]

GORDON, ALEXANDER, of Glengerack, born 1698, son of Charles Gordon and his wife Margaret Duff, fought at the Battle of Sheriffmuir, surrendered in Banff in 1716. [JAB.100]

GORDON, ALEXANDER, in Scardargue, fought at Sheriffmuir in 1715. [JAB.100]

GORDON, General ALEXANDER, of Auchintoul, Aberdeenshire, his estates in the parishes of Turriff and Auchterless were forfeited in 1715, escaped to Bordeaux, France, in 1716, at the Jacobite Court in Urbino, Italy, 1719. [JU][NRS.664]

GORDON, ALEXANDER, Earl of Huntly, at the Jacobite Court in Urbino, Italy, 171. [JU]

GORDON, ALEXANDER, a servant, 1719-1735. [SI.362]

GORDON, CHARLES, of Abergeldie, son of ... Gordon of Minmore, a Jacobite in 1715. [JAB.101]

GORDON, CHARLES, a prisoner at Carlisle in December 1716. [SUL.Cheap.ms5.537]

GORDON, CHARLES, of Buthlaw, son of William Gordon and his wife Elizabeth Martin, an Advocate in Aberdeen, a Jacobite in 1715, died 23 December 1751. [JAB.102]

GORDON, CHARLES, of Tilphoudie, son of John Gordon and his wife Elizabeth Duguid, was killed at the Battle of Sheriffmuir in 1715. [JAB.102]

GORDON, FRANCIS, of Craig, born 1653, son of Francis Gordon and his wife Elizabeth Menzies, a Jacobite, was captured in Dunfermline, Fife, on 24 October 1715, died in Carlisle in September 1715. [JAB.103][CRA.127]

GORDON, FRANCIS, born 1680, son of Francis Gordon of Craig and his wife Agnes Ogilvie, fought at Sheriffmuir in 1715, died 1727 in England. [JAB.103]

GORDON, GEORGE, in the Mill of Kincardine, son of John Gordon, a Jacobite, was captured in Dunfermline, Fife, on 24 October 1715, imprisoned in Stirling and in Carlisle, died 1716. [CRA.51][JAB.105][SUL.Cheap.ms.5.537]

GORDON, GEORGE, of Sauchen, a Jacobite in 1715.
[CRA.39][JAB.105]

GORDON, GEORGE, of Glastirem, son of Patrick Gordon, a
Jacobite who surrendered in Banff in March 1716, and died in
1721. [CRA.40][JAB.105]

GORDON, GEORGE, of Buckie, Banffshire, a Jacobite, escaped
capture at Dunfermline, Fife, surrendered in March 1716, died
1729. [JAB.104]

GORDON, GEORGE, of Carnousie, Banffshire, son of Sir George
Gordon of Edinglassie and his wife Jean Forbes, the Jacobite Cess
Collector of Banff in 1715. [JAB.104]

GORDON, HARRY, son of John Gordon of Avoche and his wife
Isobel Farquharson, a Jacobite who surrendered in Banff in March
1716. [JAB.107]

GORDON, JAMES, of Barnes, Premnay, Aberdeenshire, son of
George Gordon of Shellagreen, a Jacobite in 1715, a Captain, died
before 1739. [CRA.71][JAB.108]

GORDON, JAMES, in the Mains of Esslemont, Aberdeenshire, a
Jacobite in 1715. [JAB.33]

GORDON, JAMES, of Ellon, Aberdeenshire, son of Alexander
Gordon, a Jacobite in 1715, died 27 February 1732.
[JAB.10][CRA.192]

GORDON, Reverend JAMES, a Roman Catholic priest, born 1664,
son of Patrick Gordon of Glastirem, a Jacobite in 1715, died 1746
at Thornhill. [JAB.214]

GORDON, JAMES, son of James Gordon of Auchlyne, and his wife
Rachel Burnett, was killed at the Battle of Sheriffmuir in 1715.
[JAB.106]

GORDON, JAMES, a brewer in Aberdeen, a Jacobite captured in Dunfermline, Fife, on 24 October 1715, imprisoned in Edinburgh and in Carlisle, released. [TNA.SP54.12.152][JAB.106][SUL.Cheap.5.537]

GORDON, JAMES, Dean of Guild in Aberdeen, a Jacobite in 1715, died in January 1728. [JAB.107]

GORDON, Dr JAMES, of Hilton, son of Dr John Gordon of Colleston, a surgeon, was captured at Sheriffmuir in 1715, died 1755. [JAB.108][CAT.II.205]

GORDON, JAMES, of Letterfourie, born 1660, son of John Gordon and his wife Janet Seton, fought at Sheriffmuir in 1715, died in 1748. [JAB.109]

GORDON, Sir JAMES, of Park, son of Sir John Gordon and his wife Helen Ogilvy, a Jacobite who surrendered in Banff in March 1716, died 15 December 1727 at Pool Wells. [JAB.110]

GORDON, JAMES, born 1650, son of Robert Gordon of Chapelton, minister of Rhynie, Aberdeenshire, a Jacobite, deposed in 1716. [JAB.228][F.6.330]

GORDON, Colonel JOHN, of Glenbucket, Donside, Aberdeenshire, born 1678, a Jacobite in 1715, died in Boulogne, France, in 1747. [HMC.Stuart.i.507]

GORDON, JOHN, from Coldstone, Aberdeenshire, a Jacobite, died in Lancaster Prison on 7 January 1716. [LBR][JAB.113]

GORDON, JOHN, son of Adam Gordon of Balgowan, a Jacobite who escaped via Banff to France in 1716, settled in Rouen. [JAB.97][CRA.116]

GORDON, JOHN, of Achanacy, a Jacobite prisoner in Banff in November 1716. [JAB.110]

GORDON, Dr JOHN, son of Dr John Gordon of Colliestone and his wife Katherine Fullarton, a Jacobite in 1715, died 1735. [JAB.113]

GORDON, JOHN, a Captain in Mar's Battalion, a prisoner at Preston in 1715. [CS.V.113]

GORDON, JOHN, from Cromar, Aberdeenshire, was captured at Preston in 1715. [TNA.SP35.7.2][JAB.113]

GORDON, JOHN, of Dumeath, son of Patrick Gordon, a Jacobite prisoner in London 1716. [TNA.SP35.7.1][JAB.114]

GORDON, JOHN, son of Sir James Gordon of Lesmoir and his wife Jane Gordon, a Jacobite in 1715. [JAB.115]

GORDON, Dr JOHN, son of James Gordon of Seaton and his wife Marjorie Forbes, Professor of Civil Law at King's College, Aberdeen, a Jacobite in 1715, died in September 1741. [JAB115]

GORDON, JOHN, a Captain in Mar's Regiment, fought at Sheriffmuir in 1715, captured. [CAT.II.205] [NRS.GD1.53.72]

GORDON, JOHN, a Jacobite imprisoned in Edinburgh Castle, 1715. [NRS.RH15.123.40]

GORDON, LUDOVICK, son of Reverend James Gordon, minister at Kinoir, a Jacobite, deposed in 1716. [JAB.229][F.6.330]

GORDON, PATRICK, born 1694, son of John Gordon of Aberlour, Morayshire, and his wife Jean Gordon, a Jacobite who was captured at Dunfermline, Fife, on 24 October 1715, imprisoned in Stirling and in Carlisle, died in Aberlour during 1760. [JAB.117][SUL.Cheap.5.537]

GORDON, PATRICK, born 1692, son of John Gordon of Auchleuchries, and his wife Elizabeth Grant, a Jacobite in 1715, escaped to the continent in 1716. [JAB.118]

GORDON, PATRICK, in Bogs, North Rhynie, Aberdeenshire, a Jacobite in 1715. [JAB.118]

GORDON, PATRICK, a Lieutenant of the Earl of Panmure's Regiment of Foot in 1715. [NRS.GD45.1.201]

GORDON, PETER, in Drumbulg, a Jacobite in 1715. [JAB.119]

GORDON, RICHARD, born 1687, son of John Gordon of Seatoun, Regent of King's College, Aberdeen, a Jacobite in 1715, died 9 November 1763. [JAB.120]

GORDON, ROBERT, son of Sir James Gordon of Lesmoir and his wife Jane Gordon, a Jacobite in 1715. [JAB.115]

GORDON, ROBERT, of Cluny, son of Robert Gordon of Cluny, a Jacobite in 1715. [CRA.68][JAB.120]

GORDON, ROBERT, a Lieutenant in Mar's Regiment, was captured at the Siege of Preston in 1715. [CS.V.161]

GORDON, ROBERT, son of Patrick Gordon of Hallhead, a Jacobite in 1715, later a wine merchant and Jacobite agent in Bordeaux, France, died in 1738. [JAB.121][HMC.Stuart pp.V.425-428]

GORDON, ROBERT, a farmer from the Brae of Scurdargue, fought at the Battle of Sheriffmuir in 1715. [JAB.101]

GORDON, ROBERT, a Jacobite at Sheriffmuir, 1715. [NRS.RH2.4.308/86]

GORDON, ROBERT, of Gordonstoun, 1715.

GORDON, THOMAS, born 1666 in Aberdeen, a Jacobite and an officer of the Royal Navy, was commissioned as a Captain Commodore of the Russian Navy in 1719, Governor of Cronstadt from 1733 until his death on 16 March 1741. [NRS.GD24.1.854.21][HS.9.1/25]

GORDON, WILLIAM, Viscount Kenmuir, son of Alexander Gordon and his wife Marion McCulloch, captured at Preston in 1715, beheaded on Tower Hill, London, on 24 February 1716, estate forfeited in 1715. [SP.V.129][NRS.E638][NRS.GD1.53.72.1]

GORDON, WILLIAM, of Craigwillie, a Jacobite who surrendered on 13 March 1716. [JAB.121/183]

GORDON, WILLIAM, of Goval, son of James Gordon of Seaton, a Jacobite in 1715, died in 1733. [JAB.121]

GORDON, WILLIAM, a merchant from Kintore, Aberdeenshire, fought in Kintore's Squadron in 1715. [JAB.122]

GORDON, WILLIAM, son of William Gordon of Farskane and his wife Helen Duff, a Jacobite in 1715, escaped to Paris in 1716, later a merchant in Norway. [JAB.122]

GORTIE, GEORGE, was transported via Liverpool aboard the Scipio bound for Antigua on 30 March 1716. [CTB.31.204]

GOURLAY, JOHN, treasurer of Perth and the Commissary, carried arms, 1715. [NRS. B59.30]

GRAEME, WILLIAM, at the Jacobite Court at Urbino, Italy, 1717. [JU]

GRAHAM, ...of Inchbrakie, a prisoner at Carlisle on 31 October 1715. [CS.V.64]

GRAHAM, DAVID, imprisoned at Preston, then transported via Liverpool aboard the Goodspeed bound for Virginia on 28 July 1716, landed in Maryland in October 1716. [SPC.1716.310] [CTB.31.209][CS.V.160][HM.388] [NRS.GD1.53.72]

GRAHAM, FERGUS, son of Mossknows, a prisoner at Preston 1in 1715, was transported via Liverpool aboard the Elizabeth and Anne bound to Jamaica or Virginia on 29 June 1716, landed at

York, Virginia. [SPC.1716.310][CTB.31.208][VSP.1.185]
[NRS.GD1.53.72]

GRAHAM, JAMES, son of Graham of Mossknowes, a prisoner at
Preston in 1715. [CS.V.160]

GRAHAM, JAMES, was transported via Liverpool aboard the Anne
bound for Virginia on 31 July 1716. [SPC.1716.310][CTB.31.209]

GRAHAM, JAMES, of Garvock, Perthshire, a Jacobite in 1715.
[NRS.B59.20.1]

GRAHAM, JAMES, of Braco, Perthshire, a Jacobite agent from
1715 to 1716.

GRAHAM, OLIVER, a maltman and burgess of Perth, carried arms,
surrendered in 1715. [NRS.B59.30.36/37/40]

GRAHAM, Major THOMAS, a Jacobite at Dunfermline and later at
Sheriffmuir in 1715. [MHP.297][JAB.104]

GRAHAM, THOMAS, in Dowallie, a Jacobite prisoner at Blackness,
Stirling, and Carlisle. [CAT.II.239]

GRAHAM, WALTER, a Jacobite prisoner at Carlisle in December
1716. [SUL.Cheap.5.537]

GRAHAM, WILLIAM, Viscount Dundee, son of David Graham, a
Jacobite in 1715, died 1724. [SP.II.332]

GRAHAM, WILLIAM, from Dowallie, Perthshire, a Jacobite
prisoner, was marched via Blackness and Stirling to Carlisle in
September 1716. [CAT.II.239]

GRANGER, ..., Jacobite Supervisor of Excise in Perth, 1715.
[NRS.B59.30.36]

GRANT, DANIEL, Adjutant of McIntosh's Regiment, a prisoner at Preston, was transported via Liverpool aboard the Goodspeed bound for Virginia on 28 July 1716, landed in Maryland in October 1716. [SPC.1716.310][CS.V.162][CTB.31.209][HM.389] [NRS.GD1.53.72]

GRANT, JOHN, of Glenmoriston, Urquhart, Inverness-shire, estate forfeited in 1715. [NRS.E633]; a Jacobite at Sheriffmuir, 1715. [NRS.RH2.4.308/170];

GRANT, ROBERT, a farmer from Cushnie, Aberdeenshire, was transported via Liverpool aboard the Elizabeth and Anne bound for Jamaica or Virginia on 29 June 1716, landed in Virginia. [SPC.1716.310][JAB.151][CTB.31.208][VSP.1.186]

GRANT, WILLIAM, was transported via Liverpool aboard the Friendship bound for Virginia on 24 May 1716, landed in Maryland in August 1716. [SPC.1716.311][HM.386]

GRANT, ..., of Rothiemurcus, 1715.

GRAY, ALEXANDER, son of Provost Thomas Hay of Aberdeen, minister at Footdee, Aberdeen, a Jacobite in 1715, deposed in 1716. [F.6.27][JAB.229]

GRAY, ANDREW, from Waterton, Aberdeenshire, fought at the Battle of Sheriffmuir in 1715. [JAB.83]

GRAY, JOHN, a soldier of the Perth company in 1715. [NRS.B59.30.17]

GRAY, JOHN, a bailie of Fraserburgh, Aberdeenshire, a Jacobite in 1715. [JAB.218]

GRAY, PATRICK, Convenor of the Trades of Aberdeen, a Jacobite in 1715, died 1736. [JAB.123]; a wright in Aberdeen, testament, 13 November 1736, Comm. Aberdeen. [NRS]

GRAY, WILLIAM, a farmer from Aberdeenshire, a Jacobite, was captured at Burntisland, Fife, on 11 January 1716. [JAB.13]

GREGORY, JOHN, an Ensign of the Earl of Panmure's Regiment of Foot in 1715. [NRS.GD45.1.201]

GREGORY, MALCOLM, from Aboyne, Aberdeenshire, Captain of the Earl of Panmure's Regiment of Foot in 1715. [NRS.GD45.1.201]

GRIERSON, GILBERT, son of Grierson of Lag, Dumfries-shire, a prisoner at Preston and in London in 1716. [CS.V.160/186] [NRS.GD1.53.72]

GRIERSON, JAMES, of Lag, the younger, a prisoner at Preston, 1715. [NRS.GD1.53.72]

GRIERSON, WILLIAM, the younger of Lag, Dumfries-shire, estate forfeited in 1715. [NRS.E643]

GRINSELL, ADAM, a soldier of the Perth company in 1715. [NRS.B59.30.17]

GRUB, JOHN, an Episcopalian preacher in Kirkden and in Carmyllie, Angus, a Jacobite in 1715, deposed in 1717. [HHA.170][F.V.300]

GRUDER, WILLIAM, a subaltern, a prisoner at Preston, 1715. [NRS.GD1.53.72]

GUILD, THOMAS, born 1687, son of Thomas Guild in Glamis, Angus, a Jacobite in 1715, was transported via Liverpool aboard the <u>Susannah</u> bound for South Carolina, on 7 May 1716, later a planter in Colleton County, S.C., probate 1737, S.C. [SPC.1716.309][CTB.31.206]

GUNN. JOHN, born 1692, a servant to James Moir of Stonywood, Aberdeenshire, a Jacobite in 1715, died 1767. [JAB.161]

GUTHRIE, ALEXANDER, an Episcopalian preacher in Arbroath, Angus, a Jacobite in 1715. [HHA.170]

GUTHRIE, GIDEON, born 1663, an Episcopalian preacher in Brechin, Angus, in Fetteresso, Kincardineshire, in 1715, a Jacobite in 1715, deposed in 1716. [NRS.CH2.575.1][F.V.465]

GUTHRIE, JAMES, an Episcopalian preacher in Guthrie, Angus, a Jacobite in 1715. [HHA.170][F.V.437]

GUTHRIE, JOHN, was transported via Liverpool aboard the Susannah bound for South Carolina on 7 May 1716. [SPC.1716.309][CTB.31.206]

GUTHRIE, JOHN, was transported via Liverpool aboard the Wakefield bound for South Carolina on 21 May 1716. [SPC.1716.309][CTB.31.205]

GUTHRIE, ROBERT, was transported via Liverpool aboard the Wakefield bound for South Carolina on 21 May 1716. [SPC.1716.309][CTB.31.205]

HALKET, GEORGE, schoolmaster of Rathen, Aberdeenshire, a Jacobite in 1715. [JAB.123]

HALL, DAVID, a merchant from Edinburgh, a prisoner at Preston and in London 1716. [CS.V.161/186] [NRS.GD1.53.72]

HAMILTON, BASIL, of Baldoun, a prisoner at Preston in 1715, estate forfeited, 1715.
[CS.V.43/160/186][NRS.E614][NRS.GD1.53.72.1]

HAMILTON, EZEKIAL, an Episcopalian chaplain at the Jacobite Court at Urbino, Italy, in 1716. [JU]

HAMILTON, JOHN, of Pumpherston, a prisoner at Preston and in London in 1716. [CS.V.160/186] [NRS.GD1.53.72]

HAMILTON, JOHN, the janitor of King's College, Aberdeen, a Jacobite in 1715. [JAB.210]

HAMILTON, JOHN, of Gibston, a Jacobite, was captured at Dunfermline, Fife, on 24 October 1715, a prisoner in Stirling and in Carlisle, discharged. [JAB.124][TNA.SP35.2.14][SUL.Cheap.pp5.537]

HAMILTON, Lieutenant, a Jacobite at Sheriffmuir, 1715. [NRS.RH2.4.308/170];

HANDYSIDE, ROBERT, was transported via Liverpool aboard the Two Brothers bound for Jamaica on 26 April 1716, landed on Montserrat in June 1716. [SPC.1716.313][CTB.31.206][CTP.CC.43]

HANTON, JAMES, a soldier of the Perth company in 1715. [NRS.B59.30.17]

HARESTANES, MATTHEW, a prisoner in Preston and in London in 1716. [CS.V.160/186] [NRS.GD1.53.72]

HARDY, ANDREW, a vintner and burgess of Perth, a Lieutenant, surrendered. [NRS.B59.30.36/37/40]

HARPER, ADAM, son of Reverend William Harper and his wife Elizabeth Innes, minister of Boharm, Banffshire, a Jacobite in 1715, resigned in 1716, died on 14 May 1726. [JAB.229]

HAY, ALEXANDER, son of Thomas Hay and his wife Jean King, Conjunct Sheriff Clerk of Aberdeen, a Jacobite in 1715. [JAB.130]

HAY, ALEXANDER, of Arnbath, son of Alexander Hay, a Jacobite in 1715. [JAB.126][CRA.109]

HAY, ALEXANDER, born 1698, son of Alexander Hay of Arnbath, Tough, Aberdeenshire, and his wife Christian Abernethy, a Jacobite who was captured at Dunfermline, Fife, on 24 October

1715, and imprisoned in Stirling and in Carlisle.
[JAB.127][SUL.Cheap.5.537][CRA.109]

HAY, CHARLES, of Rannes, born 1688, son of James Hay and his wife Margaret Gordon, a Jacobite who surrendered in Banff during March 1716, died in London in 1751. [JAB.131]

HAY, JAMES, at the Jacobite Court in Urbino, Italy, 1717; a. gentleman at the Jacobite court, 1718-1727. [JU][SI.366]

HAY, JOHN, of Cromlix, Dunblane, Perthshire, son of the Earl of Kinnoull, born 1691, Jacobite Governor of Perth in 1715, estate forfeited in 1715, escaped to St Germains in France in 1716, a Groom of the Bedchamber at the Jacobite Court in Urbino, Italy, 1717, was created Earl of Inverness in 1719, settled in St Germains, died on 24 September 1740. [JU][JP.68][MHP.303] [NRS.E623][SP.V.231][NRA.B59.30.6/35] [SP.V.231]

HAY, JOHN, of Muldavit, son of William Hay and his wife Helen Crichton, a Jacobite who surrendered at Banff in March 1716, died 1720. [JAB.21]

HAY, JOHN, was transported via Liverpool aboard the Friendship bound for Virginia on 24 May 1716, landed in Maryland in August 1716. [SPC.1716.311][HM.386]

HAY, JOHN, a barber in Aberdeen, a Jacobite in 1715. [JAB.213]

HAY, Mrs MARJORY, Countess of Inverness, at the Jacobite Court in Urbino, Italy, 1718. [JU]; Lady of the Queen's Bedchamber 1719-1722. [SI.361]

HAY, THOMAS, Viscount Duplin, son of George Hay of Balhousie, a Jacobite in 1715, a prisoner in 1716, died on 5 January 1719. [SP.V.231]

HAY, THOMAS, Earl of Kinnoull, a Jacobite imprisoned in 1715, died 1719. [NRS.GD45.1.193]

HAY, WALTER, of Lickleyhead, a Jacobite in 1715, died in 1725, testament, 10 December 1725, Comm. Aberdeen. [NRS] [JAB.129]

HAY, WILLIAM, brother of Provost Hay of Perth, fought at Sheriffmuir in 1715, a prisoner at Carlisle in December 1716, escaped. [CAT.II.205][JAB.129][SUL.Cheap.5.537]

HAY, WILLIAM, a messenger in Aberdeen, a Jacobite in 1715. [JAB.213]

HAY, WILLIAM, minister at Rothiemay, a Jacobite in 1715, was deposed in 1716, died in January 1718. [JAB.230][F.6.332]

HAY, WILLIAM, enrolled in the Russian Navy in 1717, a Captain from 1718 to 1724, later a Jacobite agent in Russia. [TNA.SP91/107.fos.87-89].

HENDERSON, CHARLES, was transported via Liverpool aboard the Elizabeth and Anne bound for Jamaica or Virginia on 29 June 1716, landed in Virginia. [SPC.1716.310][CTB.31.208][VSP.I.186]

HENDERSON, ROBERT, a farmer from Cushnie, Aberdeenshire, was transported via Liverpool aboard the Hockenhill bound for St Kitts on 25 June 1716, mutinied and landed on Sint Maartens in September 1716. [SPC.1716.312][JAB.21][CTB.31.205]

HENDERSON, WILLIAM, was transported via Liverpool aboard the Wakefield bound for South Carolina on 21 April 1716. [SPC.1716.309][CB.31.205]

HENDERSON, WILLIAM, quartermaster of Strathmore's Regiment, a prisoner at Preston in 1715, was transported via Liverpool aboard the Wakefield bound for South Carolina on 21 April 1716. [SPC.1716.309][CTB.31.205][CS.V.162] [NRS.GD1.53.72]

HENDRY, JAMES, was transported via Liverpool aboard the Friendship bound for Virginia on 24 May 1716, landed in Maryland in August 1716. [SPC.1716.311][HM.386]

HEPBURN, ALEXANDER, born 1657 in Buchan, Aberdeenshire, minister at St Fergus, Aberdeenshire, a Jacobite in 1715, deposed in 1716, died in Peterhead, Aberdeenshire, in 1737. [JAB.230]

HEPBURN, JAMES, son to Hepburn of Keith, [NRS.GD1.53.72.1]

HEPBURN, JOHN, son of Robert Hepburn of Keith, Banffshire, a prisoner at Preston later in London 1716. [CS.V.160/186]

HEPBURN, ROBERT, of Keith, Banffshire, a prisoner at Preston and in London in 1716. [CS.V.186][NRS.RH2.4.305.28]

HEPBURN, WILLIAM, a vintner and merchant in Aberdeen, a Jacobite in 1715, testament, 24 January 1751, Comm. Aberdeen, [NRS][JAB.13]

HERD, JOHN, was transported via Liverpool aboard the Susannah bound for South Carolina on 7 May 1716. [SPC.1716.309][CTB.31.206]

HERRING, JAMES, a tailor in Perth, carried arms, a prisoner in 1715. [NRS.B59.30.36]

HILL, JAMES, was transported via Liverpool aboard the Friendship bound for Virginia on 24 May 1716, landed in Maryland in August 1716. [SPC.1726.311][HM.387][MdArch.34.164]

HOLLAND, THOMAS, was transported via Liverpool aboard the Elizabeth and Anne bound for Jamaica or Virginia on 29 June 1716. [SPC.1716.310][CTB.31.208]

HOME, ALEXANDER, Earl of Home, a Jacobite was imprisoned in 1715, died in 1720. [SP]

HOME, FRANCIS, from Wedderburn, Duns, Berwickshire, was transported via Liverpool aboard the Elizabeth and Anne bound for Jamaica or Virginia on 29 June 1716, landed in Virginia in August 1716, settled in Rappahannock, Virginia. [NRS.GD1.53.72.1] [SPC.1716.310][CTB.31.208] [VSP.I.185][VMHB.38.106][CS.V.160]

HOME, GEORGE, of Wedderburn, Berwickshire, estate forfeited in 1715. [NRS.E659]

HOME, GEORGE, of Whitfield, parish of Coldingham, Berwickshire, estate forfeited in 1715. [NRS.E660]

HOME, GEORGE, born 1698, son of George Home of Wedderburn, Wedderburn Castle, Duns, Berwickshire, captured at Preston in 1715, emigrated to America in 1721, settled in Rappahannock, Culpepper County, Virginia, Crown Surveyor of Virginia, died 1760. [NRS.GD267.1.3][VMHB.20.397][UT.91][CS.V.160]

HOME, THOMAS, a prisoner at Preston, was transported via Liverpool aboard the Goodspeed bound for Virginia on 28 July 1716, landed in Maryland in August 1716. [NRS.GD1.53.72.1] [SPC.1716.310][CTB.31.209][HM.389][CS.V.160]

HORN, JOHN, of Westhall, Oyne, Aberdeenshire, son of Reverend James Horn and his wife Isabella Leslie, a Jacobite in 1715. [CRA.84][JAB.132][TNA.SP54.9.43]

HOUSTOUN, JOHN, of Houstoun, 1715. [NRS.GD220.5.455.26]

HUME, ALEXANDER, a prisoner at Preston, 1715. [NRS.GD1.53.72.1]

HUME, GEORGE, of Whitfield, the elder, a prisoner at Preston and in London, 1716. [CS.V.161/186] [NRS.GD1.53.72]

HUME, GEORGE, the younger, a prisoner at Preston, 1715. [NRS.GD1.53.72]

HUME, JAMES, of Ayton, Berwickshire, son of Charles Hume the Earl of Home, a Jacobite prisoner at Preston and in London in 1716, estate forfeited, 1715, died 6 December 1764. [CS.V.160/186][SP.III.479]NRS.E613][NRS.GD1.53.72.1]

HUME, ..., a Cornet, was killed at the Siege of Preston on 12 November 1715. [CS.V.133]

HUNTER, JOHN, was transported via Liverpool aboard the Elizabeth and Anne bound for Jamaica or Virginia on 29 June 1716. [SPC.1716.310][CTB.31.208]

HUNTER, PATRICK, was transported via Liverpool aboard the Friendship bound for Virginia on 24 May 1716, landed in Maryland in August 1716. [SPC.1716.311][CTB.31.207][HM.387]

HUNTER, WILLIAM, born 1662, son of Robert Hunter and his wife Mary Muschet, minister of Banff, a Jacobite in 1715, deposed in 1716, died 1730. [JAB.230][F.6.276]

HUTCHISON, JOHN, a merchant and late Provost of Arbroath, Angus, a Jacobite in 1715, a prisoner in Edinburgh and in Carlisle, escaped to Bordeaux, France, in 1716. [JAB.156][TNA.SP54.12.147][NRS.GD45.14.219.6] [CRA.230] [NRS.AC9.23M2; AC13.1.163]

HUTTON, WILLIAM, a mason and a burgess of Perth, a soldier in the Perth company in 1715. [NRS.B59.30.10.40]

IDELL, WILLIAM, minister at Coull, Aberdeenshire, a Jacobite in 1715, deposed in 1716. [F.6.90][JAB.231]

INNES, Sir GEORGE, of Coxton, son of Sir Alexander Innes and his wife Jean Rollo, fought at Sheriffmuir in 1715 and died in Scone, Perthshire in 1715. [JAB.134]; testament, 3 September 1723, Comm. Aberdeen. [NRS]

INNES, JAMES, son of Sir Alexander Innes of Coxton, a Jacobite in 1715, escaped to France in 1716. [JAB.134][OR.98]

INNES, JAMES, was transported via Liverpool aboard the Africa bound for Barbados on 15 July 1716. [SPC.1716.312][CTB.31.209]

INNES, JOHN, of Sinnahard, son of John Innes of Towie and his wife Anne Hay, Captain of Mar's Regiment, a prisoner at Preston in 1715, died in 1725. [JAB.135][CS.V.161] [NRS.GD1.53.72]; testaments 15 December 1718, and 5 December 1728, Comm. Aberdeen. [NRS]

INNES, JOHN, born 1649, minister at Gamrie, Banffshire, a Jacobite in 1715, was deposed in 1716, died 14 June 1731. [JAB.231][F.6.259]; testament, 25 March 1741, Comm. Aberdeen. [NRS]

IRVINE, ADAM, of Bruckley, son of Reverend Robert Irvine and his wife Agnes Murray, a Jacobite in 1715. [JAB.135][CRA.173]

IRVINE, ALEXANDER, of Drum, Tarland, Aberdeenshire, son of Alexander Irvine of Murthill and his wife Jane Irvine, fought at Sheriffmuir in 1715, escaped abroad in 1716, died 1735. [CRA.31][JAB.136]

IRVINE, ALEXANDER, of Crimond, Aberdeenshire, son of James Irvine of Artamford and his wife Margaret Sutherland, a Jacobite in 1715, died in 1746. [CRA.33]

IRVINE, JAMES, son of Robert Irvine and his wife Barbara Mitchell, the Sheriff Clerk of Kincardineshire, a Jacobite in 1715. [JAB.137]

IRVINE, JOHN, born 1652, a Roman Catholic priest, a Jacobite in 1715, died at Gordon Castle on 17 April 1717. [JAB.215]

IRVINE, JOHN, of Kincausie, son of John Irvine and his wife Elizabeth Ramsay, a Jacobite in 1715. [JAB.137]

IRVINE, WILLIAM, of Artamford, son of James Irvine and his wife Margaret Sutherland, a Jacobite in 1715. [JAB.137]

IRVINE, WILLIAM, born 1660, son of Alexander Irvine of Fortie, an Episcopalian chaplain, a Jacobite in 1715, a prisoner at Preston and in London, escaped, died in Edinburgh on 19 December 1725. [CS.V.52][JAB.232][CRA.190]

IRVING, JAMES, a prisoner at Carlisle, Cumberland, in December 1716. [SUL.Cheap.5.537

IRVING, WILLIAM, of Knockhill, a prisoner at Preston and in London in 1716. [CS.V.186] [NRS.GD1.53.72.1]

JACK, HENRY, a soldier in the Perth company in 1716. [NRS.B59.30.17]

JACK, JOHN, a soldier in the Perth company in 1716. [NRS.B59.30.17]

JACKSON, JOHN, a maltman and a burgess of Perth, a Jacobite in 1716. [NRS.B59.30.37/40]

JAFFREY, ANDREW, minister of Alford, Aberdeenshire, until deposed in 1716, a Jacobite in 1715. [F.6.118]

JAFFRAY, ANDREW, of Ardtannies, son of Alexander Jaffray and his wife Sarah Cant, a merchant in Aberdeen, a Jacobite in 1715. [JAB.138]

JOHNSON, WILLIAM, was transported via Liverpool aboard the Goodspeed bound for Virginia on 28 July 1716, landed in Maryland in October 1716. [SPC.1716.310][CTB.31.209][HM.388]

JOHNSTON, JAMES, was transported via Liverpool aboard the Elizabeth and Anne bound for Jamaica or Virginia on 29 June 1716, landed in Virginia in August 1716. [SPC.1716.310][CTB.31.208][VSP.1.186]

JOHNSTON, JOHN, a butcher in Perth, carried arms, surrendered in 1715. [NRS.B59.30.36]

JOHNSTON, Sir JOHN, of Keith-hall, fought at Sheriffmuir in 1715, died in Edinburgh in 1724. [CRA.98]

JOHNSTON, JOHN, son of Sir John Johnston, died at Sheriffmuir in 1715. [CRA.98]

JOHNSTON, JOHN, from Aberdeen, was transported via Liverpool settled in New Windsor, S.C., died in March 1744, probate 1744, South Carolina. [CTB.31.206][APB.3.122]

JOHNSTON, JOHN, son of Dugald Johnston in Ardnamurchan, Inverness-shire, Jacobite in 1715. [NRS.SC54.22.17.1-2]

JOHNSTON, Sir JOHN, of Caskieben, Aberdeenshire, son of John Johnston, fought at Sheriffmuir in 1715, died in Edinburgh in 1724. [JAB.138][CRA.230]

JOHNSTON, JOHN, son of Sir John Johnston of Caskieben, was killed at Sheriffmuir in 1715. [JAB.139][CRA.230]

JOHNSTON, JOHN, of Boginjoss, son of John Johnston and his wife Margaret Alexander, a Jacobite in 1715. [JAB.139]

JOHNSTON, JOHN, was transported via Liverpool aboard the Elizabeth and Anne bound for Jamaica or Virginia on 29 June 1716, landed in Virginia in August 1716. [SPC.1716.310][CTB.31.208][VSP.1.186]

JOHNSTON, ROBERT, was transported via Liverpool aboard the Elizabeth and Anne bound for Jamaica or Virginia on 29 June 1716, landed in Virginia in August 1716. [SPC.1716.310][CTB.31.208][VSP.1.186]

JOHNSTON, ROBERT, of Wamphrey, Dumfries-shire, a prisoner at Preston in 1715. [CS.V.160] [NRS.GD1.53.72]

JOHNSTON, WILLIAM, portioner of Drumcrief, a prisoner at
Preston in 1715. [CS.V.160] [NRS.GD1.53.72]

JOLLIE, WILLIAM, a Jacobite in 1715. [JAB.217]

KEIR, JAMES, a soldier of the Perth company in 1715.
[NRS.B59.30.10/17]

KEITH, ALEXANDER, of Northfield, son of George Keith, a Jacobite
in 1715. [JAB.139]

KEITH, GEORGE, born 1694, son of William Keith the Earl
Marischal, fought at Sheriffmuir in 1715, estates forfeited in
1715, escaped to France, died in Potsdam, Prussia, on 28 May
1778. [SP.V.64][NRS.E647]

KEITH, GEORGE, son of Sir William Keith of Ludquharn,
Aberdeenshire, an advocate in Aberdeen, a Jacobite in 1715, died
on 24 September 1738, testaments, 30 November 1738 and 7
September 1742, Comm. Aberdeen. [NRS][JAB.140]

KEITH, JAMES, an Episcopalian minister at Belhelvie,
Aberdeenshire, 1715-1716, a Jacobite in 1715. [F.6.47][JAB.233]

KEITH, JAMES FRANCIS EDWARD, born 16 June 1696 in Inverugie,
Aberdeenshire, son of William Keith the Earl Marischal, a Jacobite
in 1715, escaped in 1716, participated in the 1719 Rising, an
officer in the Spanish Army from 1721, later joined the Russian
Army in 1730 reaching the rank of Field Marshal and Governor of
the Ukraine, finally in 1747 entered Prussian service, died at
Hochkirchen on 14 October 1758. [UAL.GB231, ms3295][Scottish
National Portrait Gallery]

KEITH, JOHN, a tenant farmer in Aboyne, Aberdeenshire, a
Jacobite in 1715. [JAB.206]

KEITH, JOHN, son of the Earl of Kintore, fought at Sheriffmuir in 1715. [CRA.98]

KEITH, WILLIAM, the Earl of Kintore, Aberdeenshire, son of Sir John Keith, fought at Sheriffmuir in 1715, died 5 December 1718. [CRA.98][JAB.144][SP.V.241]

KEITH, Sir WILLIAM, of Ludquharn, Aberdeenshire, a Jacobite in 1715, escaped to France in 1716. [JAB.141]

KENNEDY, ALEXANDER, was transported via Liverpool aboard the Two Brothers bound for Jamaica on 26 April 1716, landed on Montserrat in June 1716. [SPC.1716.313][CTB.31.205][CTP.CC43]

KENNEDY, DANIEL, was transported via Liverpool aboard the Goodspeed bound for Virginia on 28 July 1716, landed in Maryland in October 1716. [SPC.1716.310][CTB.31.209][HM.389]

KENNEDY, JOHN, a gentleman, a Jacobite in 1715, was tried in Liverpool on 7 February 1716. [CS.V.95]

KENNEDY, JOHN, was transported via Liverpool aboard the Two Brothers bound for Jamaica on 26 April 1716, landed on Montserrat in June 1716. [SPC.1716.313][CTB.31.205][CTP.CC43]

KENNEDY, JOHN, was transported via Liverpool aboard the Scipio bound for Antigua on 30 March 1716. [SPC.1716.310][CTB.31.204]

KENNEDY, JOHN, was transported via Liverpool aboard the Elizabeth and Anne bound for Jamaica or Virginia on 29 June 1716, landed in Virginia. [SPC.1716.310][CTB.31.208][VSP.1.185]

KENNEDY, MALCOLM, a Jacobite in 1715, in Knock, Coll, April 1716. [NRS.SC54.22.17.1]

KENNEDY, MALCOLM, was transported via Liverpool aboard the Wakefield bound for South Carolina on 21 April 1716. [SPC.1716.309][CTB.31.205]

KENNEDY, MURDOCH, a Jacobite in 1715, in Knock, Coll, 1716. [NRS.SC54.22.17.1]

KENNEDY, RORIE, a laborer, a Jacobite in 1715, was executed at Preston on 9 February 1716. [CS.V.192]

KENNY, JOHN, was transported via Liverpool aboard the Goodspeed bound for Virginia on 28 July 1716, landed in Maryland in October 1716. [SPC.1716.310][HM.388]

KER, DUNCAN, a carter and a burgess of Perth, a soldier of the Perth company in 1715, a prisoner. [NRS.B59.30.17/37/40]

KER, HENRY, an Ensign of Strathmore's Battalion, a prisoner at Preston in 1715. [CS.V.162] [NRS.GD1.53.72]

KER, ROBERT, a prisoner at Preston, 1715. [NRS.GD1.53.72.1]

KERR, WILLIAM, of Arbivinal, a prisoner at Carlisle, in December 1716. [SUL.Cheap.5.537]

KIDD, ALEXANDER, was transported via Liverpool aboard the Elizabeth and Anne bound for Jamaica or Virginia on 29 June 1716, landed in Virginia. [SPC.1716.310][CTB.31.208][VSP.1.185]

KID, JAMES, a precentor and schoolmaster in Arbroath, Angus, a Jacobite in 1715. [HHA.171]

KINARTY, JOHN, of Dowly, Perthshire, a Jacobite in 1715, died in Lancaster Prison on 23 March 1716. [LBR]

KINLOCH, Sir JAMES, of Ogilvy's Regiment, fought at Sheriffmuir in 1715. [MHP.294]

KINLOCH, JOHN, a Jacobite in 1715. [MHP.303][NRS.GD1.931]

KINLOCH, Dr, brother to Kilrie, a prisoner in Carlisle in December 1716. [SUL.Cheap.5.537]

KINNAIRD, CHARLES, 1715. [HMC.Stuart.i.525]

LAING, HENRY, a glover and a burgess of Perth, a soldier of the Perth company in 1715. [NRS.B59.30.17/40]

LAING, WILLIAM, a soldier of the Perth company in 1715. [NRS.B59.30.17]

LAMONT, DUNCAN, a Jacobite in 1715, in Ardchiavaig, Ross, Mull, 1716. [NRS.SC54.22.17.2]

LAMONT, MALCOLM, a Jacobite in 1715, in Kinlochscriden, Broloss, Mull, 1716. [NRS.SC54.22.17.2]

LAMONT, MURDOCH, a Jacobite in 1715, in Carsaig, Broloss, Mull, 1716. [NRS.SC54.22.17.2]

LAMONT, NEIL, a Jacobite in 1715, on Iona, Argyll, in 1716. [NRS.SC54.22.17.2]

LAUDER, DAVID, was transported via Liverpool aboard the Goodspeed bound for Virginia on 28 July 1716, landed in Maryland in October 1716. [SPC.1716.310][CTB.31.209][HM.388]

LAUDER, GEORGE, was transported via Liverpool aboard the Elizabeth and Anne bound for Jamaica or Virginia on 29 June 1716, landed in Virginia. [SPC.1716.310][CTB.31.208][VSP.1.186]

LAUDER, JAMES, an Episcopalian minister in Perthshire, a Jacobite in 1715. [NRS.B59.20.1]

LAUDER, ..., of Killilung, a prisoner at Preston in 1715. [CS.V.161] [NRS.GD1.53.72]

LAW, ALEXANDER, minister at Kearn, Aberdeenshire, a Jacobite in 1715, deposed in 1716. [F.6.121][JAB.333]

LAW, WILLIAM, minister at Slains, Aberdeenshire, a Jacobite in
1715, deposed in 1716. [JAB.233]

LAWRENCE, JAMES, the beadle of the parish of St Vigean's,
Angus, a Jacobite in 1715, deposed in April 1716.
[HHA.170][NRS.CH2.15.3]

LAWRY, THOMAS, was transported via Liverpool aboard the
Friendship bound for Virginia on 24 May 1716, landed in
Maryland in August 1716. [SPC.1716.311][HM.386]

LAWTON, ALEXANDER, was transported via Liverpool aboard the
Hockenhill bound for St Kitts on 25 June 1716, mutinied and
landed on Sint Maartens in September 1716.
[SPC.1716.312][CTB.31.207][JAB.21]

LEITH, ALEXANDER, of Freeland, Rayne, Aberdeenshire, born
1664, son of James Leith and his wife Margaret Strachan, Colonel
of Glenbucket's Regiment, a Jacobite in 1715, died 1754.
[CRA.78][JAB.146]

LEITH, GEORGE, servant to the Earl of Errol, a Jacobite in 1715.
[JAB.217]

LEITH, JOHN, of Leith-hall, son of James Leith, a Jacobite in 1715.
[JAB.14][TNA.SP54.12]

LEITH, PATRICK, minister at Lumphanan, Aberdeenshire, from
168- until deposed in 1716, a Jacobite in 1715. [F.6.106][JAB.233]

LEMON, JOHN, was transported via Liverpool aboard the
Susannah bound for South Carolina on 7 May 1716.
[SPC.1716.309][CTB.31.206]

LESLIE, ALEXANDER, Major of the Earl of Panmure's Regiment of
Foot in 1715, escaped to Bordeaux, France, by 1719.
[NRS.GD45.1.201]

LESLIE, CHARLES, an Episcopalian chaplain at the Jacobite Court at Urbino, Italy, in 1716. [JU]

LESLIE, CHARLES, born 1667, natural son of .....Leslie of Pitcaple, a Jacobite in 1715, died in Old Rayne, Aberdeenshire, 1728. [JAB.147]

LESLIE, JAMES, son of Reverend Alexander Leslie and his wife Helen Seymour, a Jacobite in 1715, died 1730. [JAB.147]

LESLIE, JOHN, a soldier of the Perth company in 1715. [NRS.B59.30.17]

LESLIE, JOHN, in Tullibardine's Regiment, fought at Sheriffmuir in 1715, captured. [CAT.II.206]

LESLIE, JOHN, a baillie of Aberdeen, a Jacobite in 1715, testament, 18 September 1730, Comm. Aberdeen [NRS][JAB.147]

LESLIE, ROBERT, in Montpellier, France, 1716. [HMC.Stuart pp.ii.102]

LESLIE, WILLIAM, born 1651, son of George Leslie of Little Folla and his wife Isabella Cheyne, minister at Ellon, Aberdeenshire, a Jacobite in 1715, died 1722. [JAB.235]

LIDDELL, GEORGE, son of Duncan Liddell and his wife Jean Montgomery, Professor of Mathematics at Marischal College, Aberdeen, a Jacobite in 1715. [JAB.148][TNA.SP54.12.39]

LINDSAY, ALEXANDER, a baker in Perth, carried arms in 1715, a prisoner. [NRS.B59.30.36/37/40]

LINDSAY, COLIN, the Earl of Balcarres, born 1652, son of Alexander Lindsay and his wife Anna Mackenzie, fought at Sheriffmuir in 1715, died in 1723. [SP.I.522]

LINDSAY, HENRY, son of Reverend David Lindsay in Rescobie, Angus, minister of Dunnichen, Angus, from 1682, a Jacobite in 1715, deposed in 1716, died 1720. [F.V.282]

LINDSAY, JAMES, was transported via Liverpool aboard the Elizabeth and Anne bound for Jamaica or Virginia on 29 June 1716, landed in Virginia. [SPC.1716.310][CTB.31.208][VSP.I.186]

LINDSAY, JOHN, of Pitscandly, parish of Rescobie, Angus, a prisoner at Carlisle in December 1716, estates forfeited in 1715. [SUL.Cheap.5.537][NRS.E652]

LINDSAY, JOHN, born 14 November 1691, son of Colin Lindsay the Earl of Balcarres, fought at Sheriffmuir in 1715. [SP.I.522]

LINDSAY, ROBERT, a Jacobite in 1715. [CRA.28]

LINDSAY, ROBERT, an Episcopalian preacher in Edzell, Angus, a Jacobite in 1715, deposed in 1716. [NRS.CH2.575.1][F.V.390]

LINDSAY, WILLIAM, a goldsmith in Aberdeen, Jacobite tax collector in 1715. [JAB.208]

LISTER, JOHN, of Clerkseat, son of Alexander Lister, a burgess of Aberdeen, a Jacobite in 1715. [JAB.148]

LIVINGSTON, ANDREW, minister at Kelg, Aberdeenshire, from 1683 until he was deposed in 1716, a Jacobite in 1715. [F.6.128][JAB.235]

LIVINGSTONE, JAMES, Earl of Linlithgow and Callander, son of Alexander Livingstone and his wife Anne Graham, a Jacobite in 1715, fought at Sheriffmuir in 1715, escaped to the continent in 1716, estate forfeited in 1715, settled in Avignon, Urbino, and died in Rome on 25 April 1723. [NRS.E644] [JCR.43][SI.365] [SP.V.450; II.363]

LIVINGSTONE, WILLIAM, Viscount Kilsyth, fought at Sheriffmuir in 1715, estate forfeited, died in Rome 1733. [SI.365] [NRS.E640]

LIVINGSTON, WILLIAM, minister at Deer, Aberdeenshire, a Jacobite in 1715, died in 1751. [JAB.235]

LOCKHART, GEORGE, of Carnwath, Lanarkshire, born 1673, a prisoner in 1715, escaped to Holland, a Jacobite agent in Scotland from 1718 to 1727. [NRS.GD220.5.453.16; GD220.5.642.1; GD220.5.623.3]

LOCKHART, Captain PHILIP, brother of George Lockhart of Carnwath, Lanarkshire, a Jacobite in 1715, was captured, court-martialled, and shot at Preston.
[MHP.296][CS.V.161/175][CAT.II.217] [NRS.GD1.53.72]

LOGAN, JOHN, a Jacobite in 1715. [JAB.217]

LONGMUIR, WILLIAM, schoolmaster of Rothiemay, a Jacobite in 1715. [JAB.148]

LOW, ABRAHAM, was transported via Liverpool aboard the Friendship bound for Virginia on 24 May 1716, landed in Maryland in August 1716. [SPC.1716.311][HM.386]

LOW, JAMES, was transported via Liverpool aboard the Friendship bound for Virginia on 24 May 1716, landed in Maryland in August 1716. [SPC.1716.311][HM.386]

LOW, ROBERT, sr., a soldier of the Perth company in 1715. [NRS.B59.30.17]

LOW, ROBERT, Jr., a soldier of the Perth company in 1715. [NRS.B59.30.17]

LOWRIE, ALEXANDER, a prisoner at Preston in 1715. [CS.V.160] [NRS.GD1.53.72]

LUMSDEN, DAVID, of Cushnie, Aberdeenshire, born 1682, son f Alexander Lumsden and his wife Elizabeth Leith, a Jacobite in 1715, died on 23 December 1718. [JAB.150][CRA.112]

LUMSDEN, HARRY, of Auchindoir, Aberdeenshire, born 1685, son of Alexander Lumsden and his wife Agnes Gordon, a Lieutenant of Mar's Battalion, a prisoner at Preston, was transported via Liverpool aboard the Friendship bound for Virginia on 24 May 1716, landed in Maryland in August 1716, returned to Scotland, died at Kildrummy, Aberdeenshire, on 8 June 1754. [SPC.1716.311][HM.387][JAB.152][CS.V.161][CRA.113] [NRS.GD1.53.72]

LUNAN, ALEXANDER, born 1647, son of Reverend William Lunan, minister of Daviot, Inverness-shire from 1672 until he was deposed in 1716, a Jacobite in 1715, died 1731. [F.6.156]

LUNDY, CHARLES, was transported via Liverpool aboard the Scipio bound for Antigua on 30 March 1716. [SPC.1716.310][CTB.31.204]

LUTHEART, WILLIAM, an Excise officer from Dumfries, a prisoner at Preston in 1715. [CS.V.160] [NRS.GD1.53.72]

LYON, JOHN, born 1690, 5th Earl of Strathmore, Commander of Tullibardine's Regiment, was killed at Sheriffmuir on 13 November 1715. [MHP.298][SP.VIII.306]

LYON, JAMES, son of Frederick Lyon late minister at Airlie, Angus, fought at Sheriffmuir in 1715, a prisoner. [CAT.II.205]; was transported aboard the pink Marlborough of Leith master John Hutton, from Leith to London in December 1715. [NRS.RH2.4.308]

LYON, PATRICK, of Auchterhouse, Angus, a Lieutenant Colonel of the Earl of Strathmore's Regiment, son of the Earl of Strathmore, was killed at the Battle of Sheriffmuir on 13 November 1715. [MHP.293[JAB.10][CAT.II.205][SP.VIII.303]

LYON, PATRICK, minister at Kinghorn, Fife, a Jacobite in 1715, deposed in 1716. [NRS.GD124.9.85][F.V.94]

LYON, PATRICK, schoolmaster of Dundee Grammar School, and an Episcopalian, was deposed on 1 May 1716. [NRS.CH2.103.8][DCA.Town Council Minutes, 1 May 1716]

LYON, PHILIP, was transported via Liverpool aboard the Wakefield bound for South Carolina on 21 April 1716. [SPC.1716.309][CTB.31.205]

LYON, PATRICK, of Auchterhouse, Lieutenant Colonel of the Earl of Panmure's Regiment of Foot in 1715. [NRS.GD45.1.201]

LYON, ROBERT, an Ensign of the Earl of Panmure's Regiment of Foot in 1715. [NRS.GD45.1.201]

LYON, WILLIAM, a Lieutenant of Strathmore's Battalion, a prisoner at Preston, was transported via Liverpool aboard the Elizabeth and Anne bound for Jamaica or Virginia on 29 June 1716, landed in Virginia. [SPC.1716.310][CTB.31.208] [CS.V.162][VSP.I.186] [NRS.GD1.53.72]

LYON, WILLIAM, a magistrate of Dundee, a Jacobite in 1715. [NRS.RH2.4.308/170]

LYON, ..., son of the Reverend George Lyon minister of Tannadice, Angus, "hung as a rebel in 171...".[F.V.305]

MCALISTER, PHILIP, a Jacobite in 1715, on Iona, Argyll, in 1716. [NRS.SC54.22.17.2]

MCCALLAN, ALLAN VCEWAN, a Jacobite in 1715, in Drumnatorran, Sunart, 1716. [NRS.SC54.22.17.1]

MCALLAN OIG CAMERON, EWAN, a Jacobite in 1715, in Camisean, Sunart, 1716. [NRS.SC54.22.17.1]

MCALLANVE {?}, ALEXANDER, a Jacobite in 1715, in Achanaha, Ardnamurchan, 1716. [NRS.SC54.22.17.1]

MCARTNA, ARCHIBALD, a Jacobite in 1715, in Asopoll, Ross, Mull, 1716. [NRS.SC54.22.17.2]

MCBANE, FERGUS, a Captain of Macintosh's Regiment, a prisoner at Preston in 1715. [NRS.GD1.53.72]

MCBEAN, ANGUS, Captain of McIntosh's Regiment, a prisoner at Preston, was transported via Liverpool aboard the Anne bound for Virginia on 31 July 1716.
[SPC.1716.310][CTB.31.209][CS.V.162]

MCBEAN, DANIEL, was transported via Liverpool aboard the Anne bound for Virginia on 31 July 1716.
[SPC.1716.309][CTB.31.206]

MCBEAN, FRANCIS, was transported via Liverpool aboard the Goodspeed bound for Virginia on 28 July 1716, landed in Maryland in October 1716. [SPC.1716.310][CTB.31.209][HM.388]

MCBEAN, JOHN, a Subaltern of McIntosh's Regiment, a prisoner at Preston, was transported via Liverpool aboard the Elizabeth and Anne bound for Jamaica or Virginia on 29 Jun 1716.
[SPC.1716.310][CTB.31.208][CS.V.162] [NRS.GD1.53.72]

MCBEAN, JOHN, was transported via Liverpool aboard the Friendship bound for Virginia on 24 May 1716, landed in Maryland in August 1716.
[SPC.1716.311][HM.387][MdArch.34.164]

MCBEAN, JOHN, was transported via Liverpool aboard the Anne bound for Virginia on 31 July 1716. [CTB.31.209]

MCBEAN, LACHLAN, was transported via Liverpool aboard the Wakefield bound for South Carolina on 21 April 1716. [SPC.1716.309][CTB.31.205]

MCBEAN, LOUGHLIN, was transported via Liverpool aboard the Wakefield bound for South Carolina on 21 April 1716. [CTB.31.205]

MCBEAN, WILLIAM, was transported via Liverpool aboard the Friendship bound for Virginia on 24 May 1716, landed in Maryland on 20 August 1716. [SPC.1716.311][HM.386]

MCBHODICH, HUGH, a Jacobite in 1715, in Beach, Broloss, Mull, 1716. [NRS.SC54.22.17.2]

MCBHODICH, JOHN, a Jacobite in 1715, in Bunessan, Ross, Mull, 1716. [NRS.SC54.22.17.2]

MCBRAYNE, LACHLAN, was transported via Liverpool aboard the Wakefield bound for South Carolina on 21 April 1716. [SPC.1716.309]

MCCALLUM, DONALD, was transported via Liverpool aboard the Susannah bound for South Carolina on 7 May 1716. [SPC.1716.309][CTB.31.206]

MCCALLUM, DUNCAN, was transported via Liverpool aboard the Susannah bound for South Carolina on 7 May 1716. [SPC.1716.309][CTB.31.206]

MCCALLUM, JOHN, was transported via Liverpool aboard the Two Brothers bound for Jamaica on 26 April 1716, landed on Montserrat in June 1716. [SPC.1716.313][CTB.31.205][CTP.CC.43]

MCCALLUM, JOHN, a laborer, a prisoner at Preston, was condemned on 25 January 1716. [CS.V.193]

MCCALLUM, JOHN, was transported via Liverpool aboard the Goodspeed bound for Virginia on 28 July 1716, landed in Maryland in October 1716. [SPC.1716.310][HM.389]

MCCALLUM, MALCOLM, was transported via Liverpool aboard the Goodspeed bound for Virginia on 28 July 1716, landed in Maryland in October 1716. [SPC.1716.310][HM.388][CTB.31.209]

MCCANN, EDWARD, was transported via Liverpool aboard the Two Brothers bound for Jamaica on 26 April 1716, landed on Montserrat in June 1716. [SPC.1716.313][CTP.CC.43]

MCCHARLES VCQUARRIE, HECTOR, a Jacobite in 1715, in Keil, Coll, 1716. [NRS.SC54.22.17.1]

MCCLASER, ALEXANDER, was transported via Liverpool aboard the Two Brothers bound for Jamaica on 26 April 1716, landed on Montserrat in June 1716. [SPC.1716.313][CTP.CC.43][CTB.31.206]

MCCLELLAN, ROBERT, of Barscob, was a prisoner at Preston and in London. [CS.V.160/186][NRS.GD1.53.72.1]

MCCLOCHRIET, ARCHIBALD, a Subaltern, captured at Preston, 1715. [NRS.GD1.53.72]

MCCOAN, JOHN, a Jacobite in 1715, in Crogan, Kinlochbuy, Mull, 1716. [NRS.SC54.22.17.2]

MCCOLL, DONALD, a tenant of Duncan Stewart in Swordle, Ardnamurchan, fought at Sheriffmuir in 1715. [NRS.S54.22.17.1]

MCCOLL, DUNCAN NA CRONIE, a Jacobite in 1715, may have fought at Sheriffmuir, later in Glenborrodale. Ardnamurchan, Inverness-shire. [NRS.SC54.22.17.1-2]

MCCOLL, SORLE, a Jacobite in 1715, in Tarbert, Ardnamuchan, 1716. [NRS.SC54.22.17.1]

MCCONACHIE, JOHN MCILVRA or MCPHERSON, a Jacobite in 1715, at Braynanalt, Ardnamurchan, 1716. [NRS.SC54.22.17.1]

MCCOLL, JOHN, a Jacobite in 1715, in Glenborodale, Ardnamurchan, in 1716. [NRS.SC54.22.17.1]

MCCORRARE, JOHN DOW, a Jacobite in 1715, in Totmore, Coll, 1716. [NRS.SC54.22.17.1]

MCCOY, DANIEL, was transported via Liverpool aboard the Scipio bound for Antigua on 30 March 1716. [SPC.1716.310][CTB.31.204]

MCCOY, DONALD, was transported via Liverpool aboard the Susannah bound for South Carolina on 7 May 1716. [SPC.1716.310][CTB.31.204]

MCCOY, HUGH, was transported via Liverpool aboard the Wakefield bound for South Carolina on 21 April 1716. [SPC.1716.309][CTB.31.205]

MCCOY, JOHN, was transported via Liverpool aboard the Hockenhill bound for St Kitts on 25 June 1716, mutinied and landed on Sint Maartens in September 1716. [SPC.1716.309] [JAB.21][CTB.31.205]

MCCOY, JOHN, was transported via Liverpool aboard the Wakefield bound for South Carolina on 21 April 1716. [CTB.31.205]

MCCOY, JOHN, was transported via Liverpool aboard The Two Brothers bound for Jamaica on 26 April 1716, landed on Montserrat in June 1716. [SPC.1716.310][CTP.CC.43][CTB.31.204]

MCCOY, PATRICK, was transported via Liverpool aboard the Goodspeed bound for Virginia on 28 July 1716, landed in Maryland in October 1716. [SPC.1716.310][HM.389] [CTB.31.209]

MCCOY, PAUL, was transported via Liverpool aboard the Scipio bound for Antigua on 30 March 1716.[SPC.1716.310][CTB.31.204]

MCCRAING, HECTOR, son of Clandullie McCraing, a Jacobite in 1715, in Kilbrenan, Torloisk, 1716. [NRS.SC54.54.22.17.2]

MCCULLO, DAVID, a soldier of the Perth company in 1715. [NRS.B59.30.17]

MCCULLOCH, ROBERT, was transported via Liverpool aboard The Two Brothers bound for Jamaica on 26 April 1716, landed on Montserrat in June 1716. [SPC.1716.313][CTP.CC.43][CTB.31.206]

MCDANELL, DANIEL, was transported via Liverpool aboard the Scipio bound for Antigua on 30 March 1716. [SPC.1716.310]

MCDARRAN, ARCHIBALD, was transported via Liverpool aboard the Friendship bound for Virginia on 24 May 1716, landed in Maryland in August 1716. [SPC.1716.311][HM.387]

MCDERMOTT, ANGUS, was transported via Liverpool aboard the Two Brothers bound for Jamaica on 26 April 1716, landed on Montserrat in June 1716. [SPC.1716.313][CTP.CC.43][CTB.31.206]

MCDERMOTT, ANGUS, was transported via Liverpool aboard the Goodspeed bound for Virginia on 28 July 1716, landed in Maryland in October 1716. [SPC.1716.310][CTB.31.209][CTP.CC.43]

MCDERMOTT, JOHN, was transported via Liverpool aboard the Scipio bound for Antigua on 30 March 1716. [SPC.1716.310] [CTB.31.204]

MCDHOIL, alias MCLEAN, ALLAN, a Jacobite in 1715, in Suij, Ross, Mull, 1716. [NRS.SC54.22.17.2]

MCDHOIL, ANGUS, a Jacobite in 1715, in Carsaig, Brloss, Mull,, 1716. [NRS.SC54.22.17.2]

MCDHOIL VCEARLINE, EWAN, a Jacobite n 1715, in Torraston, Coll, 1716. [NRS.SC54.22.17.1]

MCDHOIL, FERQUHAR VAIN, a Jacobite in 1715, in Breckachie, Coll, in 1716. [NRS.SC54.22.17.1]

MCDHOIL OIG VCGOWN, JOHN, a Jacobite in 1715, in Anaheilt, Sunart, 1716. [NRS.SC54.22.17.1]

MCDHOIL, JOHN VCINNISH, a Jacobite in 1715, in sSallachan, Morvern, 1716. [NRS.SC54.22.17.2]

MCDHOIL VOIR VCALESTER, a Jacobite in 1715, in Gorteneorn, Ardnamurchan, 1716. [NRS.SC54.22.17.1]

MCDHOUILL, JOHN, a workman in Auchnellan, Sunart, Inverness-shire, a Jacobite in 1715. [NRS.SC54.22.17.1-2]

MCDIARMID, ALEXANDER, a Jacobite in 1715, a workman in Achinellan, Sunart, 1716. [NRS.SC54.22.17.1]

MCDONACHIE, ANGUS, a Jacobite in 1715, in Ballihogh, Coll, in 1716. [NRS.SC54.22.17.1]

MACDONALD, ALASTAIR, born 1698, a Jacobite in 1715, escaped to France, died in 1746.

MACDONALD, ALEXANDER, of Glencoe, parish of Lismore and Appin, Argyll, estate forfeited in 1715. [NRS.E675]

MCDONALD, ALEXANDER, of Glengarry, a Jacobite at Sheriffmuir, 1715. [NRS.RH2.4.308/170][TNA.SP54.8.94]

MACDONALD, ALLAN, born 1675, 14TH Chief of Clanranald, of Ormiclate House, South Uist, fought at Killiecrankie in 1689, and with his clan at Sheriffmuir in 1715, of Ormiclate House, South Uist, died of wounds on 14 November 1715 at Drummond Castle, Perthshire. [JP.31][NRS.RH2.4.308/170]

MCDONALD, ALLAN, of Clanranald, at the Jacobite Court in Urbino, Italy, 1717 [JU]

MCDONALD, ANGUS, in Balliscate, Aros, Mull, a Jacobite in 1715, fought at Sheriffmuir. [NRS.SC54.22.17.1-2]

MCDONALD, ANGUS ROY, a Jacobite in 1715, in Arnabost, Coll, 1716. [NRS.SC54.22.17.1]

MCDONALD, ARCHIBALD, possibly from Perthshire, petitioned for transportation in 1716. [CAT.II.240]

MCDONALD, ARCHIBALD, a Jacobite in 1715, at Kilmorie, Ardnamurchan in 1716. [NRS.SC54.22.17.1]

MCDONALD, ARCHIBALD, a Jacobite in 1715, in Camisnagaell, Ardnamuchan, 1716. [NRS.SC54.22.17.1]

MCDONALD, COLL, was transported via Liverpool aboard the Wakefield bound for South Carolina on 21 April 1716. [SPC.1716.309][CTB.31.205]

MXDONALD, COLL, of Keppoch, 1716. [NRS.RH2.4.310.154]

MCDONALD, DENIS, was transported via Liverpool aboard the Two Brothers bound for Jamaica on 26 April 1716, landed on Montserrat in June 1716. [SPC.1716.313][CTP.CC.43][CTB.31.205]

MACDONALD, Sir DONALD, of Sleat, son of Sir Donald MacDonald and his wife Mary Douglas, fought with his clan at the Battle of Sheriffmuir, 16 September 1715, his estates in Inverness-shire were forfeited in 1715, was created Lord Sleat by King James, died 1718. [JP.167][MHP.297][NRS.E656][NRS.RH2.4.308]

MCDONALD, DONALD, a Jacobite in 1715, Baillie of Canna, in Tarbert, Canna, 1716. [NRS.SC54.22.17.1]

MCDONALD, DONALD MCINNISH VCEAN DHOIL, a Jacobite in 1715, in Pennimolloch, 1716. [NRS.SC54.22.17.2]

MACDONALD, DONALD, a gentleman, was executed in Preston on 9 February 1716. [CS.V.192]

MCDONALD, DONALD, was transported via Liverpool aboard the Wakefield bound for South Carolina on 21 April 1716. [SPC.1716.309][CTB.31.205]

MCDONALD, DONALD, was transported via Liverpool aboard the Scipio bound for Antigua on 30 March 1716. [CTB.31.204]

MCDONALD, EVAN, of Dowly, Perthshire, a Jacobite, died in Lancaster Prison on 29 March 1716. [LBR]

MCDONALD, JAMES, was transported via Liverpool aboard the Susannah bound for South Carolina on 7 May 1716. [SPC.1716.309][CTB.31.206]

MCDONALD, JOHN, of Dalchoisnie, Inverness-shire, a Subaltern of Nairne's Regiment, a prisoner at Preston. [CAT.II.210][CS.V.161] [NRS.GD1.53.72]

MCDONALD, JOHN, son of Alexander McDonald, a Jacobite in 1715, in Achanaha, Ardnamurchan, in 1716. [NRS.SC54.22.17.1]

MCDONALD, JOHN, was transported via Liverpool aboard the Susannah bound for South Carolina on 7 May 1716. [SPC.1716.309][CTB.31.206]

MCDONALD, JOHN, was transported via Liverpool aboard the Wakefield bound for South Carolina on 21 April 1716. [SPC.1716.309][CTB.31.205]

MCDONALD, JOHN,, was transported via Liverpool aboard the Friendship bound for Virginia on 24 May 1716, landed in Maryland on 20 August 1716. [SPC.1716.311][HM.387]

MCDONALD, JOHN, from Moy, Inverness-shire, died in Lancaster Prison on 15 February 1715. [LBR]

MCDONALD, LACHLAN, a Jacobite in 1715, in Bunessan, Ross, Mull, 1716. [NRS.SC54.22.17.2]

MCDONALD, NEIL, a Jacobite at the Battle of Sheriffmuir in 1715, in Breacachadh, Coll, in 1716. [NRS.SC54.22.54]

MACDONALD, RONALD, of Clanranald, South Uist, estate forfeited in 1715, participated in the 1719 Rising. [NRS.E648][NRS.GD201/1/204]

MCDONAL, RONALD, a Jacobite in 1715, in Camisnagaell, Ardnamurchan, 1716. [NRS.SC54.22.17.1]

MCDONALD, RORY, was transported via Liverpool aboard the Susannah bound for South Carolina on 7 May 1716. [SPC.1716.309][CTB.31.206]

MCDONALD, WILLIAM, was transported via Liverpool aboard the Two Brothers bound for Jamaica on 26 April 1716, landed on Montserrat in June 1716. [SPC.1716.313][CTP.CC.43][CTB.31.206]

MCDONALD, WILLIAM, was transported via Liverpool aboard the Susannah bound for South Carolina on 7 May 1716. [SPC.1716.313][CTB.31.206][CTP.CC.43]

MCDONALD, WILLIAM, from Moy, Inverness-shire, a Jacobite, died in Lancaster Prison on 9 May 1716. [LBR]

MCDONALD, ..., of Shian, a Jacobite at Sheriffmuir, 1715. [NRS.RH2.4.308/170];

MCDONALD, ..., of Sarlil, a Jacobite at Sheriffmuir, 1715. [NRS.RH2.4.308/170]

MCDONALD, ..., of Kiltry, a Jacobite at Sheriffmuir, 1715.
[NRS.RH2.4.308/170];

MCDONALD, ..., of Auchtira, a Jacobite at Sheriffmuir, 1715.
[NRS.RH2.4.308/170];

MACDONELL, ALASTAIR, of Glengarry, son of Ranald MacDonell and his wife Flora MacLeod, fought at Killiecrankie in 1689, and at Sheriffmuir with his clan in 1715, was created Lord MacDonell in 1716, died in 1724. [JP.85]

MACDONELL, ALLAN, a Jacobite, died in Lancaster Prison on 24 March 1716. [LBR]

MCDONELL, COLL, of Keppoch, at the Jacobite Court in Urbino, Italy, 171. [JU]

MCDONELL, DENIS, was transported via Liverpool aboard the Two Brothers bound for Jamaica on 26 April 1716, landed on Montserrat in June 1716. [SPC.1716.313][CTP.CC.43]

MACDONELL, DONALD, of Tullochcroisk, a Subaltern of Charles Murray's Regiment, fought at Preston, taken prisoner, tried 23 January 1716 and executed at Preston on 9 February 1716. [MHP.303][CAT.II.211][CS.V.161]

MCDONELL, JOHN, from Benvie, Perthshire, a Jacobite, died in Lancaster Prison on 16 May 1716. [LBR]

MCDOUGALL, ALEXANDER, was transported via Liverpool aboard the Friendship bound for Virginia on 24 May 1716, landed in Maryland in August 1716. [SPC.1716.311][HM.387]

MCDUGALL, HUGH, was transported via Liverpool aboard the Goodspeed bound for Virginia on 28 July 1716, landed in Maryland in October 1716. [SPC.1716.310][HM.389] [CTB.31.209]

MCDOUGALL, JOHN, of Lorn, Kilbride parish, Argyll, estate forfeited in 1715. [NRS.E683]

MCDOUGALL, JOHN, of Dunollie, husband of Mary McDonald, 1715. [NRS.RH2.4.308.92]

MCDOWAL, DONALD, a subaltern of Murray's Regiment, a prisoner at Preston in 1716. [NRS.GD1.53.72]

MCDUFFIE, EWAN, a Jacobite in 1715, a workman in Anaheilt, Sunart, 1716. [NRS.SC54.22.17.1]

MCDUFFIE, EWAN, a Jacobite in 1715, in Strontian, Sunart, 1716. [NRS.SC54.22.17.1]

MCDULLEN, ROBERT, a prisoner at Preston in 1715. [CS.V.160] [NRS.GD1.53.72]

MCEACHERN, ANGUS, a Jacobite in 1715, in Ferinish Carnacalloch, Morvern, 1716. [NRS.SC54.22.17.2]

MCEACHERN, DONALD, a Jacobite in 1715, a tenant in Ranochanmore, Sunart, 1716. [NRS.SC54.22.17.1]

MCEACHERN, DONALD, a Jacobite in 1715, in Penguila , Morvern, 1716. [NRS.SC54.22.17.2]

MCEACHERN, DUNCAN, a Jacobite in 1715, in Kilfhinichen, Broloss, Mull, 1716. [NRS.SC54.22.17.2]

MCEACHERN, DUNCAN, a Jacobite in 1715, in Achanaha, Morvern, 1716. [NRS.SC54.22.17.2]

MCEACHERN, EWAN, a Jacobite in 1715, in Kingastill, Morvern, 1716. [NRS.SC54.22.17.2]

MCEACHERN, JOHN, a Jacobite in 1715, in Beach, Morvern, 1716. [NRS.SC54.22.17.2]

MCEACHERN, NEIL, a Jacobite in 1715, on Iona, Argyll, in 1716. [NRS.SC54.22.54]

MCEACHERN, NEIL, a Jacobite in 1715, an officer in Derrigave, Sunart, 1716. [NRS.SC54.22.17.1]

MCEAN, ALEXANDER VCREILL, a Jacobite in 1715, in Hyenish, Mull, Argyll. [NRS.SC54.22.17.1-2]

MCEAN, ARCHIBALD, a Jacobite in 1715, in Laga, Ardnamurchan, 1716. [NRS.SC54.22.17.1]

MCEAN, DONALD bane, a Jacobite in 1715, in Achalinan, Morvern, 1716. [NRS.SC54.22.17.2]

MCEAN, EWAN VCDOIL DHU, a Jacobite in 1715, in Crossaboll, Coll, in 1716. [NRS.SC54.22.17.1]

MCEAN, RORIE MCEWAN, a Jacobite in 1715, in Crossaboll, Coll, 1716. [NRS.SC54.22.17.1]

MCEAN, JOHN VCGILPATRICK, a Jacobite in 1715, in Crossaboll, Coll, in 1716. [NRS.SC54.22.17.1]

MCEAN, JOHN MCINNISH, a Jacobite in 1715, in Keylliemore, Aros, Mull, 1716. [NRS.SC54.22.17.2.]

MCEAN, JOHN VCALESTAR, a Jacobite in 1715, in Keylliemore, Aros, Mull, 1716. [NRS.SC54.22.17.2.]

MCEAN, MALCOLM VCJUNIFFE, a Jacobite in 1715, in Kinlochscridan, Broloss, Mull,, 1716. [NRS.SC54.22.17.2]

MCEAN, ..., of Glencoe, a Jacobite at Sheriffmuir, 1715. [NRS.RH2.4.308/170];

MCEOIN, JOHN VCILLCHALLUM, a Jacobite in 1715, on Creich on the Ross of Mull, Argyll, in 1716. [NRS.SC54.22.17.2]

MCERRICHER, COLIN ROY MCILVRA, a Jacobite in 1715, in Sunopole, Morenish, 1716. [NRS.SC54.22.17.2.]

MCEWAN, JOHN, a merchant in Dunkeld, Perthshire, a Subaltern of Murray's Battalion, fought at Preston in 1715, taken prisoner, tried 1 February 1716 – guilty, may have died at Lancaster. [CAT.II.211]

MCEWAN, JOHN, was transported via Liverpool aboard the Goodspeed bound for Virginia on 28 July 1716, landed in Maryland in October 1716. [SPC.1716.310][HM.388] [CTB.31.209]

MCEWAN, MALCOLM, oig, in Ardchiavaig, Ross, Mull, Argyll, a Jacobite in 1715. [NRS.SC54.22.17.2]

MCFADEN, DONALD BANE, a Jacobite in 1715, in Poity, Ross, Mull, 1716. [NRS.SC54.22.17.2]

MCFARLAN, ANGUS, a Jacobite in 1715, on Iona, Argyll, in 1716. [NRS.SC54.22.54]

MCFARLAN, ARCHIBALD, in Kilvickeon, Ross, Mull, Argyll, a Jacobite in 1715. [NRS.SC54.22.17-2]

MCFARLAN, DONALD, a Jacobite in 1715, in Ardlun, Ross, Mull, 1716. [NRS.SC54.22.17.2]

MCFARLANE, JOHN, was transported via Liverpool aboard the Two Brothers bound for Jamaica on 26 April 1716, landed on Montserrat in June 1716. [SPC.1716.313][CTP.CC.43][CTB.31.206]

MCFARLAN, JOHN, a Jacobite in 1715, on Iona, Argyll, in 1716. [NRS.SC54.22.17.1-2]

MCFARLAND, JOHN, a Jacobite in 1715, in Suij, Ross, Mull, 1716. [NRS.SC54.22.17.2]

MCFARLAN, LACHLAN, a Jacobite in 1715, on Iona, Argyll, in 1716. [NRS.SC54.22.17.2]

MCFINLAY VCEAN, DONALD, a Jacobite in 1715, in Ormsaigbeg, Ardnamurchan, 1716. [NRS.SC54.22.17.1]

MCGHIE, Dr CHARLES, a physician at the Jacobite Court at Urbino, Italy, in 1716. [JU]

MCGIBBON, ALEXANDER, an Ensign of Strathmore's Regiment, taken prisoner at Preston, 1715. [CS.V.162] [NRS.GD1.53.72]

MCGIBBON, DUNCAN, was transported via Liverpool aboard the Two Brothers bound for Jamaica on 26 April 1716, landed on Montserrat in June 1716. [SPC.1716.313][CTB.31.206]

MCGIE, JAMES, from Waterton, Aberdeenshire, fought at Sheriffmuir in 1715. [JAB.83]

MCGILLIVRAY, ALEXANDER, was transported via Liverpool aboard the Wakefield bound for South Carolina on 21 April 1716. [SPC.1716.309][CTB.31.205]

MCGILLIVRAY, DANIEL, was transported via Liverpool aboard the Elizabeth and Anne bond for Jamaica or Virginia on 29 June 1716, landed in Virginia. [SPC.116.310.][CTB.31.208][VSP.I.186]

MCGILLIVRAY, DONALD, was transported via Liverpool aboard the Susannah bound for South Carolina on 7 May 1716. [SPC.1716.309][CTB.31.206]

MCGILLIVRAY, DONALD, from Dunlichtie, Inverness-shire, a Jacoite, died in Lancaster Prison on 21 May 1716. [LBR]

MCGILLIVRAY, FARQUHAR, from Dunlichtie, Inverness-shire, died in Lancaster Prison on 22 January 1716. [LBR]

MCGILLIVRAY, FARQUHAR, a Captain of McIntosh's Regiment, captured at Preston, was transported via Liverpool aboard the Friendship bound for Virginia on 24 May 1716, landed in Maryland on 20 August 1716. [SPC.1716.311][CS.V.162][HM.386]

MCGILLIVRAY, FARQUHAR, from Dallashie, Inverness-shire, a Jacobite, died in Lancaster Prison on 5 Marsh 1716. [LBR]

MCGILLIVRAY, FERGUS, was transported via Liverpool aboard the Susannah bound for South Carolina on 7 May 1716. [SPC.1716.309][CTB.31.206]

MCGILLIVRAY, JAMES, was transported via Liverpool aboard the Wakefield bound for South Carolina on 21 April 1716. [SPC.1716.309][CTB.31.205]

MCGILLIVRAY, JOHN, was transported via Liverpool aboard the Scipio bound for Antigua on 30 March 1716. [SPC.1716.310][CTB.31.204]

MCGILLIVRAY, JOHN, a laborer, a prisoner at Preston, was condemned on 25 January 1716, [CS.V.193], and possibly transported via Liverpool aboard the Wakefield bound for South Carolina on 21 April 1716. [SPC.1716.309][CTB.31.205]

MCGILLIVRAY, JOHN, from Dunlichtie, Inverness-shire, a Jacobite, died in Lancaster Prison on 16 January 1716. [LBR]

MCGILLIVRAY, LAUCHLIN, son of Daniel McGillivray in Inverness-shire, was transported via Liverpool aboard the Wakefield bound for South Carolina on 21 April 1716, died 1736 in South Carolina, probate 1737, S.C.

MCGILLIVRAY, OWEN, was transported via Liverpool aboard the Wakefield bound for South Carolina on 21 April 1716. [SPC.1716.309][CTB.31.205]

MCGILLIVRAY, WILLIAM, an Ensign of McIntosh's Regiment, captured at Preston in 1715, [CS.V.162][, possibly was transported via Liverpool aboard the Elizabeth and Anne bound for Jamaica or Virginia on 29 June 1716, landed in Virginia. [SPC.1716.310][CTB.31.208][VSP.1.185]

MCGILLIVRAY, WILLIAM, was transported via Liverpool aboard the Friendship bound for Virginia on 24 May 1716, landed in Maryland in August 1716. [SPC.1716.311][HM.388]

MCGIVEN, ALEXANDER, was transported via Liverpool aboard the Goodspeed bound for Virginia on 28 July 1716, landed in Maryland in October 1716. [SPC.1716.310][HM.389] [CTB.31.209]

MCGLASHAN, NEIL, the chamberlain to the Duke of Atholl, fought at Sheriffmuir, a prisoner in 1715. [CAT.ii.206]

MCGREGOR or DRUMMOND, ALEXANDER born 1660, a plotter, died in Dunblane in 1749. [JP.96]

MCGREGOR, ALEXANDER, participated in the assault on Edinburgh Castle in 1715. [TNA.SP54.8.36]

MCGREGOR, ALEXANDER, a Captain of Logie's Regiment, captured at Preston in 1715. [CS.V.161] [NRS.GD1.53.72]

MCGREGOR, ALEXANDER, in Reinacharn, Glengairn, a Jacobite in 1715. [JAB.207]

MCGREGOR, CALLUM, in Reinacharn, Glengairn, a Jacobite in 1715. [JAB.207]

MCGREGOR, DONALD, a servant of Alexander Robertson of Struan, Perthshire, a Jacobite in 1715. [NRS.B59.20.1]

MCGREGOR, DONALD, from Balquhidder, Perthshire, a Jacobite, died in Lancaster Prison on 19 April 1716. [LBR]

MCGREGOR, DUNCAN, was transported via Liverpool aboard the Susannah bound for South Carolina on 7 May 1716. [SPC.1716.309][CTB.31.206]

MCGREGOR, GREGOR, was transported via Liverpool aboard the Anne bound for Virginia on 31 July 1716. [SPC.1716.310][CTB.31.209]

MCGREGOR, GREGOR, of Glengyle, born 1689, a Subaltern of Logie's Regiment, was captured at Preston, at the Jacobite Court in Urbino, Italy, 1715, died in 1777.[CS.V.161] [JU][CS.V.161]

MCGREGOR, JOHN, in Reinacharn, Glencairn, a Jacobite in 1715. [JAB.207]

MCGREGOR, JOHN, from Moy, Inverness-shire, a Jacobite, died in Lancaster Prison on 28 April 1716. [LBR]

MCGREGOR, JOHN, was captured at Preston in 1715, condemned on 30 January 1716, [CS.V.194]; and possibly was transported via Liverpool aboard the Goodspeed bound for Virginia on 28 July 1716, landed in Maryland in October 1716. [SPC.1716.310][CTB.31.209][HM.388]

MCGREGOR, JAMES MHOR, son of Rob Roy McGregor, fought at Sheriffmuir in 1715, died in France in 1789.

MCGREGOR, MALCOLM, was transported via Liverpool aboard the Susannah bound for South Carolina on 7 May 1716. [SPC.1716.309][CTB.31.206]

MACGREGOR, ROB ROY, of Craigrostan and Ardess, Buchanan, Stirlingshire, fought at the Battle of Sheriffmuir in 1715, estate forfeited in 1715, surrendered in 1717, escaped from imprisonment at Logerait on 7 June 1717, participated in the 1719 Rising, died in Balquhidder. [MHP.292/298/306][SP.VI.264][NRS.E635]

MACGREGOR, or DRUMMOND, Sir WILLIAM, of Balhaldies, born 1698, a Jacobite in 1715, fought at Sheriffmuir, died in Paris in 1765. [JP.97][NLS.GB233.ms3186-9]

MCGRUTHER, WILLIAM, was transported via Liverpool aboard the Elizabeth and Anne bound for Jamaica or Virginia on 29 June 1716, landed in Virginia. [SPC.1716.310][CTB.31.208][VSP.I.186]

MCGUIRE, WILLIAM, a Subaltern of Macintosh's Regiment, a prisoner at Preston, 1715. [NRS.GD1.53.72]

MCHARDY, JOHN, was transported via Liverpool aboard the Goodspeed bound for Virginia on 28 July 1716. [SPC.1716.310][HM.389] [CTB.31.209]

MCHARDY, JOHN, in Glencairn, a Jacobite in 1715. [JAB.207]

MCHENRY, GORDON, the Jacobite Cess Collector in Aberdeen, 1715. [JAB.154]

MCIAN VCDHOIL, LACHLAN, a Jacobite in 1715, in Torraston, Coll, 1716. [NRS.SC54.22.17.1]

MCILEISE, DONALD, in Ardnamurchan, a Jacobite in 1715. [NRS.SC54.22.17.1-2]

MCILEISE, DONALD, son of Donald McIleise, a Jacobite in 1715, in Suaradimore, Ardnamurchan, in 1716. [NRS.SC54.22.17.1]

MCILEISE, DUNCAN, servant to Duncan Stewart in Swordle, Ardnamurchan, Inverness-shire, fought at Sheriffmuir in 1715. [NRS.SC54.22.17.1-2]

MCILEISE, JOHN, a Jacobite in 1715, in Tobermory, Torloisk, 1716. [NRS.SC54.54.22.17.2]

MCILESPIE, EWAN, a Jacobite in 1715, in Crossaboll, Coll, 1716. [NRS.SC54.22.17.1]

MCILESEPIE, JOHN, a Jacobite in 1715, in Potoranald, Coll, 1716. [NRS.SC54.22.17.1]

MCILLICHALLUM, DONALD VCDHOIL, a Jacobite in 1715, in Cragart, Treshnish, 1716. [NRS.SC54.22.17.2.]

MCILLEPHADRISH, JOHN, a Jacobite in 1715, in Achalinan, Morvern, 1716. [NRS.SC54.22.17.2]

MCILMARTIN, MALCOLM, a Jacobite in 1715, in Gruline, Glen Forsa, Mull, 1716. [NRS.SC54.22.17.2]

MCILMICHAEL, EWAN, a Jacobite in 1715, in Glenboradell, Ardnamurchan, 1716. [NRS.SC54.22.17.1]

MCILVORIE, JOHN, a Jacobite in 1715, in Knock , Morvern, 1716. [NRS.SC54.22.17.2]

MCILVOYLE, DONALD, a Jacobite in 1715, in Achachossnich, Ardnamurchan, 1716. [NRS.SC54.22.17.1]

MCILVRA, ALEXANDER, of Pennighael, Carsaig, Broloss, Mull, Argyll, a Jacobite in 1715. [NRS.SC54.22.17.2]

MCILVRA, ARCHIBALD, a Jacobite in 1715, on Iona, Argyll, in 1716. [NRS.SC54.22.17.2]

MCILVRA, ARCHIBALD, a Jacobite in 1715, in Kilpatrick, Broloss, 1716. [NRS.SC54.22.17.2]

MCILVRA, DONALD, a Jacobite in 1715, In Achateny, Ardnamurchan, in 1716. [NRS.SC54.22.17.1]

MCILVRA, JOHN, a Jacobite in 1715, in Girgadill, Ardnamuchan, 1716. [NRS.SC54.22.17.1]

MCILVRA, JOHN, a Jacobite in 1715, in Ledmore, Aros, Mull, 1716. [NRS.SC54.22.17.2.]

MCILVRA, PATRICK, a Jacobite in 1715, in Suaradilmore, Ardnamurchan, in 1716. [NRS.SC54.22.17.1]

MCINLEA, ARCHIBALD, a Jacobite in 1715, in Arivolcheyne, Morenish, 1716. [NRS.SC54.22.17.2.]

MCINLIER, DUNCAN, was transported via Liverpool aboard the Two Brothers bound for Jamaica on 26 April 1716, landed on Montserrat in June 1716. [SPC.1716.313][CTP.CC.43]

MCINLISTER, ANGUS, a Jacobite in 1715, on Iona, Argyll, in 1716. [NRS.SC54.22.54]

MCINLISTER, ARCHIBALD, a Jacobite in 1715, on Iona, Argyll, in 1716. [NRS.SC54.22.54]

MCINLISTER, DONALD, a Jacobite in 1715, on Iona, Argyll, in 1716. [NRS.SC54.22.54]

MCINLISTER, DUNCAN, a Jacobite in 1715, on Iona, Argyll, in 1716. [NRS.SC54.22.17.2]

MCINLISTER, JOHN, a Jacobite in 1715, on Iona, Argyll, in 1716. [NRS.SC54.22.17.2]

MCINLISTER, MALCOLM, a Jacobite in 1715, on Iona, Argyll, in 1716. [NRS.SC54.22.17.2]

MCINLISTER, NEIL, a Jacobite in 1715, on Iona, Argyll, in 1716. [NRS.SC54.22.17.2]

MCINNES, JOHN, was transported via Liverpool aboard the
Susannah bound for South Carolina on 7 May 1716.
[SPC.1716.309][CTB.31.206]

MCINNISH, ARCHIBALD, a Jacobite in 1715, on Iona, Argyll, in
1716. [NRS.SC54.22.17.1]

MCINNISH, ARCHIBALD VCILLESPIE, a Jacobite in 1715, in Finarie,
Morvern, 1716. [NRS.SC54.22.17.2]

MCINNISH, DONALD MCILLICHALLUM, in Achatashenaig, Aross,
Mull, Argyll, a Jacobite in 1715. [NRS.SC54.22.17.2]

MCINNISH, DUNCAN VAIN, in Achaluachrich, Morvern, Inverness-
shire, a Jacobite in the McLean Regiment in 1715, fought at
Sheriffmuir. [NRS.SC54.2.17.2]

MCINISH, DUSHIE VCERICHER, a Jacobite in 1715, on Creich, Ross
of Mull, Argyll, in 1716. [NRS.SC54.22.54]

MCINNISH, EWAN, a Jacobite in 1715, in Kinlochteacus, Morvern,
1716. [NRS.SC54.22.17.2]

MCINTOSH, ALEXANDER, was transported via Liverpool aboard
the Goodspeed bound for Virginia on 28 July 1716, landed in
Maryland in October 1716. [SPC.1716.310][HM.388]
[CTB.31.209]

MCINTOSH, ALEXANDER, was transported via Liverpool aboard
the Wakefield bound for South Carolina on 21 April 1716.
[SPC.1716.309][CTB.31.205]

MCINTOSH, ANGUS, from Dellerish, Inverness-shire, died in
Lancaster Prison on 16 January 1716. [LBR]

MCINTOSH, ANGUS, was transported via Liverpool aboard the
Two Brothers bound for Jamaica on 26 April 1716, landed on
Montserrat in June 1716. [SPC.1716.313][CTB.31.206]

MCINTOSH, BENJAMIN, a Subaltern of McIntosh's Regiment, was captured at Preston in 1715. [CS.V.162] [NRS.GD1.53.72]

MCINTOSH, DONALD, from Dellarie, Inverness-shire, died in Lancaster Prison on 2 April 1716. [LBR]

MCINTOSH, DONALD, from Dunlichtie, Inverness-shire, died in Lancaster Prison on 9 April 1716. [LBR]

MCINTOSH, DONALD, from Dellarsie, Inverness-shire, died in Lancaster Prison on 23 April 1716. [LBR]

MCINTOSH, DONALD, a Subaltern in McIntosh's Regiment, was captured at Preston in 1715, [CS.V.162], possibly transported via Liverpool aboard the Wakefield bound for South Carolina on 21 April 1716. [SPC.1716.309][CTB.31.205] [NRS.GD1.53.72]

MCINTOSH, DUNCAN, in Tullibardine's Regiment, fought at Sheriffmuir, a prisoner in 1715. [CAT.II.206]

MCINTOSH, DUNCAN, a Captain of McIntosh's Regiment, a prisoner at Preston, [CS.V.162], possibly transported via Liverpool aboard the Wakefield bound for South Carolina on 21 April 1716. [SPC.1716.309][CTB.31.205] [NRS.GD1.53.72]

MCINTOSH, DUNCAN, an Ensign of McIntosh's Regiment, a prisoner at Preston, [CS.V.162], possibly transported via Liverpool aboard the Susannah bound for South Carolina on 7 May 1716. [SPC.1716.309][CTB.31.206] [NRS.GD1.53.72]

MCINTOSH, EVAN, from Moy, Inverness-shire, a Jacobite, died in Lancaster Prison on 1 March 1716. [LBR]

MCINTOSH, EWEN, was transported via Liverpool aboard the Susannah bound for South Carolina on 7 May 1716. [SPC.1716.309][CTB.31.206]

MCINTOSH, FERGUS, a Captain of McIntosh's Regiment, a prisoner at Preston, 1715. [CS.V.162] [NRS.GD1.53.72]

MCINTOSH, GEORGE, a prisoner at Preston, executed in Lancaster on 18 February 1716. [CS.V.194]

MCINTOSH, JAMES, was transported via Liverpool aboard the Wakefield bound for South Carolina on 21 April 1716. [SPC.1716.309][CTB.31.205]

MCINTOSH, JAMES, a laborer, a prisoner at Preston in 1715, was condemned on 23 January 1716. [CS.V.192]

MCINTOSH, JAMES, was transported via Liverpool aboard the Susannah bound for South Carolina on 7 May 1716. [SPC.1716.309][CTB.31.206]

MCINTOSH, JAMES, an Ensign of McIntosh's Regiment, captured at Preston in 1715. [CS.V.162] [NRS.GD1.53.72]

MCINTOSH, JAMES, was transported via Liverpool aboard the Goodspeed bound for Virginia on 28 July 1716, landed in Maryland in October 1716. [SPC.1716.310][HM.389] [CTB.31.209]

MCINTOSH, JAMES, was transported via Liverpool aboard the Elizabeth and Anne bound for Jamaica or Virginia on 29 June 1716, landed in Virginia. [SPC.1716.310][CTB.31.208][VSP.I.186]

MCINTOSH, JOHN, a Major of McIntosh's Regiment, a prisoner at Preston in 1715. [CS.V.161] [NRS.GD1.53.72]

MCINTOSH, JOHN, an Ensign of McIntosh's Regiment, a prisoner at Preston in 1715. [CS.V.162] [NRS.GD1.53.72]

MCINTOSH, JOHN, a Subaltern of Macintosh's Regiment, 1715, a prisoner at Preston. [NRS.GD1.53.72]

MCINTOSH, JOHN, was transported via Liverpool aboard the Wakefield bound for South Carolina on 21 April 1716. [CTB.31.205]

MCINTOSH, JOHN, an Advocate, Aide de Camp, and Lieutenant of McIntosh's Regiment, a prisoner at Preston. [CS.V.162] [NRS.GD1.53.72]

MCINTOSH, JOHN, was transported via Liverpool aboard the Susannah bound for South Carolina on 7 May 1716. [CTB.31.206] [SPC.1716.309]

MCINTOSH, JOHN, in Tullibardine's Regiment, fought at Sheriffmuir, a prisoner in 1715. [CAT.II.206]

MCINTOSH, JOHN, was transported via Liverpool aboard the Elizabeth and Anne bound for Jamaica or Virginia on 29 June 1716, landed in Virginia. [SPC.1716.310][CTB.31.208][VSP.I.185]

MACINTOSH, JOHN, a soldier of the Perth company in 1715. [NRS.B59.30.17]

MACKINTOSH, LAUCHLAN, son of Lauchlan Mackintosh and his wife Magdalene Lindsay, a Captain in McIntosh's Regiment, captured at Preston in 1715, possibly transported via Liverpool aboard the Goodspeed bound for Virginia on 28 July 1716, landed in Maryland in October 1716. [NRS.GD1.53.72] [SPC.1716.310][CTB.31.209][HM.388][CS.V.162]

MACKINTOSH, LAUCHLAN, 20th Chief of Clan Chattan, a Jacobite Colonel in 1715, fought at Preston, was created Lord Mackintosh in 1717. [JP.98]

MCINTOSH, LAUCHLAN, an Ensign in McIntosh's Regiment, a prisoner in Preston, possibly transported via Liverpool aboard the

Scipio bound for Antigua on 30 March 1716.
[SPC.1716.310][CTB.31.204] [NRS.GD1.53.72]

MCINTOSH, MALCOLM, was transported via Liverpool aboard the
Scipio bound for Antigua on 30 March 1716.
[SPC.1716.310][CTB.31.204]

MCINTOSH, ROBERT, in Tullibardine's Regiment, fought at
Sheriffmuir, a prisoner in 1715. [CAT.II.206]

MCINTOSH, THOMAS, was transported via Liverpool aboard the
Elizabeth and Anne bound for Jamaica or Virginia on 29 June
1716. [SPC.1716.310][CTB.31.208]

MCINTOSH, WILLIAM, a Captain of McIntosh's Regiment, a
prisoner at Preston in 1715. [CS.V.162] [NRS.GD1.53.72]

MCINTOSH, WILLIAM, the younger of Borlum, Brigadier General,
at Sheriffmuir. [MHP.295]

MCINTOSH, WILLIAM, of Borlum, Inverness-shire, born 1662,
Colonel of McIntosh's Regiment, a prisoner at Preston and in the
Tower of London, 1715, his estates in Alvie and Dores, Inverness-
shire, were forfeted in 1715, he escaped to France, died 1743.
[CS.V.161/186][NRS.E666] [NRS.GD1.53.72]

MCINTOSH, WILLIAM, was transported via Liverpool aboard the
Wakefield bound for South Carolina on 21 April 1716.
[SPC.1716.309]

MCINTOSH, WILLIAM, was transported via Liverpool aboard the
Susannah bound for South Carolina on 7 May 1716.
[SPC.1716.309][CTB.31.206]

MCINTOSH, WILLIAM, was transported via Liverpool aboard the
Scipio bound for Antigua on 30 March 1716. [SPC.1716.309]

MCINTOSH, WILLIAM, was transported via Liverpool aboard the Anne bound for Virginia on 31 July 1716. [SPC.1716.309]

MCINTYRE, ARCHIBALD, a Jacobite in 1715, in Potmore, Coll, 1716. [NRS.SC54.22.17.1]

MCINTYRE, DENIS, was transported via Liverpool aboard the Two Brothers bound for Jamaica on 26 April 1716, landed on Montserrat in June 1716. [SPC.1716.313][CTP.CC.43][CTB.31.205]

MCINTYRE, FYNLAY, of Lakan, Inverness-shire, died in Lancaster Prison on 14 February 1716. [LBR]

MCINTYRE, GILBERT, a Jacobite in 1715, in Laga, Ardnamurchan, 1715. [NRS.SC54.22.17.1]

MCINTYRE, FINLAY, was transported via Liverpool aboard the Goodspeed bound for Virginia on 28 July 1716, landed in Maryland in October 1716. [SPC.1716.310][CTB.31.209][HM.389]

MCINTYRE, HUGH, was transported via Liverpool aboard the Goodspeed bound for Virginia on 28 July 1716, landed in Maryland in October 1716. [SPC.1716.310][CTB.31.209][HM.389]

MCINTYRE, JOHN, was transported via Liverpool aboard the Two Brothers bound for Jamaica on 26 April 1716, landed on Montserrat in June 1716. [SPC.1716.313][CTP.CC.43][CTB.31.205]

MCINTYRE, JOHN, was transported via Liverpool aboard the Friendship bound for Virginia on 24 My 1716, landed in Maryland in August 1716. [HM.387]

MCINTYRE, MALCOLM, a Jacobite in 1715, on Iona, Argyll, in 1716. [NRS.SC54.22.17.2]

MCKAY, DONALD, a Jacobite in 1715, in Achaforses,, Morvern, 1716. [NRS.SC54.22.17.2]

MACKAY, HENRY, a gentleman, a prisoner at Preston, 1715. [CS.V.163]

MACKAY, JOHN, was transported via Liverpool aboard the Elizabeth and Anne bound for Jamaica or Virginia on 29 June 1716. [CTB.31.208]

MCKAY, ROBERT, a tenant of the Earl of Mar, imprisoned in Cumberland Gaol in 1716. [JRS.210]

MCKEELS, DANIEL, was transported via Liverpool aboard the Susannah bound for South Carolina on 7 May 1716. [SPC.1716.309][CTB.31.206]

MCKENN, DANIEL, was transported via Liverpool aboard the Two Brothers bound for Jamaica on 26 April 1716. [CTB.31.205]

MCKENNY, ALEXANDER, was transported via Liverpool aboard the Elizabeth and Anne bound for Jamaica or Virginia on 29 June 1716, landed in Virginia. [SPC.1716.310][CTB.31.208][VSP.I.185]

MCKENNY, COLIN, was transported via Liverpool aboard the Scipio bound for Antigua on 30 March 1716. [SPS.1716.310][CTB.31.204]

MCKENNY, JOHN, was transported via Liverpool aboard the Goodspeed bound for Virginia on 28 July 1716, landed in Maryland in October 1716. [SPC.1716.310][HM.388]

MCKENRIG, HENRY, a Jacobite in 1715, on Iona, Argyll, in 1716. [NRS.SC54.22.54]

MACKENZIE, ALEXANDER, of Applecross, estate forfeited, 1715. [NRS.E611]; a Jacobite at Sheriffmuir, 1715. [NRS.RH2.4.308/170];

MACKENZIE, ALEXANDER, of Davochmaluach, Ross-shire, estate forfeited in 1715. [NRS.E624]

MACKENZIE, ALEXANDER, born around 1664, minister of Newtyle, Angus from 1685 to 1695, Episcopal preacher there during 1715, died in Edinburgh on 20 September 1722. [F.V.272]

MACKENZIE, ALEXANDER, of Fraserdale, Kirkhill, Inverness-shire, fought at Sheriffmuir in 1715, estate forfeited in 1715, a prisoner in Carlisle in December 1716. [MHP.297][NRS.E631][SUL.Cheap.5.537]

MACKENZIE, COLIN, of Kildon, a Captain who fought at Sheriffmuir in 1715, a prisoner. [CAT.II.205][SUL.Cheap.5.537]

MCKENZIE, DONALD, of Kilcowie, parish of Suddy, Ross-shire, estate forfeited, 1715. [NRS.E679]; a Jacobite at Sheriffmuir, 1715. [NRS.RH2.4.308/170];

MCKENZIE, DONALD, a Jacobite in 1715, tenant in Ranochanmore, Snart, 1716. [NRS.SC54.22.17.1]

MCKENZIE, GEORGE, of Nuthill, Fife, estate forfeited in 1715. [NRS.E685]

MACKENZIE, GEORGE, at the Jacobite Court in Urbino, Italy, 1718. [JU]

MACKENZIE, GEORGE, son of Delvine, Perthshire, a Jacobite in 1715, a prisoner in Perth, freed in 1725. [MHP.303]

MCKENZIE, HENDRY, a Jacobite in 1715, in Iona, Argyll, 1716. [NRS.SC54.22.17.2]

MCKENZIE, JAMES, of Dalmore, Kindrochit, son of Kenneth McKenzie, a Jacobite in 1715, dead by 1733. [CRA.55][JAB.153]

MCKENZIE, Sir JOHN, of Coull, letter, 1715. [NRS.GD1.616.12]; Jacobite Tax collector in Inverness, Governor of Inverness, 1715. [NRS.GD241.380.13]; estate forfeited in 1715. [NRS.E622]

MACKENZIE, JOHN, of Avoch, estate forfeited, 1717. [NRS.E612]

MACKENZIE, JOHN, uncle to Fairburn, a Jacobite at Sheriffmuir, 1715. [NRS.RH2.4.308/170];

MACKENZIE, JOHN, son of MacKenzie of Delvin, a Jacobite at Sheriffmuir, 1715. [NRS.RH2.4.308/170]

MACKENZIE, Sir KENNETH, of Coull, Jacobite Governor of Inverness, 1715. [NRS.RH2.4.307.83; SP54.8.69]

MCKENZIE, KENNETH, of Dalmore, Kindrochit, a Jacobite in 1715.

MCKENZIE, KENNETH, fought at Sheriffmuir in 1715, a prisoner. [CAT.II.205]

MCKENZIE, KENNETH, a gentleman who was tried in Liverpool on 7 February 1716. [CS.V.195]

MACKENZIE, RODERICK, of Fairburn in the parishes of Urray and Loch Broom, Ross-shire, estate forfeited in 1715. [NRS.E629]; a Jacobite at Sheriffmuir, 1715. [NRS.RH2.4.308/170];

MCKENZIE, THOMAS, was transported via Liverpool aboard the Hockenhill bound for St Kitts on 25 June 1716, mutinied and landed on Sint Maartens in September 1716. [SPC.1716.312][CTB.31.217][JAB.21]

MACKENZIE, WILLIAM, Marquis of Seaforth, son of Kenneth Mackenzie and his wife Frances Herbert, fought at Sheriffmuir with his clan in 1715, his estates were forfeited in 1715, he escaped to France, died on the Isle of Lewis on 8 January 1740. [JP.163][SP.VII.511][NRS.655][NRS.RH2.4.308/170]

MCKENZIE, WILLIAM, was transported via Liverpool aboard the Wakefield bound for South Carolina on 21 April 1716; later a merchant and planter in Charleston, S.C., probate 1738 South Carolina. [SM.I.44][SPC.1716.309][CTB.31.205]

MCKENZIE, ..., of Torridon, captured at Sheriffmuir, was transported aboard the pink Marlborough of Leith master John Hutton, from Leith to London in December 1715. [NRS.RH2.4.308]

MACKENZIE, ..., of Dalmaluack, a Jacobite at Sheriffmuir, 1715. [NRS.RH2.4.308/170];

MACKENZIE, ...of Auchladonnell, the younger, a Jacobite at Sheriffmuir, 1715. [NRS.RH2.4.308/170]

MACKENZIE, ..., of Balmackie, a Jacobite at Sheriffmuir, 1715. [NRS.RH2.4.308/170];

MACKENZIE, ..., of Brae?, the younger, a Jacobite at Sheriffmuir, 1715. [NRS.RH2.4.308/170]

MACKENZIE, ..., of Granard, a Jacobite at Sheriffmuir, 1715. [NRS.RH2.4.308/170];⁻

MACKENZIE, ..., of Suddy, a Jacobite at Sheriffmuir, 1715. [NRS.RH2.4.308/170];

MACKENZIE, ..., of Culdrone, a Jacobite at Sheriffmuir, 1715. [NRS.RH2.4.308/170];

MACKENZIE, ..., of Echilly, a Jacobite at Sheriffmuir, 1715. [NRS.RH2.4.308/170];

MACKENZIE, ..., of Avoch, a Jacobite at Sheriffmuir, 1715. [NRS.RH2.4.308/170];

MCKINGDON, CHARLES, a Jacobite in 1715, in Ardnacallich, Ulva, 1716. [NRS.SC54.22.17.1]

MCKINLAY, DONALD, a Jacobite in 1715, in Beach, Broloss, 1716. [NRS.SC54.22.17.2]

MCKINNON, Sir JOHN, of that Ilk, born 1682, fought at Sheriffmuir in 1715, 29th Chief of MacKinnon, his estates on Mull and Skye were forfeited in 1715, died in 1756 in Kilmorie, Skye. [NRS.E645]

MCKINNON, JOHN, a gentleman, a prisoner at Preston in 1715, condemned on 1 February 1716. [CS.V.194]

MCKINNON, NEIL MCDHOIL, in Balevulin, Tiree, a Jacobite in 1715. [NRS.SC54.22.17.1-2]

MCINTAILOR, ARCHIBALD, a Jacobite in 1715, in Esa, Borloisk, 1716. [NRS.SC54.54.22.17.2]

MCKINVINE, CHARLES, son of Neil McKinvine, a Jacobite in 1715, on Bouge, Toresay, Mull, in 1716. [NRS.SC54.22.17.1-2]

MCKINVINE, DONALD, a Jacobite in 1715, in Peinalbanich, Mishnish, 1716. [NRS.SC54.54.22.17.2]

MCKINVINE, FINLAY, a Jacobite in 1715, in Peinalbanach, Mishnish, 1716. [NRS.SC54.54.22.17.2]

MCKINVINE, JOHN ROY, a Jacobite in 1715, in Diskaig, Toresay, Mull, 1716. [NRS.SC54.22.17.2]

MCKINVINE, LACHLAN, a Jacobite in 1715, in Fracadill, Morinish, 1716. [NRS.SC54.22.17.2.]

MCKINVINE, LACHLAN, son of Hector McKinvine, in Sorn, Mishnish, a Jacobite in 1715, in Sorn, Mishnish, 1716. [NRS.SC54.54.22.17.2]

MCKINVINE, NEIL, a Jacobite in 1715, on Iona, Argyll, 1716. [NRS.SC54.22.17.2]

MCKUARIG, ..., A Jacobite in 1715, in Achanalia, Sunart, 1716. [NRS.SC54.22.17.1]

MCLACHLAN, ALEXANDER, a Jacobite in 1715, in Laudale, Morvern, 1716. [NRS.SC54.22.17.2]

MCLACHLAN, ALEXANDER, of Tullibardine's Regiment, a prisoner at Sheriffmuir in 1715. [CAT.II.206]

MCLACHLAN, CHARLES, in Balliphuill, Tiree, a Jacobite in 1715. [NRS.SC54.22.17.1-2]

MCLACHLAN, JOHN, a Jacobite in 1715, in Laudale, Morvern, 1716. [NRS.SC54.22.17.2]

MCLACHLAN, DONALD, a Jacobite in 1715, in Kinlochteacus, Morvern, 1716. [NRS.SC54.22.17.2]

MCLACHLAN, DUGALD, a Jacobite in 1715, in Drumnine, Morvern, 1716. [NRS.SC54.22.17.2]

MCLACHLAN, EWN, on Tiree, a Jacobite in 1715, was killed at Sheriffmuir. [NRS.SC54.22.17.1-2]

MCLACHLAN, NEILE VCPHADRICK, a Jacobite in 1715, in Pennigaile, Broloss, Mull, 1716. [NRS.SC54.22.17.2]

MCLAGAN, ANDREW, a merchant and burgess of Perth, a prisoner in 1715. [NRS.B59.30.36/37/40]

MCLAREN, ALEXANDER, was transported via Liverpool aboard the Scipio bound for Antigua on 30 March 1716. [SPC.1716.310][CTB.31.204]

MCLAREN, DONALD, possibly from Balquhidder, Stirlingshire, a Jacobite in 1715, imprisoned at Blackness, Stirling, and Carlisle. [CAT.II.239]

MCLAREN, alias MACGREGOR, DUNCAN, piper to the Duke of Atholl, a Jacobite in 1715, imprisoned at Blackness, Stirling, and Carlisle. [CAT.II.215/239]

MCLAREN, JAMES, was transported via Liverpool aboard the Scipio bound for Antigua on 30 March 1716. [SPC.1716.310][CTB.31.204]

MCLAREN, JOHN, was transported via Liverpool aboard the Susannah bound for South Carolina on 7 May 1716. [SPC.1716.309][CTB.31.206]

MCLAREN, PATRICK, a wright and a burgess of Perth, a Jacobite in 1715, carried arms, a prisoner. [NRS.B59.30.36/40]

MCLAREN, PATRICK, was transported via Liverpool aboard the Susannah bound for South Carolina on 7 May 1716. [SPC.1716.309][CTB.31.206]

MCLAREN, WALTER, was transported via Liverpool aboard the Hockenhill bound for St Kitts on 25 Jun 1716, mutinied and landed on Sint Maartens in September 1716. [SPC.1716.312][CTB.31.207][JAB.21]

MCLAUGHLAN, ARCHIBALD, a Subaltern in Logie's Regiment, a prisoner at Preston, possibly transported via Liverpool aboard the Elizabeth and Anne bound for Jamaica or Virginia on 29 June 1716. [SPC.1716.310][CTB.31.208]

MCLAUGHLAN, JOHN, was transported via Liverpool aboard the Friendship bound for Virginia on 24 May 1716. [SPC.1716.311]

MCLEA, DONALD, a servant in Tour na Moine, Ardnamurchan, Inverness-shire, a Jacobite in 1715. [NRS.SC54.22.17.1-2]

MCLEA, DUNCAN, a Jacobite in 1715, in Achalinn, Morvern, 1716. [NRS.SC54.22.17.2]

MCLEA, EWAN MCILLECHALLUM, a Jacobite in 1715, in Acharanich, Morvern, 1716. [NRS.SC54.22.17.2]

MCLEA, JOHN, a Jacobite in 1715, in Achabeg, Morvern, 1716. [NRS.SC54.22.17.2]

MCLEAN, ALEXANDER, a tenant of Weem, a prisoner in Blackness, Stirling, and Carlisle, possibly transported via Liverpool aboard the Wakefield bound for South Carolina on 21 April 1716. [SPC.1716.309][CTB.31.205][CS.V.162][CAT.II.239]

MCLEAN, Captain ALLAN, captured in Edinburgh having attempted to capture the castle, 1715. [Wodrow pp, x]

MCLEAN, ALLAN, an Ensign of McIntosh's Regiment, a prisoner at Preston in 1715, possibly transported via Liverpool aboard the Friendship bound for Virginia on 24 May 1716, landed in Maryland in August 1716. [SPC.1716.311][HM.386] [NRS.GD1.53.72]

MCLEAN, ALLAN, in How, Tiree, possibly killed at Sheriffmuir, 1715. [NRS.SC54.22.17.1-2]

MCLEAN, ALLAN, a Jacobite in 1715, in Sorn, Mishnish, 1716. [NRS.SC54.54.22.17.2]

MCLEAN, ALLAN, in Sorn, Mishnish, Mull, Argyll, a Jacobite in 1715, fought at Sheriffmuir. [NRS.SC54.22.17.1-2]

MCLEAN, ALLAN, a Jacobite in 1715, in Univee, Morenish, 1716. [NRS.SC54.22.17.2.]

MCLEAN, ANGUS OGE, a Jacobite in 1715, at Uige, Coll, in 1716. [NRS.SC54.22.17.1]

MCLEAN, CHARLES, in Killinnaig, Mull, Argyll, a Jacobite in 1715. [NRS.SC54.22.17.1-2]

MCLEAN, CHARLES, in Suy, Ross, Mull, Argyll, a Jacobite in 1715. [NRS.SC54.22.17.1-2]

MCLEAN, CHARLES, a Jacobite in 1715, in Adacha, Ross, Mull, 1716. [NRS.SC54.22.17.2]

MCLEAN, CHARLES, a Jacobite in 1715, in Sheba, Ross, Mull, 1716. [NRS.SC54.22.17.2]

MCLEAN, DANIEL, was transported via Liverpool aboard the Two Brothers bound for Jamaica on 26 April 1716, landed on Montserrat in June 1716. [SPC.1716.313][CTB.31.205][CTP.CC.43]

MCLEAN, DONALD, a Jacobite in 1715, in Kilchreist, Morinish, in Mull, Argyll, 1716. [NRS.SC54.22.17.1-2]

MCLEAN, DONALD, son of Neil McEan VcEachine McLean, in Gott, Mull, Argyll, a Jacobite in 1715. [NRS.SC54.22.17.1-2]

MCLEAN, DONALD, a Jacobite in 1715, in Kinlochteacus, Morvern, 1716. [NRS.SC54.22.17.2]

MCLEAN, EWAN, a Jacobite in 1715, in Sorn, Mishnish, 1716. [NRS.SC54.54.22.17.2]

MCLEAN, HECTOR, a Jacobite in 1715, on Errald on Mull, Argyll, in 1716. [NRS.SC54.22.54]

MCLEAN, HECTOR, a Jacobite in 1715, on Creich, Ross of Mull, Argyll, in 1716. [NRS.SC54.22.54]

MCLEAN, HECTOR, a Jacobite in 1715, in Univee, Morenish, 1716. [NRS.SC54.22.17.2.]

MCLEAN, HECTOR, a Jacobite in 1715, in Lephine, Mishnish, 1716. [NRS.SC54.54.22.17.2]

MCLEAN, Sir HECTOR, a Jacobite in 1715, was created Lord Maclean in 1716, died in Paris in 1751. [JP.102]

MCLEAN, HECTOR, IN Cornaigbeg, a Jacobite at Sheriffmuir in 1716. [NRS.SC54.22.17.1-2]

MCLEAN, HECTOR ROY, in Baliphetrish, Mull, Argyll, a Jacobite in 1715. [NRS.SC54.22.17.1-2]

MCLEAN, JOHN, a trumpeter, a letter, 1715. [NRS.GD1.616.12]

MCLEAN, JOHN, Adjutant to Lord Seaforth, fought at Sheriffmuir, a prisoner in 1715. [CAT.II.205]; was transported aboard the pink Marlborough of Leith master John Hutton, from Leith to London in December 1715. [NRS.RH2.4.308]

MCLEAN, JOHN, a Jacobite in 1715, in Glenleid, Morvern, 1716. [NRS.SC54.22.17.2]

MCLEAN, JOHN, a Jacobite in 1715, in Achabeg, Morvern, 1716. [NRS.SC54.22.17.2]

MCLEAN, Sir JOHN, a Jacobite at Sheriffmuir, 1715. [NRS.RH2.4.308/170]; was imprisoned in Gordon Castle in February 1716, later taken to Aberdeen or to Edinburgh Castle. [NRAS.771, bundle I836]

MCLEAN, JOHN, was transported via Liverpool aboard the Wakefield bound for South Carolina on 21 April 1716. [SPC.1716.309][CTB.31.205]

MCLEAN, JOHN, in Creich, Ross, Mull, Argyll, a Jacobite in 1715. [NRS.SC54.22.17.1-2]

MCLEAN, JOHN, a Jacobite, 1715, in Univee, Morinish, 1716. [NRS.SC54.22.17.2.]

MCLEAN, JOHN, In Mingarie, Quinish, Mull, Argyll, a Jacobite in 1715. [NRS.SC54.22.17.1-2]

MCLEAN, JOHN, was transported via Liverpool aboard the
Friendship bound for Virginia on 24 May 1716, landed in
Maryland in August 1716. [HM.387]

MCLEAN, JOHN, in Clenleid, Morvern, Inverness-shire, a Jacobite
in McLean's Regiment in 1715, fought at Sheriffmuir.
[NRS.SC54.22.17.1-2]

MCLEAN, LACHLAN, in Cahors, France, 1718. [HMC.Stuart vii.73]

MCLEAN, LAUCHLAN, a Captain of McIntosh's Regiment, a
prisoner at Preston in 1715. [CS.V.162] [NRS.GD1.53.72]

MCLEAN, LACHLAN, in Kilvickeown, Mull, Argyll, 1716, a Jacobite
in 1715. [NRS.SC54.22.17.1-2]

MCLEAN, LACHLAN, in Grisopoll, Coll, a Jacobite in 1715.
[NRS.SC54.22.17.1-2]

MCLEAN, LACHLAN, brother of Hector McLean on Muck, a
Jacobite in 1715. [NRS.SC54.22.17.1-2]

MCLEAN, LACHLAN, a Jacobite in 1715, in Aren, Aros, 1716.
[NRS.SC54.22.17.2.]

MCLEAN, NEIL BANE, a Jacobite in 1715, in Ballihogh, Coll, in
1716. [NRS.SC54.22.17.1]

MCLEAN, NEIL, a Jacobite in 1715, in Lealt Barr, Morvern, 1716.
[NRS.SC54.22.17.2]

MCLEAN, PETER, was transported via Liverpool aboard the Scipio
bound for Antigua on 30 March 1716.
[SPC.1716..310][CTB.31.204]

MCLEAN, ..., of Borara, a Jacobite at Sheriffmuir, 1715.
[NRS.RH2.4.308/170];

MCLEAR, ALEXANDER, was transported via Liverpool aboard the Two Brothers bound for Jamaica on 26 April 1716, landed on Montserrat in June 1716. [SPC.1716.313][CTB.31.205][CTP.CC.43]

MCLEISH, JOHN, a messenger in Muthill, Perthshire, a Jacobite in 1715. [NRS.B59.20.1]

MCLEOD, ALEXANDER, servant to Douglas of Glendervie, captured at Sheriffmuir, was transported aboard the pink Marlborough of Leith master John Hutton, from Leith to London in December 1715. [NRS.RH2.4.308]

MCLEOD, JOHN, was transported via Liverpool aboard the Wakefield bound for South Carolina on 21 April 1716. [SPC.1716.309][CTB.31.205]

MCLEOD, MALCOLM, the younger, a Jacobite in 1715, in Balliterach, Mishnish, 1716. [NRS.SC54.54.22.17.2]

MCLEAN, MURDOCH, a Jacobite in 1715, in Sorn, Mishnish, 1716. [NRS.SC54.54.22.17.2]

MCLEOD, alias MCNEIL VCKINLAY, DONALD, a Jacobite in 1715, in Ballihterach, Mishnish, 1716. [NRS.SC54.54.22.17.2]

MACLEROY, WILLIAM, a Captain of Macintosh's Regiment, a prisoner in 1715. [NRS.GD1.53.72]

MACLERUY, WILLIAM, an Ensign of Macintosh's Regiment, a prisoner at Preston, 1715. [NRS.GD1.53.72]

MCMILLAN, ARCHIBALD, a Jacobite in 1715, in Bunessan, Ross, Mull, 1716. [NRS.SC54.22.17.2]

MCMILLAN, JOHN more, a Jacobite in 1715, in Ardealanis, Ross, Mull, 1716. [NRS.SC54.22.17.2]

MCMURDOCH, DONALD, a Jacobite in 1715, in Cliad, Coll, 1716. [NRS.SC54.22.17.1-2]

MCNABB, ALEXANDER, was transported via Liverpool aboard the Two Brothers bound for Jamaica on 26 April 1716, landed on Montserrat in June 1716. [SPC.1716.313][CTB.31.206][CTP.CC.43]

MCNAB, JOHN, in Suie, Argyll, a Jacobite in 1715. [JRA.2.315]

MCNABB, JOHN, was transported via Liverpool aboard the Two Brothers bound for Jamaica on 26 April 1716, landed on Montserrat in June 1716. [SPC.1716.313][CTB.31.206][CTP.CC.43]

MCNABB, THOMAS, was transported via Liverpool aboard the Friendship bound for Virginia on 24 May 1716, landed in Maryland in August 1716. [HM.387][SPC.1716.311]

MCNAIRN, JOHN, a prisoner at Preston in 1715. [CS.V.160] [NRS.GD1.53.72]

MCNAUGHTON, DONALD, in Tullibardine's Regiment, fought at Sheriffmuir in 1715, a prisoner. [CAT.II.206]

MCNAUGHTON, DUNCAN, was transported via Liverpool aboard the Susannah bound for South Carolina on 7 May 1716. [SPC.1716.309][CTB.31.206]

MCNAUGHTON, MALCOLM, was transported via Liverpool aboard the Elizabeth and Anne bound for Jamaica or Virginia on 29 June 1716, landed in Virginia. [SPC.1716.310][CTB.31.208][VSP.I.185]

MCNEIL, ALLEN, fought at the Battle of Sheriffmuir in 1715, on Coll, Argyll, by 1716. [NRS.SC54.22.54]

MCNEIL, ALLEN oig, a Jacobite in 1715, in Brechachie, Coll, in 1716.. [NRS.SC54.22.17.1]

MCNEIL VCDHOIL, ANGUS, a Jacobite in 1715, in Kinlochscridan, Broloss, Mull, 1716. [NRS.SC54.22.17.2]

MCNEIL VOIRE, ANGUS, a Jacobite in 1715, in Ardvarginis, Brolass, Mull, 1716. [NRS.SC54.22.17.2]

MCNEIL VANE, CHARLES, a Jacobite in 1715, in Trialan, Coll, 1716. [NRS.SC54.22.17.1]

MCNEILL, DONALD, son of John McInish Vain McNeill, a Jacobite in 1716, in Aros, Mull, 1716. [NRS.SC54.22.17.2.]

MCNEILL, JOHN MCQUARRIE, a Jacobite in 1715, in Kilvickeon, Ulva, 1716. [NRS.SC54.22.17.1]

MCNIVEN, JOHN, a horse-hirer and burgess of Perth, a Jacobite in 1715, carried arms, a prisoner. [NRS.B59.30.36/37/40]

MCNORMER, DUNCAN, was transported via Liverpool aboard the Two Brothers bound for Jamaica on 26 April 1716, landed on Montserrat in June 1716. [SPC.1716.313][CTB.31.206][CTP.CC.43]

MCOLONY, ARCHIBALD RIOCH, a Jacobite in 1715, a workman in Anaheilt, Sunart, 1716. [NRS.SC54.22.17.1]

MCPHADEN, ANGUS, a Jacobite in 1715, in Brechachie, Coll, in 1716. [NRS.SC54.22.17.1]

MCPHAIL, ANGUS, a Jacobite in 1715, in Ardtorinish, Morvern, 1716. [NRS.SC54.22.17.2]

MCPHAIL, DONALD, a Jacobite in 1715, in Ferinish Carnakalloch, Morvern, 1716. [NRS.SC54.22.17.2]

MCPHAIL, DUNCAN, was transported via Liverpool aboard the Elizabeth and Anne bound for Jamaica or Virginia on 29 June 1716, died at sea. [SPC.1716.310][CTB.31.208]

MCPHAIL, LUDOVIC, from Alvie, Inverness-shire, died in Lancaster Prison on 7 May 1716. [LBR]

MCPHAIL, PAUL, a Jacobite in 1715, in Strone, Morvern, 1716. [NRS.SC54.22.17.2]

MCPHATRISH, NEIL, a Jacobite in 1715, in Couin, Quinish, Mull, 1716. [NRS.SC54.22.17.2]

MCPHERSON, ALEXANDER, was transported via Liverpool aboard the Wakefield bound for South Carolina on 21 April 1716. [SPC.1716.309][CTB.31.205]

MCPHERSON, ALEXANDER, was transported via Liverpool aboard the Two Brothers bound for Jamaica on 26 April 1716, landed on Montserrat in June 1716. [SPC.1716.313][CTB.31.206][CTP.CC.43]

MCPHERSON, ANGUS, was transported via Liverpool aboard the Susannah bound for South Carolina on 7 May 1716. [SPC.1716.309][CTB.31.206]

MCPHERSON, DANIEL, was transported via Liverpool aboard the Scipio bound for Antigua on 30 March 1716. [SPC.1716.310][CTB.31.204]

MCPHERSON, DONALD, was transported via Liverpool aboard the Susannah bound for South Carolina on 7 May 1716. [SPC.1716.309][CTB.31.206]

MCPHERSON, DONALD, was transported via Liverpool aboard the Wakefield bound for South Carolina on 21 April 1716. [SPC.1716.309][CTB.31.205]

MCPHERSON, DUNCAN, was transported via Liverpool aboard the Susannah bound for South Carolina on 7 May 1716. [SPC.1716.309][CTB.31.206]

MCPHERSON, JOHN, was transported via Liverpool aboard the

Susannah bound for South Carolina on 7 May 1716.
[SPC.1716.309][CTB.31.206]

MCPHERSON, alias MCPHUIL VCLACHLAN, JOHN, a Jacobite in
1715, in Langapole, Torloisk, 1716. [NRS.SC54.54.22.17.2]

MCPHERSON, LACHLAN, from Dunlichtie, Inverness-shire, died in
Lancaster Prison on 1 January 1716. [LBR]

MCPHERSON, MURDCH, servant to the Captain of Clanranald,
captured at Sheriffmuir, was transported aboard the pink
Marlborough of Leith master John Hutton, from Leith to London
in December 1715. [NRS.RH2.4.308]

MCPHERSON, OWEN, was transported via Liverpool aboard the
Elizabeth and Anne bound for Jamaica or Virginia on 29 June
1716, landed at York, Virginia.
[SPC.1716.310][CTB.31.208][VSP.I.185]

MCPHERSON, THOMAS, from Dellerich, Inverness-shire, died in
Lancaster Prison on 22 February 1716. [LBR]

MCPHERSON, WILLIAM, from Alvie, Inverness-shire, died in
Lancaster Prison on 22 January 1716. [LBR]

MCPHERSON, WILLIAM, was transported via Liverpool aboard the
Goodspeed bound for Virginia on 28 July 1716, landed in
Maryland in October 1716. [SPC.1716.310][HM.388][CTB.31.209]

MCQUARRIE, DONALD MORE, a Jacobite in 1715, in Breckachie,
Coll, in 1716. [NRS.SC54.22.17.1]

MCQUARRIE, DONALD, a Jacobite in 1715, in Soubie, Ulva, 1716.
[NRS.SC54.22.17.2]

MCQUARRIE, HECTOR, a Jacobite in 1715, in Ardnacallich, Ulva,
1716. [NRS.SC54.22.17.1]

MCQUARRIE, HECTOR, a Jacobite in 1715, in Ua, Ulva, 1716. [NRS.SC54.22.17.1]

MCQUARRIE, LACHLAN, of Ulva, a Jacobite in 1715, in Ardnacallich, Ulva, 1716. [NRS.SC54.22.17.2]

MCQUARRIE, PAUL, a Jacobite in 171, in Balligartan, Ulva, 1716. [NRS.SC54.22.17.2]

MCQUEEN, ALEXANDER, from Moy, Inverness-shire, died in Lancaster Prison on 7 March 1716. [LBR]

MCQUEEN, ALEXANDER, was transported via Liverpool aboard the Wakefield bound for South Carolina on 21 April 1716. [SPC.1716.309][CTB.31.205]

MCQUEEN, ALEXANDER, was transported via Liverpool aboard the Friendship bound for Virginia on 24 May 1716, landed in Maryland in August 1716. [HM.387][SPC.1716.311]

MCQUEEN, DANIEL, was transported via Liverpool aboard the Scipio bound for Antigua on 30 March 1716. [SPC.1716.310][CTB.31.204]

MCQUEEN, DAVID, was transported via Liverpool aboard the Wakefield bound for South Carolina on 21 April 1716. [SPC.1716.309][CTB.31.205]

MCQUEEN, DAVID, was transported via Liverpool aboard the Friendship bound for Virginia on 24 May 1716, landed in Maryland in August 1716. [HM.387][SPC.1716.311]

MCQUEEN, DAVID, paymaster of Macintosh's Regiment, 1715, a prisoner at Preston. [NRS.GD1.53.72]

MCQUEEN, DOUGAL, an Ensign of McIntosh's Regiment, a prisoner at Preston in 1715, possibly was transported via

Liverpool aboard the Friendship bound for Virginia on 24 May 1716, landed in Maryland in August 1716.
[HM.386][SPC.1716.311][CS.V.162] [NRS.GD1.53.72]

MCQUEEN, DUNCAN, was transported via Liverpool aboard the Wakefield bound for South Carolina on 21 April 1716.
[SPC.1716.309][CTB.31.205]

MCQUEEN, HECTOR, was transported via Liverpool aboard the Friendship bound for Virginia on 24 May 1716, landed in Maryland in August 1716. [HM.387][SPC.1716.311]

MCQUEEN, JOHN, a Subaltern in Murray's Regiment, a prisoner at Preston in 1715, possibly was transported via Liverpool aboard the Wakefield bound for South Carolina on 21 April 1716.
[SPC.1716.309][CTB.31.205][CS.V.161] [NRS.GD1.53.72]

MCQUEEN, JOHN, from Petty, Inverness-shire, died in Lancaster Prison on 2 April 1716. [LBR]

MCQUEEN, WILLIAM, paymaster of McIntosh's Regiment, a prisoner at Preston in 1715. [CS.V.162]

MCQUEEN, WILLIAM, a Subaltern in McIntosh's Regiment, a prisoner at Preston in 1715. [CS.V.162]

MCQUIN, ALEXANDER, possibly was transported via Liverpool aboard the Wakefield bound for South Carolina on 21 April 1716.
[SPC.1716.309][CTB.31.205]

MCQUIN, DANIEL, was transported via Liverpool aboard the Elizabeth and Anne bound for Jamaica or Virginia on 29 June 1716, landed at York, Virginia.
[SPC.1716.310][CTB.31.208][VSP.I.185]

MCRAW, DONALD, in Tullibardine's Regiment, fought at Sheriffmuir, a prisoner in 1715. [CAT.II.206]

131

MCRAW, HUGH, in Tullibardine's Regiment, fought at Sheriffmuir, a prisoner in 1715. [CAT.II.206]

MCRORIE or CAMPBELL, ANGUS, a Jacobite in 1715, in Arnabost, Coll, in 1716. [NRS.SC54.22.17.1]

MCRORIE, LACHLAN VCEAN VCNEIL, a Jacobite in 1715, in Harven, Treshnish, 1716. [NRS.SC54.22.17.2.]

MCROY, FARINTRAN, a Captain of Macintosh's Regiment, a prisoner at Preston, 1715. [NRS.GD1.53.72]

MCRUARIE, MORE, DONALD, a Jacobite in 1715, in Totronald, Coll, in 1716. [NRS.SC54.22.17.1-2]

MCSHOULL, PATRICK, an Ensign of McIntosh's Regiment, a prisoner at Preston in 1715. [CS.V.162] [NRS.GD1.53.72]

MCVANE, JOHN, was transported via Liverpool aboard the Susannah bound for South Carolina on 7 May 1716. [SPC.1716.309][CTB.31.206]

MCVANE, MALCOLM, was transported via Liverpool aboard the Susannah bound for South Carolina on 7 May 1716. [SPC.1716.309][CTB.31.206]

MCVANNICH, ANGUS ROY, a Jacobite in 1715, in Ostramule, Aros, Mull, 1716. [NRS.SC54.22.17.2.]

MCVANNICH, JOHN, a Jacobite in 1715, in Grisiboll Coll, in 1716. [NRS.SC54.22.17.1]

MCVURICH, DONALD, servant to the Captain of Clanranald, captured at Sheriffmuir, was transported aboard the pink Marlborough of Leith master John Hutton, from Leith to London in December 1715. [NRS.RH2.4.308]

MAITLAND, ALEXANDER, at the Jacobite Court in Urbino, Italy, died in September 1717. [JU]

MAITLAND, CHARLES, Earl of Lauderdale, born 1688, son of John Maitland, fought at Sheriffmuir in 1715, died 15 July 1744. [SP.V.311]

MAITLAND, DAVID, son of Reverend John Maitland minister at Forgue, Aberdeenshire, a Jacobite in 1715. [JAB.237]

MAITLAND, GEORGE, a Jacobite in 1715. [CRA.27]

MAITLAND, JAMES, born 1671, son of Reverend John Maitland and his wife Bethia Orr, minister at Inverkeithny, Banffshire, a Jacobite in 1715, deposed in 1715, died in 1740. [F.6.263][JAB.237]

MAITLAND, RICHARD, son of Richard Maitland minister of Inverkeithny, minister of Nigg, Ross and Cromarty, from 1674 until deposed in 1716, a Jacobite in 1715. [F.6.69][JAB.237]

MAITLAND, WILLIAM, a Jacobite in 1715, a prisoner at Preston and in London. [CS.V.10/186][NRS.GD1.53.72.1]

MALCOLM, JAMES, of Grange, Kilconquhar, Fife, estate forfeited in 1715. [NRS.E634][JSAHR.xvi.56]

MALCOLM, JAMES, a Jacobite, captured at Dunfermline, Fife, on 24 November 1715. [JAB.104]

MALCOLM, JAMES, was transported via Liverpool aboard the Elizabeth and Anne bound for Jamaica or Virginia on 29 June 1716, landed at York, Virginia. [SPC.1716.310][CTB.31.208][VSP.I.186]

MALCOLM, ROBERT, a Jacobite, captured at Dunfermline, Fife, on 24 November 1715. [JAB.104]

MALLONE, JAMES, was transported via Liverpool aboard the Goodspeed bound for Virginia on 28 July 1716, landed in Maryland in October 1716. [SPC.1716.310][HM.388][CTB.31.209]

MANN, WILLIAM, was transported via Liverpool aboard the Friendship bound for Virginia on 24 May 1716, landed in Maryland in August 1716. [HM.387][SPC.1716.311]

MARJORYBANKS, GEORGE, was transported via Liverpool aboard the Elizabeth and Anne bound for Jamaica or Virginia on 29 June 1716, landed at York, Virginia.
[SPC.1716.310][CTB.31.208][VSP.I.185]

MARR, GEORGE, a merchant in Aberdeen, a Jacobite in 1715. [JAB.213]

MARTIN, PETER, a servant to John Hamilton of Gibston, a Jacobite in 1715, imprisoned in Newgate, discharged. [JAB.126]

MARTIN, WILLIAM, was transported via Liverpool aboard the Elizabeth and Anne bound for Jamaica or Virginia on 29 June 1716, landed at York, Virginia.
[SPC.1716.310][CTB.31.208][VSP.I.185]

MARTISON, JOHN, was transported via Liverpool aboard the Friendship bound for Virginia on 24 May 1716, landed in Maryland in August 1716. [HM.387][SPC.1716.311]

MASTERTON, JOHN, a merchant in Edinburgh, a Jacobite in 1715, imprisoned at Preston and in London. [CS.V.161/186] [NRS.GD1.53.72]

MATHIE, JAMES, a maltman and a burgess of Perth, a Jacobite in 1715, carried arms, a prisoner. [NRS.B59.30.36/37/40]

MATHESON, ..., of Ormadgefield, a Jacobite at Sheriffmuir, 1715. [NRS.RH2.4.308/170];

MATTEWSON, JOHN, was transported via Liverpool aboard the
Susannah bound for South Carolina on 7 May 1716.
[SPC.1716.309][CTB.31.206]

MAULE, GEORGE, son of Patrick Maule and his wife Christian
Forbes, factor for the Earl of Panmure, a prisoner at Preston in
1715, in Carlisle Castle, a letter 7 November 1716.
[JAB.155][SUL.Cheap.5.537][NRS.E650.5]

MAULE, HARRY, of Kellie, Angus, a Jacobite in 1715, escaped to
Leiden, Holland, in 1716, died 23 June 1734.
[NRS.GD1.616.36][NRS.GD45.26.73][SP.VII.22][CRA.233]

MAULE, JAMES, Earl of Panmure, Angus, son of George Maule,
fought at Sheriffmuir in 1715, estates forfeited in 1715, escaped
via Montrose on 3 February 1716 to the Netherlands then to
France, at the Jacobite Court in Urbino, Italy, 1717, died in Paris
on 6 April 1720. [JU][NRS.GD45.26.73; GD45.14.251; E650.79]
[SP.VII.26][CRA.233]

MAULE, PATRICK, minister of Panbride, Angus, from 1680, a
Jacobite in 1715, deposed in April 1716. [NRS.GD45.1.198]
[F.V.448][HHA.171][NRS.CH2.15.3]

MAXWELL, CHARLES, of Cowhill, a Jacobite in 1715, a prisoner at
Preston and in London. [CS.V.160/186] [NRS.GD1.53.72]

MAXWELL, EDMUND/EDWARD, of Carnselloch, the younger, a
Jacobite in 1715, a prisoner at Preston and in London.
[CS.V.160/186] [NRS.GD1.53.72]

MAXWELL, GEORGE, son of Maxwell of Munshes, a Jacobite in
1715, a prisoner at Preston. [CS.V.160] [NRS.GD1.53.72]

MAXWELL, JAMES, son of Maxwell of Castlemills, a Jacobite in
1715, a prisoner at Preston. [CS.V.160] [NRS.GD1.53.72]

MAXWELL, JOHN, of Steilston, a Jacobite in 1715, a prisoner at Preston and in London. [CS.V.160/186] [NRS.GD1.53.72]

MAXWELL, Sir PATRICK, of Springkeil, a Jacobite in 1715. [SP.V.127]

MAXWELL, SAMUEL, a Jacobite in 1715, a prisoner at Preston. [CS.V.160] [NRS.GD1.53.72]

MAXWELL, WILLIAM, of Munshes, the younger, a Jacobite in 1715, a prisoner at Preston, possibly was transported via Liverpool aboard the Elizabeth and Anne bound for Jamaica or Virginia on 29 June 1716, landed at York, Virginia. [SPC.1716.310][CTB.31.208][VSP.I.186][CS.V.160] [NRS.GD1.53.72]

MAXWELL, WILLIAM, Earl of Nithsdale, born 1676, son of Robert Maxwell, a Jacobite in 1715, captured at Preston in 1715, his estates in Dumfries-shire were forfeited in 1715, he escaped from the Tower of London, at the Jacobite Court in Urbino, Italy, 1717, died in Rome on 20 March 1744. [NRS.GD1.53.72] [JU][SM.6.198][SP.III.417][NRS.E649]

MELDRUM, GEORGE, was transported via Liverpool aboard the Scipio bound for Antigua on 30 March 1716. [SPC.1716.310]

MENZIES, ALEXANDER, of Woodend, parish of Maddertie, Perthshire, Captain of Charles Murray's Regiment, fought at Preston in 1715, a prisoner, estate forfeited in 1716, tried on 11 May 1716 – found guilty. [NRS.GD1.53.72] [MHP.303][CAT.II.211][CS.V.161][NRS.E662]

MENZIES, ARCHIBALD, a Subaltern in Lord Nairne's Regiment, a Jacobite in 1715, fought at Preston, a prisoner, tried and executed at Garstang in February 1716. [MHP.303][CAT.II.210][CS.V.161/194] [NRS.GD1.53.72]

MENZIES, ARCHIBALD, was transported via Liverpool aboard the Elizabeth and Anne bound for Jamaica or Virginia on 29 June 1716, landed at York, Virginia.
[SPC.1716.310][CTB.31.208][VSP.I.185]

MENZIES, CHARLES, of Kinmundy, a solicitor, a Jacobite in 1715.
[JAB.155]

MENZIES, GEORGE, at the Jacobite Court in Urbino, Italy, 1717
[JU]

MENZIES, JAMES, of Culdares, a Captain of Murray's Regiment, fought at Preston in 1715, a prisoner, tried on 11 May 1716 – not guilty, pardoned. [CAT.II.211][CS.V.161][MHP.304]
[NRS.GD1.53.72]

MENZIES, JAMES, a maltman and burgess of Perth, a Jacobite in 1715, a soldier of the Perth company, surrendered.
[NRS.N59.30.17/36/37/40]

MENZIES, JAMES, son of the above, a burgess of Perth, a Jacobite in 1715, surrendered. [NRS.B59.30.36/37/40]

MENZIES, JOHN, a tenant of Weem's, Perthshire, in Tullibardine's Regiment, fought at Sheriffmuir, a prisoner was marched via Blackness, Stirling, to Carlisle in September 1716.
[CAT.II.206/239]

MENZIES, ROBERT, a tenant of Weems, Perthshire, in Tullibardine's Regiment, fought at Sheriffmuir, a prisoner was marched via Blackness and Stirling, to Carlisle in September 1716.
[CAT.II.206/239]

MENZIES, ROBERT, of Balnavert, a Subaltern in Murray's Regiment, a Jacobite in 1715, fought at Preston, a prisoner.
[CAT.II.210][CS.V.161]

MENZIES, ROBERT, possibly brother to Menzies of Culdares, a Subaltern in Murray's Regiment in 1715. [CAT.II.211] [NRS.GD1.53.72]

MENZIES, ROBERT, a Subaltern in Nairne's Regiment, was transported via Liverpool aboard the Elizabeth and Anne bound for Jamaica or Virginia on 29 June 1716, landed at York, Virginia. [SPC.1716.310][CTB.31.208][VSP.I.186] [NRS.GD1.53.72]

MENZIES, WILLIAM, a letter, 1715. [NRS.GD1.53.70]

MENZIES, WILLIAM, a tenant of Weems, Perthshire, in Tullibardine's Regiment, fought at Sheriffmuir, a prisoner was marched via Blackness and Stirling to Carlisle in September 1716. [CAT.II.206/239]

MENZIES, WILLIAM, a tenant of Weems, Perthshire, a Jacobite in 1715, a prisoner in Blackness, Stirling, and Carlisle. [CAT.II.239]

MENZIES, WILLIAM, of Pitfoddels, Aberdeenshire, born 1688, son of William Menzies of Pitfoddels and his wife Beatrix Fletcher, a Jacobite in 1715, fought at Sheriffmuir, surrendered on 22 February 1716, imprisoned in Edinburgh, escaped, died on 6 January 1780. [JAB.156][CRA.210][TNA.SP.54.18.157]

MERCER, JAMES, a Jacobite in 1715, a soldier in the Perth company. [NRS.B59.30.17]

MESTON, WILLIAM, born 1680 in Midmar, Aberdeenshire, son of William Meston and his wife Katherine Leonard, Professor of Philosophy at Marischal College in Aberdeen, a Jacobite in 1715, died in 1745. [JAB.158]

MICHEY, JOHN, was transported via Liverpool aboard the Elizabeth and Anne bound for Jamaica or Virginia on 29 June 1716, landed at York, Virginia. [SPC.1716.310][VSP.I.186]

MIDDLETON, Captain ALEXANDER, born 1676, son of Reverend George Middleton, a Jacobite in 1715, died 26 October 1751. [JAB.158]

MIDDLETON, Reverend GEORGE, born 1645, son of Dr Alexander Middleton the Principal of King's College, Aberdeen, a Jacobite in 1715, deposed in 1716, died in May 1726. [JAB.239]

MILL, ALEXANDER, of New Milns, a Jacobite in 1715, a prisoner at Preston and in London. [CS.V.161/186] [NRS.GD1.53.72]

MILL, DAVID, was transported via Liverpool aboard the Friendship bound for Virginia on 24 May 1716, landed in Maryland in August 1716. [HM.386][SPC.1716.311]

MILL, THOMAS, in Perth, a Jacobite in 1715. [NRS.B59.30.10]

MILLER, ROBERT, a Jacobite in 1715, Corporal of the Perth company. [NRS.B59.30.17]

MILLER, WILLIAM, Captain of Strathmore's Regiment, a prisoner at Preston in 1715. [CS.V.162] [NRS.GD1.53.72]

MILN, PATRICK, a cooper and burgess of Perth, a Jacobite in 1715, carried arms, a prisoner. [NRS.B59.36/40]

MILN, WILLIAM, a cooper and burgess of Perth, a Jacobite in 1715, carried arms, a prisoner. [NRS.B59.36/40]

MILN, WILLIAM, an Ensign of McIntosh's Regiment, a prisoner at Preston in 1715. [CS.V.162] [NRS.GD1.53.72]

MITCHELL, DAVID, was transported via Liverpool aboard the Elizabeth and Anne bound for Jamaica or Virginia on 29 June 1716, landed at York, Virginia.
[SPC.1716.310][CTB.31.208][VSP.I.185]

MITCHELL, GEORGE, was transported via Liverpool aboard the Wakefield bound for South Carolina on 21 April 1716. [SPC.1716.309][CTB.31.205]

MITCHELL, GEORGE, was transported via Liverpool aboard the Hockenhill bound for St Kitts on 21 April 1716, mutinied and landed on Sint Maartens in September 1716. [CTB.31.208][JAB.21]

MITCHELL, JAMES, was transported via Liverpool aboard the Friendship bound for Virginia on 24 May 1716, landed in Maryland in August 1716. [HM.387][SPC.1716.311]

MITCHELL, THOMAS, born in 1659, son of Thomas Mitchell and his wife Marjory Moir, a Jacobite in 1715, died on 20 December 1719. [JAB.159]

MOIR, ALEXANDER, of Scotstown, son of Dr William Moir and his wife Jean Abernethy, a Jacobite in 1715, escaped via Banff to Norway and from there to Holland, died in Scotland in 1752. [JAB.159][CRA.237]

MOIR, ALEXANDER, son of John Moir, Regent of Marischal College, Aberdeen, a Jacobite in 1715. [JAB.160]

MOIR, JAMES, of Stoneywood, born 1659, son of Dr William Moir and his wife Jean Abernethy, escaped via Banff to Norway on 8 April 1716, died in Aberdeen on 22 November 1739. [JAB.161]

MOIR, WILLIAM, a farmer in Cushnie, Aberdeenshire, a Jacobite in 1715, was transported to Virginia in 1716. [JAB.151/153]

MOIR, WILLIAM, of Invernetty, Peterhead, Aberdeenshire, born 1669, son of John Moir of Stoneywood and his wife Jean Sandilands, escaped via Banff to Norway on 8 April 1716, testament, 1744, Comm. Aberdeen. [NRS][CRA.144][JAB.162]

MOIR, WILLIAM, bursar of King's College, Aberdeen, a Jacobite in 1715. [JAB.210]

MONCRIEFF, DAVID, a soldier of the Perth company in 1715. [NRS.B59.30.17]

MONCRIEFF, GEORGE, a maltman and councillor of Perth, a Jacobite in 1715, carried arms. [NRS.B59.30.36]

MONCRIEFF, GEORGE, a writer in Perth, a Jacobite in 1715. [NRS.B59.30.37/40]

MONDELL, JOHN, was transported via Liverpool aboard the Elizabeth and Anne bound for Jamaica or Virginia on 29 June 1716, landed at York, Virginia. [SPC.1716.310][CTB.31.208] [VSP.I.185]

MONTGOMERY, NICHOLAS, was transported via Liverpool aboard the Elizabeth and Anne bound for Jamaica or Virginia on 29 June 1716. [SPC.1716.310][CTB.31.208]

MOODY, GEORGE, was transported via Liverpool aboard the Two Brothers bound for Jamaica on 26 April 1716, landed on Montserrat in June 1716. [SPC.1716.313][CTB.31.205][CTP.CC.43]

MORISON, ARCHIBALD, a Jacobite in 1715, in Kilfhinichen, Broloss, Mull, 1716. [NRS.SC54.22.17.2]

MORRISON, EDMUN, a Jacobite in 1715, on Creich, Ross of Mull, Argyll, in 1716. [NRS.SC54.22.54]

MORRISON, HECTOR, a Jacobite in 1715, in Kaolis Coll, in 1716. . [NRS.SC54.22.17.1]

MORRISON, JAMES, was transported via Liverpool aboard the Scipio bound for Antigua on 30 March 1716. [SPC.1716.310][CTB.31.204]

MORISON, JOHN, a Jacobite in 1715, in Potmore, Coll, 1716.
[NRS.SC54.22.17.1]

MORISON, RORY, a Jacobite in 1715, in Pennimore, Morenish,
1716. [NRS.SC54.22.17.2.]

MORRISON, WILLIAM, a Jacobite in 1715, in Pennimore,
Morenish, 1716. [NRS.SC54.22.17.2.]

MORTIMER, ALEXANDER, was transported via Liverpool aboard
the Friendship bound for Virginia on 24 May 1716, landed in
Maryland in August 1716. [SPC.1716.311][HM.387]

 MORTIMER, GEORGE, was transported via Liverpool aboard the
Two Brothers bound for Jamaica on 26 April 1716, landed on
Montserrat in June 1716. [SPC.1716.313][CTB.31.206][CTP.CC.43]

MOUBRAY, WILLIAM, was transported via Liverpool aboard the
Friendship bound for Virginia on 24 May 1716, landed in
Maryland in August 1716. [SPC.1716.311][HM.387]

MOWAT, WILLIAM, a merchant in Aberdeen, a Jacobite tax
collector in 1715. [JAB.208]

MURDOCH, JOHN, a carrier and burgess of Perth, a Jacobite in
1715, surrendered. [NRS.B59.30.36/37/40]

MURRAY, ALEXANDER, a merchant in Edinburgh, a prisoner at
Preston in 1715. [CS.V.161] [NRS.GD1.53.72]

MURRAY, Sir ALEXANDER, of Stanhope, letters, 1715, a prisoner
at Preston and in London in 1716. [NRS.GD1.53.72.1]
[CS.V.160/186][NLS.GB233.Adv.ms29.1.1]

MURRAY, ALEXANDER, was transported via Liverpool aboard the
Anne bound for Virginia on 31 July 1716.
[SPC.1716.310][CTB.31.209]

MURRAY, Lord CHARLES, born 24 September 1691, son of John Murray and his wife Katherine Hamilton, Colonel of Mar's Regiment, fought at Preston in 1715, taken prisoner, court martialled as having a commission in the army of King George on 28 November 1715, reprieved in 1717, died in London on 28 August 1720. [CAT.II.209/211][CS.V.161][SP.I.482][MHP.296] [NRS.GD1.53.72]

MURRAY, DAVID, was transported via Liverpool aboard the Anne bound for Virginia on 31 July 1716. [SPC.1716.310][CTB.31.209]

MURRAY, Lord GEORGE, born 4 October 1694, son of John Murray and his wife Katherine Hamilton, an officer of the Atholl Brigade in 1715, exiled to France and Italy, died in Medemblik, Holland, on 11 October 1760. [SP.I.484]

MURRAY, HENRY, was transported via Liverpool aboard the Scipio bound for Antigua on 30 March 1716. [SPC.1716.311][CTB.31.204]

MURRAY, JAMES, born 1690, son of David Murray the Viscount Stormont, and his wife Marjory Scott, a Jacobite in 1715, escaped to France in 1716, at the Jacobite Court in Urbino, Italy, 1718. [JU][JP44]; Acting Secretary of State, 1719-1721, he died in Avignon, France, in August 1770. [SI.357][JP.44][SP.VIII.205]

MURRAY, JAMES, Lord Nairn, a Jacobite, at Preston In 1715. [NRS.GD220.455.26; RH2.4.305.107]

MURRAY, JAMES, late in Rivall, a prisoner at Preston, 1715. [NRS.GD1.53.72]

MURRAY, JOHN, born 1691, a Lieutenant Colonel in Lord Charles Murray's Regiment, captured at Preston in 1715, guilty of high treason but acquitted, died in France on 11 July 1770. [JP.127] [NRS.GD1.53.72]

MURRAY, Sir PATRICK, of Ochtertyre, a Jacobite in 1715.
[TNA.SP54.8.1]

MURRAY, ROBERT, brother of Abercairny, a Jacobite in 1715, was
captured at Dunfermline, Fife, 1715. [MHP.297]

MURRAY, WILLIAM, born in the Garioch, Aberdeenshire, minister
of Inverurie, Aberdeenshire from 1679 until deposed in 1716, a
Jacobite in 1715, husband of Magdalen Gellie. [F.6.161]

MURRAY, WILLIAM, born 1688, son of the Duke of Atholl and his
wife Katherine Douglas, the Marquis of Tullibardine, a letter,
1715. [NRS.GD1.616.14]; a Jacobite in 1715, escaped to France,
participated in the '45, was captured after Culloden and died in
the Tower of London in 1746. [JP.153][MHP.303]

MURRAY, WILLIAM, born 1665, son of the Marquis of Atholl,
inherited title of Lord Nairne, was captured at Preston in 1715,
imprisoned in the Tower of London, condemned to death but
reprieved, was created Earl of Nairne in 1721, died 3 February
1726. [JP.126]

MURRAY, WILLIAM, the younger of Ochtertyre, was captured at
the Battle of Sheriffmuir, imprisoned in Edinburgh Castle in 1715.
[MHP.298][NRS.RH15.123.40][CAT.II.205]

NAIRNE, Sir DAVID, a Secretary at the Jacobite Court in Urbino,
Italy, 1717. [JU]; Secretary of the Closet, 1713-1728. [SI.357]

NAIRNE, Major DAVID, in Saintes, France. 1717.
[HMC.Stuart.v.48]

NAIRNE, GEORGE, brother to the laird of Baldovan, an Ensign of
the Earl of Panmure's Regiment of Foot in 1715.
[NRS.GD45.1.201]

NAIRNE, GEORGE, surgeon of the Earl of Panmure's Regiment of
Foot in 1715. [NRS.GD45.1.201]

NAIRNE, JOHN, the Master of Nairne, Lieutenant Colonel of
Charles Murray's Regiment, a prisoner at Preston in 1715, pled

guilty at his trial on 31 May 1715. [MHP.303][CAT.II.211/217] [NRS.GD1.53.72]

NAIRNE, Major, son of an Edinburgh baillie, was captured at Preston, court-martialled and executed in 1715. [MHP.296] [CS.V.161/175] [NRS.GD1.53.72]

NAIRNE, WILLIAM, Lord Nairne, Perthshire, a Jacobite in 1715, Colonel of Nairne's Regiment, a prisoner at Preston, estate forfeited in 1715, tried 19 January 1716, sentenced to death, pardoned. [MHP.303][CS.V.161][NRS.E684][CAT.II.210] [NRS.GD1.53.72]

NAIRNE, WILLIAM, of Baldovan, a Captain of the Earl of Panmure's Regiment of Foot in 1715, fought at Sheriffmuir, a prisoner in 1715. [NRS.GD45.1.201][CAT.II.205]

NEAVE, ALEXANDER, was transported via Liverpool aboard the Friendship bound for Virginia on 24 May 1716, landed in Maryland in August 1716. [SPC1716.311][HM.386]

NELSON, GEORGE, was transported via Liverpool aboard the Goodspeed bound for Virginia on 28 July 1716, landed in Maryland in October 1716. [SPC.1716.310][HM.386]

NEVIN, JOHN, a Jacobite in 1715, a soldier of the Perth company. [NRS.B59.30.17]

NEVERY, JAMES, was transported via Liverpool aboard the Friendship bound for Virginia on 24 May 1716, landed in Maryland in August 1716. [SPC1716.311][HM.386]

NEWLANDS, JOHN, a Jacobite in 1715, a soldier of the Perth company. [NRS.B59.30.17]

NEWTON, JONATHAN, was transported via Liverpool aboard the Susannah bound for South Carolina on 7 May 1716. [SPC.1716.309][CTB.31.206]

NICOLSON, JAMES, a prisoner at Preston and in London in 1716.
[CS.V.160/186] [NRS.GD1.53.72]

NICOLSON, JOHN, was transported via Liverpool aboard the
Scipio bound for Antigua on 30 March 1716.
[SPC.1716.311][CTB.31.204]

NICOLSON, JOHN, was transported via Liverpool aboard the
Wakefield bound for South Carolina on 21 April 1716.
[SPC.1716.309][CTB.31.205]

NIMMO, JAMES, was transported via Liverpool aboard the Scipio
bound for Antigua on 30 March 1716.
[SPC.1716.310][CTB.31.204]

NISBET, JAMES, son of James Nisbet the factor of Airth,
Stirlingshire, a Jacobite in 1715, was transported via Liverpool
aboard the Elizabeth and Anne bound for Jamaica or Virginia on
29 June 1716, landed at York, Virginia.
[SPC.1716.310][CTB.31.208] [VSP.I.185] [NRS.GD1.53.72]

NIVEN, THOMAS, a merchant in Aberdeen, a Jacobite in 1715.
[JAB.163]

NOBLE, WILLIAM, was transported via Liverpool aboard the
Elizabeth and Anne bound for Jamaica or Virginia on 29 June
1716, landed at York, Virginia. [SPC.1716.310][CTB.31.208]
[VSP.I.186]

NORIE, ROBERT, born 1647, son of Reverend Robert Norie,
minister in Dundee, a Jacobite in 1715, deposed 1716, later
Episcopal Bishop of Brechin, husband of Isabel Guthrie, died in
March 1727. [F.5.320]

OGILVIE, ARCHIBALD, of Rothiemay, born 1680, son of Sir Patrick
Ogilvie and his wife Anne Douglas, a Jacobite in 1715,

surrendered at Banff in November 1716.
[TNA.SP54.12.236][JAB.165]

OGILVIE, DAVID, son of David Ogilvie, Earl of Airlie, and his wife Grizel Lyon, a Jacobite in 1715, died 12 January 1731. [SP.I.127]

OGILVIE, HENRY, an Ensign of Strathmore's Regiment, a prisoner at Preston in 1715, was transported via Liverpool aboard the Hockenhill bound for St Kitts on 25 June 1716, mutinied and landed on Sint Maartens in September 1716.
[CS.V.162][JAB.21][SPC.1716.312][CTB.31.207] [NRS.GD1.53.72]

OGILVIE, JAMES, son of David Ogilvie, Earl of Airlie, and his wife Grizel Lyon, a Jacobite in 1715, died on 12 January 1731.
[SP.I.127]

OGILVIE, JAMES, of Boyne, son of Sir Patrick Ogilvie and his wife Anna Grant, fought at Sheriffmuir in1715, escaped to France in 1716, was a Colonel in the service of King James VIII on 9 October 1723. [JP.245][JAB.167]

OGILVIE, JOHN, bursar of King's College, Aberdeen, a Jacobite in 1715. [JAB.211]

OGILVIE, JOHN, a Jacobite in 1718. [HMC.Stuart.vii.173]

OGILVIE, PATRICK, in Aberdeen, a Jacobite in 1715. [JAB.211]

OGILVIE, WILLIAM, Chamberlain to the Earl of Errol, a Jacobite in 1715, fought at Sheriffmuir, a prisoner in Carlisle and in Edinburgh, died in Edinburgh Castle.
[TNA.SP54.12.152][JAB.168/217]

OGSTON, JAMES, was transported via Liverpool aboard the Anne bound for Virginia on 31 July 1716. [CTB.31.209]

OLIPHANT, ALEXANDER, a Jacobite in 1715, Lieutenant of the Perth company. [NRS.B59.30.11/36]

OLIPHANT, DAVID, a Jacobite in 1715, a soldier of the Perth company. [NRS.B50.30.17]

OLIPHANT, JAMES, of Gask, a Jacobite in 1715. [OG.123].

OLIPHANT, JOHN, a bailie of Dundee, Captain of the Earl of Panmure's Regiment of Foot, Grenadiers, in 1715, escaped via Bergen, Norway, to Amsterdam in June 1716, and by 1719 was in Brussels. [NRS.GD45.1.201; GD45.14.219.1/1] [NRS.RH2.4.308/170]

OLIPHANT, LAURENCE, born 1692, son of James Oliphant of Gask, Perthshire, and his wife Janet Murray, a Lieutenant in Lord Rollo's Regiment of Horse, fought at Sheriffmuir in 1715, died at Gask in 1767. [JP.138/140][MHP.294] [NRS.GD38] [NLS.GB2333.Adv.ms.82.1.1-13]

OLIPHANT, LAWRENCE, was transported via Liverpool aboard the Hockenhill bound for St Kitts on 21 April 1716, mutinied and landed on Sint Maartens in September 1716. [CTB.31.207][JAB.21][SPC.1716.312]

OLIPHANT, WILLIAM, son of Lord Patrick Oliphant and his wife Mary Crichton, a Jacobite Colonel in 1715, escaped to France in 1716, died in Scotland on 27 December 1728. [JAB.169][SP.VI.559]

ORD, JOHN, of Findochty, Moray, son of William Ord and his wife Jean Innes, a Jacobite in 1715. [JAB.170]

ORR, DUNCAN, a Jacobite in 1715, a soldier in the Perth company. [NRS.B59.30.17]

ORROCK, ALEXANDER, a Lieutenant of Strathmore's Regiment, a prisoner at Preston in 1715, was transported via Liverpool aboard the Goodspeed bound for Virginia on 28 July 1716, landed in Maryland in October 1716. [SPC.1716.310][CTB.31.209][HM.388] [NRS.GD1.53.72]

OUCHTERLONY, ALEXANDER, son of the laird of the Guynd, an Ensign of the Earl of Panmure's Regiment of Foot in 1715. [NRS.GD45.1.201]

OUCHTERLONY, JAMES, a bailie of Montrose, an Ensign of the Earl of Panmure's Regiment of Foot in 1715. [NRS.GD45.1.201]

OUCHTERLONY, JOHN, of Flemington, Angus, born 1667, son of Alexander Ouchterlony a minister in Carmyllie, Angus, minister in Aberlemno, Angus, a Jacobite in 1715, deposed in 1716, later Episcopalian Bishop of Brechin, husband of Margaret Graham, parents of Alexander Ochterlony a merchant in Philadelphia. John died in Dundee in May 1742. [F.5.277][EF.108][TBD.10/49]

OUCHTERLONY, PATRICK, a Lieutenant of the Earl of Panmure's Regiment of Foot in 1715. [NRS.GD45.1.201]

OUCHTERLONY, ROBERT, minister of Garvock, Kincardineshire, from 1685 until deposed in 1716, died 1750. [F.V.469]

OUCHTERLONY, ROBERT, of the Guynd, Angus, an Episcopalian preacher in St Vigean's, Arbroath, in 1715. [HHA.170][NRS.CH2.575.1]

OUCHTERLONY, ..., was taken prisoner at Sheriffmuir on 3 November 1715. [CAT.II.205]

PANTON, JAMES, an Ensign of the Earl of Panmure's Regiment of Foot in 1715. [NRS.GD45.1.201]

PARK, JAMES, born 1680, a shipmaster in Peterhead, Aberdeenshire, a Jacobite in 1715, died 26 May 1739. [JAB.170/217]

PARK, THOMAS, was transported via Liverpool aboard the Goodspeed bound for Virginia on 28 July 1716, landed in Maryland in October 1716. [SPC.1716.310][HM.388]

PATERSON, DAVID, from Edinburgh, died in Lancaster Prison on 15 March 1716. [LBR]

PATERSON, GEORGE, a Jacobite in 1715, a soldier of the Perth company. [NRS.B59.30.17]

PATERSON, Sir HUGH, of Bannockburn, St Ninian's, Stirlingshire, estate forfeited, 1715. [NRS.E616]

PATERSON, JAMES, a gentleman, a prisoner in Preston and in London in 1716, possibly, was transported via Liverpool aboard the Elizabeth and Anne bound for Jamaica or Virginia on 29 June 1716, landed at York, Virginia. [SPC.1716.310][CTB.31.208] [VSP.I.186] [NRS.GD1.53.72]

PATERSON, JOHN, of Craigie, a burgess of Perth, a Jacobite in 1715, Captain of the Perth company. [NRS.B59.30.17/36/37/40]

PATERSON, JOHN, of Prestonhall, a Jacobite in 1715, a prisoner at Preston and in London. [CS.V.160/186][NRS.GD1.53.72.1]

PATERSON, JOHN, the Under- Secretary to the Earl of Mar in Urbino, Italy, 1717. [JU][HMC.Stuart. vi.75]

PATERSON, ROBERT, son of John Paterson the Bishop of Ross, Principal of Marischal College, Aberdeen, a Jacobite in 1715. [JAB.239][TNA.SP54.12.39]

PATON, ALEXANDER, of Kinaldie, son of Alexander Paton and his wife Elizabeth Dunbar, a Jacobite in 1715. [JAB.171]

PATON, JAMES, of Scotston, born 1655, minister at Kettins, Angus from 1680 until arrested in 1716, died in the 1730s. [F.V.264]

PATON, JOHN, of Grandholm, born 1675, son of George Paton
and his wife Isabella Christie, a Jacobite in 1715, surrendered on
17 February 1716, a prisoner in Carlisle, died on 5 August 1739 in
Aberdeen. [JAB.173][SUL.Cheap.5.537][CRA.237]

PATON, JOHN, in Dunkeld, Perthshire, a Jacobite in 1715.
[NRS.B59.30.15]

PATULLO, JAMES [or JOHN], was transported via Liverpool aboard
the Elizabeth and Anne bound for Jamaica or Virginia on 29 June
1716, landed at York, Virginia. [SPC.1716.310][CTB.31.208]
[VSP.I.185]

PEACOCK, GEORGE, Regent of Marischal College, Aberdeen, a
Jacobite in 1715. [JAB.173]

PEARSON, JOHN, minister of Kirkmichael in Strathardle,
Perthshire, from 1687 until deposed in 1717, died in 1720.
[F.4.164]

PETER, JAMES, was transported via Liverpool aboard the
Elizabeth and Anne bound for Jamaica or Virginia on 29 June
1716, landed at York, Virginia. [SPC.1716.310][CTB.31.208]
[VSP.I.186]

PETER, JOHN, was transported via Liverpool aboard the
Friendship bound for Virginia on 24 May 1716, landed in
Maryland in August 1716. [SPC1716.310][VSP.I.185]

PHILP, GEORGE, a glover and burgess of Perth, a Jacobite in 1715,
a soldier of the Perth company, a prisoner. [NRS.B59.30.17/40]

PHILP, JOHN, son of James Philp of Almerie Close, Arbroath,
Angus, a Jacobite in 1715, escaped to the Netherlands, joined the
Dutch West India Company, Governor of Sint Maartens in the
Dutch West Indies in 1728. [NRS.RS35.15.37][Goslinga.136]

PIRIE, GEORGE, a periwig-maker in Fraserburgh, Aberdeenshire, a Jacobite in 1715. [JAB.218]

PITCAIRN, ANDREW, of Pitcairn, Fife, son of Dr Archibald Pitcairn, a Jacobite in 1715, a prisoner at Preston and in London, estate forfeited in 1715. [CS.V.161/186][NRS.E651] [NRS.GD1.53.72]

PITSCOTTIE, JAMES, Lieutenant of the Earl of Panmure's Regiment of Foot in 1715. [NRS.GD45.1.201]

PITTENDRIGH, ROBERT, a merchant in Aberdeen, a Jacobite in 1715. [JAB.174]

PLESHINGTOUN, ..., a prisoner at Preston, 1715. [NRS.GD1.53.72]

PORTEOUS, JOHN, was transported via Liverpool aboard the Elizabeth and Anne bound for Jamaica or Virginia on 29 June 1716. [SPC.1716.310][CTB.31.208]

PRESTON, ALEXANDER, a bailie and a Jacobite in Dundee, 1715. [TNA.SP54.8.129]

PRESTON, Sir JOHN, of Prestonhall, parish of Cupar, Fife, estates forfeited in 1715, he was at the Jacobite Court in Urbino, Italy, 1717. [JU][NRS.E654]

PRINGLE, ROBERT, of Sharpitlaw, a Jacobite in 1715. [NRAS.1366]

PROCTOR, JOSEPH, was transported via Liverpool aboard the Scipio bound for Antigua on 30 March 1716. [SPC.1716.310][CTB.31.204]

PROPHET, SYLVESTER, was transported via Liverpool aboard the Elizabeth and Anne bound for Jamaica or Virginia on 29 June 1716, landed at York, Virginia. [SPC.1716.310][CTB.31.208] [VSP.I.185][SG.39.4.160]

RAE, JAMES, a farmer from Cushnie, Aberdeenshire, was transported via Liverpool aboard the Elizabeth and Anne bound for Jamaica or Virginia on 29 June 1716, landed at York, Virginia. [SPC.1716.310][CTB.31.208] [VSP.I.186][JAB.151]

RAIT, FRANCIS, son of John Rait minister at Inverkeilor, Angus, minister at Kinnaird, Angus, a Jacobite in 1715. [F.V.395]

RAIT, JAMES, born 1648, Episcopalian minister at Lunan, Angus, in 1713, deposed 1717. [F.V.439/446]

RAIT, JOHN, minister at Inverkeilor and at Lunan, Angus, a Jacobite in 1715, died 1730. [HHA.170][F.V.439]

RAIT, WILLIAM, of Pitforthy, born 1653, minister of Monikie, Angus from 1680 to 1716, deposed in April 1716. [F.V.365]

RAMSAY, ALEXANDER, an Ensign in Strathmore's Regiment, a prisoner at Preston in 1715. [CS.V.162]

RAMSAY, ANDREW, an Ensign of Strathmore's Regiment in 1715, was appointed a Captain of Foot on 22 April 1726., [NRS.GD1.53.72] [JP.245]

RAMSAY, ANDREW, was transported via Liverpool aboard the Hockenhill bound for St Kitts on 21 April 1716, mutinied and landed on Sint Maartens in September 1716. [CTB.31.207][JAB.21][SPC.1716.312]

RAMSAY, DAVID, of Cairntoun, a Lieutenant of the Earl of Panmure's Regiment of Foot in 1715. [NRS.GD45.1.201] [HHA.167][HMC.Stuart.i.457]

RAMSAY, GILBERT, born 1660, son of Robert Ramsay a merchant in Aberdeen, minister at Dyce, Aberdeenshire, a Jacobite in 1715, deposed in 1716, died on 31 May 1728. [F.VI.55][JAB.240]

RAMSAY, JAMES, of Drumlochy, a Subaltern in Lord Nairne's Regiment, fought at Preston in 1715, a prisoner, estate forfeited in 1715. [MHP.303][NRS.E625][CAT.ii.210][CS.V.161] [NRS.GD1.53.72]

RAMSAY, JAMES, factor to the Earl of Kinnaird, in Perthshire, a Jacobite in 1715. [NRS.B59.30.36]

RAMSAY.JOHN, was transported via Liverpool aboard the Friendship bound for Virginia on 24 May 1716, landed in Maryland in August 1716. [SPC1716.311][MHP.303][Md.Arch.34.164][HM.387]

RAMSAY, ROBERT, from Edinburgh, a Jacobite in 1715, a prisoner at Preston. [CS.V.161] [NRS.GD1.53.72]

RAMSAY, WILLIAM, was transported via Liverpool aboard the Hockenhill bound for St Kitts on 21 April 1716, mutinied and landed on Sint Maartens in September 1716. [CTB.31.207][JAB.21][SPC.1716.312][JAB.21]

RAMSAY, WILLIAM, a Jacobite in 1715. [JAB.217]

RAMSAY, WILLIAM, a magistrate of Dundee, 1715. [RH2.4.308/170]

RANKEN, JOHN, was transported via Liverpool aboard the Wakefield bound for South Carolina on 21 April 1716. [SPC.1716.309][CTB.31.205]

RASH, JAMES, was transported via Liverpool aboard the Wakefield bound for South Carolina on 21 April 1716. [SPC.1716.309][CTB.31.205]

RATTRAY, JOHN, in Tullibardine's Regiment, fought at Sheriffmuir, a prisoner at Carlisle in December 1716. [CAT.II.206][SUL.Cheap.5.37][MHP.303]

REID, ADAM, of Edradynate, Perthshire, a Subaltern in Murray's Regiment, fought at Preston, a prisoner. [CAT.II.211][CS.V.161] [NRS.GD1.53.72]

REID, ALEXANDER, from Alford, Aberdeenshire, was transported via Liverpool aboard the Friendship bound for Virginia on 24 May 1716, settled at Reidbourne on the Chester River, Calvert County, Maryland, died on 14 October 1718.
[SPC1716.311][MSA.Maryland Provincial Court Deeds, E18/6]

REID, ALEXANDER, was transported via Liverpool aboard the Scipio bound for Antigua on 30 March 1716.
[SPC.1716.311][CTB.31.204]

REID, ADAM, of Edradynate, a Subaltern in Murray's Regiment in 1715. [CAT.II.211]

REID, DAVID, a Jacobite in 1715, a soldier of the Perth company, a prisoner in 1715. [NRS.B59.30.17/30]

REID, DONALD, from Dellarsie, Inverness-shire, died in Lancaster Prison on 25 April 1716. [LBR]

REID, GILBERT, a Subaltern in Murray's Regiment, fought at Preston, a prisoner in 1715. [CAT.II.211][CS.V.161] [NRS.GD1.53.72]

REID, JAMES, in Hoddam, Dumfries-shire, a prisoner at Preston in 1715. [CS.V.161] [NRS.GD1.53.72]

REID, JAMES, a Jacobite prisoner from Perthshire, petitioned for transportation in 1716. [CAT.II.240]

REID, Sir JOHN, of Barra, Bourtrie, a Jacobite in 1715. [CRA.99]

REID, JOHN, minister of Durris, Kincardineshire, a Jacobite in 1715, deposed in 1716, died in 1728. [F.VI.53][JAB.240]

REID, MALCOLM, was transported via Liverpool aboard the
Susannah bound for South Carolina on 7 May 1716.
[SPC.1716.309][CTB.31.206]

REID, ROBERT, son of Alexander Reid, a farmer from Mid Clova,
Kildrummy, Aberdeenshire, was transported via Liverpool aboard
the Elizabeth and Anne bound for Jamaica or Virginia on 29 June
1716. [SPC.1716.310][CTB.31.208][JRA.151][CRA.126]

REID, WILLIAM, a merchant in Aberdeen, a Jacobite in 1715.
[JAB.213]

RENTON, JAMES, of Slaithouses, a prisoner at Preston in 1715, ,
was transported via Liverpool aboard the Goodspeed bound for
Virginia on 28 July 1716, landed in Maryland in October 1716.
[SPC.1716.310][HM.389][Md.Arch.25.347][CS.V.160]
[NRS.GD1.53.72]

RHIND, ALEXANDER, was transported via Liverpool aboard the
Friendship bound for Virginia on 24 May 1716, landed in
Maryland in August 1716. [SPC. 1716.310][HM.387]
[Md.Arch.34.164]

RICHARDSON, GEORGE, a Jacobite in 1715, Lieutenant of the
Perth company. [NRS.B59.30.11]

RICHARDSON, JOHN, was transported via Liverpool aboard the
Wakefield bound for South Carolina on 21 April 1716.
[SPC.1716.309][CTB.31.205]

RICHARDSON, ROBERT, was transported via Liverpool aboard the
Wakefield bound for South Carolina on 21 April 1716.
[SPC.1716.309][CTB.31.205]

RICKART, DAVID, of Rickarton, born 1667, son of George Rickart and his wife Janet Forbes, a Jacobite in 1715, died on 29 July 1718. [JAB.174]

RIDDELL, WALTER, of Glen Riddell, a Jacobite in 1715, a prisoner at Preston and in London, estate forfeited in 1715. [CS.V.161/186][NRS.E677] [NRS.GD1.53.72]

RIDDOCH, DAVID, a maltman and a burgess of Perth, a Jacobite in 1715, carried arms, a prisoner. [NRS.B59.36/37/40]

RITCHIE, ANDREW, of Foresterhill, Aberdeenshire, a Jacobite tax collector in Aberdeen in 1715. [JAB.209]

RITCHIE, JOHN, the younger, a shipmaster in Fraserburgh, Aberdeenshire, a Jacobite in 1715. [JAB.218]

RITCHIE, JOSEPH, was transported via Liverpool aboard the Scipio bound for Antigua on 30 March 1716. [SPC.1716.310][CTB.31.204]

RITCHIE, MALCOLM, a tenant of the Earl of Aboyne, Aberdeenshire, a Jacobite in 1715. [JAB.207]

ROBB, JAMES, was transported via Liverpool aboard the Susannah bound for South Carolina on 7 May 1716. [SPC.1716.309][CTB.31.206]

ROBB, JOHN, was transported via Liverpool aboard the Susannah bound for South Carolina on 7 May 1716. [SPC.1716.309][CTB.31.206]

ROBB, THOMAS, was transported via Liverpool aboard the Susannah bound for South Carolina on 7 May 1716. [SPC.1716.309][CTB.31.206]

ROBERTSON, ALEXANDER, from Alvie, Inverness-shire, died in Lancaster Prison on 29 April 1716. [LBR]

ROBERTSON, ALEXANDER, of Struan, Perthshire, Chief of the Clan Robertson, born 1670, son of Alexander Robertson and his wife Marion Baillie, fought at Killiecrankie in 1689, fled to France, returned to Scotland, fought at Sheriffmuir in 1715, captured but escaped and returned to France, his estate was forfeited in 1715. died on 18 April 1749 at Rannoch, Perthshire.
[JP.156][MHP.303][NRS.E658]

ROBERTSON, ALEXANDER, minister at Fortingall, Perthshire, a Jacobite in 1715, deposed in 1716, died 27 February 1722.
[F.IV.178]

ROBERTSON, ALEXANDER, of Blairfettie, Perthshire, a Jacobite in 1715, a prisoner at Preston. [CAT.II.240]

ROBERTSON, ALEXANDER, of Drumachine, Captain of Nairne's Regiment, fought at Preston in 1715, a prisoner.
[CAT.II.210][CS.V.161] [NRS.GD1.53.72]

ROBERTSON, ALEXANDER, was transported via Liverpool aboard the Scipio bound for Antigua on 30 March 1716. [SPC.1716.310]

ROBERTSON, ALEXANDER, an Episcopalian preacher in Fochabers, Moray, a Jacobite in 1715. [JAB.241]

ROBERTSON, ALEXANDER, son of Reverend Thomas Robertson, minister at Longside, Aberdeenshire, a Jacobite in 1715, deposed in 1716. [JAB.241]

ROBERTSON, DANIEL, was transported via Liverpool aboard the Scipio bound for Antigua on 30 March 1716.
[SPC.1716.310][CTB.31.204]

ROBERTSON, DANIEL, was transported via Liverpool aboard the Two Brothers bound for Jamaica on 26 April 1716, landed on Montserrat in June 1716. [SPC.1716.313][CTB.31.205][CTP.CC.43]

ROBERTSON, DONALD, in Tullibardine's Regiment, fought at Sheriffmuir, a prisoner in Blackness, Stirling, and Carlisle in 1716. [CAT.II.206/239]

ROBERTSON, DONALD, of Eastertyre, parish of Logerait, Perthshire, estate forfeited in 1715. [NRS.E671]

ROBERTSON, DONALD, a Subaltern in Nairne's Regiment, fought at Preston, a prisoner in 1715, acquitted. [CAT.II.210][CS.V.161] [NRS.GD1.53.72]

ROBERTSON, DONALD, brother of Drumachine, a Jacobite in 1715, a Captain in Murray's Regiment, fought at Preston, a prisoner, tried and executed at Lancaster on 18 February 1716. [MHP.303][CAT.II.211][CS.V.161/194] [NRS.GD1.53.72]

ROBERTSON, DONALD, the younger, a Jacobite in 1715, a prisoner at Preston, acquitted on 1 February 1716. [CS.V.194][CAT.II.210]

ROBERTSON, DONALD, a servant to Alexander Robertson of Struan, Perthshire, a Jacobite in 1715, was marched via Blackness and Stirling prisons to Carlisle in September 1716. [NRS.B59.20.1][CAT.II.239]

ROBERTSON, DONALD, was transported via Liverpool aboard the Friendship bound for Virginia on 24 May 1716, landed in Maryland in August 1716. [SPC.1716.311][HM.387]

ROBERTSON, DUNCAN, was transported via Liverpool aboard the Two Brothers bound for Jamaica on 26 April 1716, landed on Montserrat in June 1716. [SPC.1716.313][CTB.31.205][CTP.CC.43]

ROBERTSON, DUNCAN, of Struan, Perthshire, to Russia in 1717, a Colonel in Russian service, died 1718. [CC.99]

ROBERTSON, FRANCIS, was transported via Liverpool aboard the Scipio bound for Antigua on 30 March 1716. [SPC.1716.310]

ROBERTSON, GEORGE, a cordiner in Aberdeen, a Jacobite tax collector in 1715. [JAB.209]

ROBERTSON, GEORGE, a Jacobite in 1715, a prisoner at Carlisle in December 1716. [SUL.Cheap.5.537]

ROBERTSON, GILBERT, an Ensign of the Earl of Panmure's Regiment of Foot in 1715. [NRS.GD45.1.201]

ROBERTSON, GILBERT, a dyer and a burgess of Perth, a Jacobite in 1715, carried arms, a prisoner. [NRS.B59.36/37/40]

ROBERTSON, JAMES, of Blairfettie, Perthshire, the younger, a Subaltern in Charles Murray's Regiment, fought at Preston in 1715, a prisoner, his estate in Atholl, Perthshire, was forfeited in 1715. [MHP.303][CAT.II.211][CS.V.161][NRS.E665]

ROBERTSON, JAMES, a Jacobite in 1715. [JAB.217]

ROBERTSON, JAMES, a Jacobite prisoner, petitioned for transportation n 1716, transported via Liverpool aboard the Susanna bound for South Carolina on 7 May 1716. [CAT.II.240][CTB.31.206]

ROBERTSON, JAMES, a Subaltern of Murray's Regiment, a prisoner at Preston in 1715. [CAT.II.211][CAT.II.211] [NRS.GD1.53.72]

ROBERTSON, JAMES, a Captain of Nairne's Regiment, fought at Preston, a prisoner. [CAT.II.210] [NRS.GD1.53.72]

ROBERTSON, JAMES, was transported via Liverpool aboard the Scipio bound for Antigua on 30 March 1716. [SPC.1716.310]

ROBERTSON, JAMES, was transported via Liverpool aboard the Two Brothers bound for Jamaica on 26 April 1716, landed on

Montserrat in June 1716.
[SPC.1716.313][CTB.31.206][CTP.CC.43]

ROBERTSON, JAMES, was transported via Liverpool aboard the
Friendship bound for Virginia on 24 May 1716, landed in
Maryland in August 1716. [SPC.1716.311][HM.387]

ROBERTSON, JAMES, of Dounie, Perthshire, a Jacobite in 1715.
[NRS.B59.20.1]

ROBERTSON, JOHN, Lieutenant of Tullibardine's Regiment, a
prisoner at Sheriffmuir in 1715. [CAT.II.206]

ROBERTSON, JOHN, of Tullibardine's Regiment, a prisoner at
Sheriffmuir in 1715. [CAT.II.206/239][SUL.Cheap.5.537]

ROBERTSON, JOHN, was marched from the prisons at Blackness
and Stirling to Carlisle, brother of Alexander Robertson of
Straloch, a Jacobite in 1715. [CAT.II.239]

ROBERTSON, JOHN, of Eastertyre, a Subaltern in Murray's
Regiment in 1715, a prisoner at Preston. [CAT.II.211][CS.V.161]

ROBERTSON, JOHN, from Logerait, Perthshire, died in Lancaster
Prison on 29 April 1716. [LBR]

ROBERTSON, JOHN, of Guay, a Captain of Murray's Regiment in
1715. [CAT.II.211][CS.V.161] [NRS.GD1.53.72]

ROBERTSON, JOHN, a Subaltern of Murray's Regiment, a prisoner
at Preston in 1715. [CAT.II.211]

ROBERTSON, JOHN, a soldier of the Perth company in 1715.
[NRS.B59.30.17]

ROBERTSON, JOHN, a gentleman, a prisoner at Preston, was
condemned on 1 February 1716. [CS.V.194] [NRS.GD1.53.72]

ROBERTSON, JOHN, was transported via Liverpool aboard the Scipio bound for Antigua on 30 March 1716. [SPC.1716.310][CTB.31.204]

ROBERTSON, JOHN, was transported via Liverpool aboard the Two Brothers bound for Jamaica on 26 April 1716, landed on Montserrat in June 1716. [SPC.1716.313][CTB.31.206][CTP.CC.43]

ROBERTSON, JOHN, was transported via Liverpool aboard the Friendship bound for Virginia on 24 May 1716, landed in Maryland in August 1716. [SPC.1716.311][HM.387]

ROBERTSON, JOHN, an Episcopalian minister in Strathdon, Aberdeenshire, was deposed in 1717. [JAB.241]

ROBERTSON, LEONARD, was transported via Liverpool aboard the Friendship bound for Virginia on 24 May 1716, landed in Maryland in August 1716. [SPC.1716.311][HM.387]MdArch.34.164]

ROBERTSON, PATRICK, of Blairchroisk, Captain of Charles Murray's Regiment, a prisoner at Preston, 1715. [MHP.303][CAT.II.211][CS.V.161] [NRS.GD1.53.72]

ROBERTSON, PATRICK, of Dungarthle, Perthshire, an officer of the Atholl Regiment, was captured crossing the Forth in October 1715, was marched via Blackness and Stirling to Carlisle in September 1716, sentenced to death but not executed. [CAT.II.197/239]

ROBERTSON, PATRICK, a Jacobite prisoner, petitioned for transportation n 1716, was transported via Liverpool aboard the Friendship bound for Virginia on 24 May 1716. [CAT.II.240][SPC.1716.311]

ROBERTSON, ROBERT BHAN, born 1673, fought at Sheriffmuir in 1715.

ROBERTSON, ROBERT, a Subaltern in Nairne's Regiment, a prisoner at Preston in 1715. [CAT.II.210][CS.V.161] [NRS.GD1.53.72]

ROBERTSON, ROWLAND, was transported via Liverpool aboard the Goodspeed bound for Virginia on 28 July 1716, landed in Maryland in October 1716. [SPC.1716.310][CTB.31.209][HM.389]

ROBERTSON, THOMAS, of Tullibardine's Regiment, a prisoner at Sheriffmuir in 1715. [CAT.II.206][SUL.Cheap.5.537]

ROBERTSON, THOMAS, in Ballantrum, a Jacobite prisoner in 1715, was marched via prisons in Blackness and Stirling to Carlisle. [CAT.II.239]

ROBERTSON, WILLIAM, son of Reverend Thomas Robertson, was captured at Dunfermline, Fife, on 24 October 1715, was marched from Blackness and Stirling to Carlisle in September 1716, discharged in 1717.
[JAB.175][TNA.SP54.8.95/54.12.152][SUL,Cheap.5.537]

ROBERTSON, ..., school-master of Kinnell, Angus, a Jacobite in 115, was deposed in March 1716. [NRS.CH2.15.3]

ROBINSON, DAVID, was transported via Liverpool aboard the Susannah bound for South Carolina on 7 May 1716. [SPC.1716.309][CTB.31.206]

ROBINSON, DONALD, was transported via Liverpool aboard the Susannah bound for South Carolina on 7 May 1716. [SPC.1716.309][CTB.31.206]

ROBINSON, JAMES, was transported via Liverpool aboard the Susannah bound for South Carolina on 7 May 1716. [SPC.1716.309][CTB.31.206]

ROBINSON, JAMES, was transported via Liverpool aboard the Elizabeth and Anne bound for Jamaica or Virginia on 29 June 1716, landed at York, Virginia.
[SPC.1716.310][CTB.31.208][VSP.1.186]

ROBINSON, JOHN, was transported via Liverpool aboard the Hockenhill bound for St Kitts on 25 June 1716, mutinied and landed on Sint Maartens in September 1716.
[SPC.1716.310][CTB.31.186][JAB.21]

ROBINSON, JOHN, was transported via Liverpool aboard the Susannah bound for South Carolina on 7 May 1716.
[SPC.1716.309][CTB.31.206]

ROBINSON, JOHN, was transported via Liverpool aboard the Elizabeth and Anne bound for Jamaica or Virginia on 29 June 1716, landed at York, Virginia.
[SPC.1716.310][CTB.31.208][VSP.1.186]

ROBINSON, ROBERT, was transported via Liverpool aboard the Elizabeth and Anne bound for Jamaica or Virginia on 29 June 1716, landed at York, Virginia.
[SPC.1716.310][CTB.31.208][VSP.1.186]

ROCH, THOMAS, a mason and a burgess of Perth, a Jacobite in 1715, carried arms, a prisoner. [NRS.B59.30.10/36/37/40]

ROLLO, JAMES, son of Robert Rollo of Powhouse, Stirlingshire, a Jacobite in 1715, a prisoner in Carlisle in December 1716.
[MHP.303][SUL.Cheap.5.537]

ROLLO, ROBERT, of Powhouse, in the parishes of Airth and St Ninian's, Stirlingshire, estates forfeited, a Jacobite in 1715, a prisoner in Carlisle in December 1716. [MHP.303][NRS.E653] [SUL.Cheap.5.537]

ROPER, THOMAS, schoolmaster in Rhynie, Aberdeenshire, a Jacobite in 1715. [JAB.175]

RORIE, JOHN, Deacon of the Shoemakers and a burgess of Perth, a Jacobite in 1715, carried arms, a prisoner. [NRS.B59.30.36/40]

ROSE, ALEXANDER, the Episcopalian Bishop of Edinburgh, a Jacobite, 1714. [BL.Add.ms38851]

ROSE, ALEXANDER, of Lethenty, son of Reverend John Rose and his wife Isobel Udny, a Jacobite in 1715. [JAB.175]

ROSE, ALEXANDER, born 1653, son of David Rose of Earlsmill, minister at Cairnie, a Jacobite in 1715, deposed in 1716. [JAB.242][F.6.303]

ROSE, DAVID, schoolmaster of Cairnie, a Jacobite in 1715. [JAB.243]

ROSE, HUGH, of Clava, in the parishes of Nairn and Croy, in the sheriffdoms of Inverness and Nairn, were forfeited in 1715. [NRS.E669]

ROSE, JOHN, of Alanbuie, a Jacobite, surrendered at Banff in September 1716. [JAB.176]

ROSS, ANDREW, a Jacobite in 1715, a soldier of the Perth company. [NRS.B59.30.17]

ROSS, CHARLES, was transported via Liverpool aboard the Wakefield bound for South Carolina on 21 April 1716. [SPC.1716.309][CTB.31.205]

ROSS, DAVID, Deacon of the Bakers and a burgess of Perth, a Jacobite in 1715, carried arms. [NRS.B59.30.36]

ROSS, HUGH, was transported via Liverpool aboard the Scipio bound for Antigua on 30 March 1716. [SPC.1716.310][CTB.31.204]

ROSS, JOHN, a burgess of Edinburgh, son of the Archbishop of Edinburgh, fought at Sheriffmuir in 1715, marched from Dunblane via Stirling and Edinburgh to Carlisle in 1716. [CAT.II.205][SUL.Cheap.5.537]

ROSS, JOHN, at the Mill of Denety, son of Alexander Ross, a Jacobite in 1715. [JAB.176]

ROSS, JOHN, was transported via Liverpool aboard the Friendship bound for Virginia on 24 May 1716, landed in Maryland in August 1716. [SPC.1716.311][HM.387]

ROSS, PATRICK, a barber and a burgess of Perth, a Jacobite in 1715, Ensign of the Perth company. [NRS.B59.10.36/37/40]

ROSS, PATRICK, an Episcopalian minister in Arbroath, Angus, a Jacobite in 1715. [JAB.243]

ROSS, PETER, tailor in Braemar, Aberdeenshire, was captured at Burntisland, Fife, on 11 January 1716. [JAB.13]

ROSS, ROBERT, a baker in Perth, a Jacobite in 1715, carried arms, a prisoner. [NRS.B59.30.36]

ROSS, THOMAS, was transported via Liverpool aboard the Susannah bound for South Carolina on 7 May 1716. [SPC.1716.309][CTB.31.206]

RUNCIMAN, ANDREW, a Jacobite in 1715, Corporal of the Perth company. [NRS.B59.30.17]

RUTHERFORD, ANDREW, a surgeon in Jedburgh, Roxburghshire, a Jacobite in 1715, a prisoner in Carlisle in December 1716. [SUL.Cheap.5.537]

RUTHERFORD, GEORGE, of Fairnetoun the younger, a Jacobite in 1715, a prisoner in Preston and in London, was transported via

Liverpool aboard the Elizabeth and Anne bound for Jamaica or Virginia on 29 June 1716. [SPC.1716.310][CTB.31.208] [NRS.GD1.53.72]

RUTHERFORD, JAMES, was transported via Liverpool aboard the Goodspeed bound for Virginia on 28 July 1716, landed in Maryland in October 1716. [SPC.1716.310][HM.389]

RUTHERFORD, JOHN, was transported via Liverpool aboard the Elizabeth and Anne bound for Jamaica or Virginia on 29 June 1716, landed in York, Virginia. [SPC.1716.310][CTB.31.208][VSP.1.186]

SANDILANDS, PATRICK, born 1682, son of Patrick Sandilands and his wife Margaret Ord, the Sheriff Depute of Aberdeenshire, a Jacobite in 1715, escaped in April 1716. [JAB.178][CRA.243]

SANGSTER, ANDREW, was transported via Liverpool aboard the Wakefield bound for South Carolina on 21 April 1716. [CTB.31.205]

SCOTT, Dr, a prisoner at Carlisle in December 1716. [SUL.Cheap.5.537]

SCOTT, ALEXANDER, a ship-master in Aberdeen, a Jacobite in 1715. [JAB.179]

SCOTT, DAVID, a wright and a burgess of Perth, a Jacobite in 1715, carried arms, a prisoner. [NRS.B59.30.36/37/40]

SCOTT, JAMES, a Jacobite in 1715, a soldier of the Perth company, a prisoner. [NRS.B59.30.17/36]

SCOTT, JOHN, the elder, a wheelwright, a soldier of the Perth company, a prisoner. [NRS.B59.30,17/37]

SCOTT, JOHN, the younger, a tailor and burgess of Perth, a Jacobite in 115, carried arms, a prisoner. [NRS.B59.30.36/37/40]

SCOTT, JOHN, the youngest, a tailor and a burgess of Perth, a Jacobite in 1715, carried arms, a prisoner. [NRS.B59.30.36/37/40]

SCOTT, JOHN, was transported via Liverpool aboard the Two Brothers bound for Jamaica on 26 April 1716, landed on Montserrat in June 1716. [SPC.1716.313][CTB31.206][CTP.CC.43]

SCOTT, ROBERT, a Jacobite in 1715, Ensign of the Perth company. [NRS.B59.30.10/17/36]

SCOTT, WALTER, of Wall, a Jacobite in 1715, a prisoner in Preston and in London, possibly transported via Liverpool aboard the Scipio bound for Antigua on 30 March 1716. [NRS.GD1.53.72] [SPC.1716.310][CTB.31.204]

SCOTT, WILLIAM, a Jacobite in 1715, a soldier of the Perth company. [NRS.B59.30.17]

SCOTT, WILLIAM, of Ancrum, a Jacobite in 1715, [NRS.GD259.2.31]; a prisoner in London, 1716. [CS.V.186]

SCRYMGEOUR, GEORGE, a Captain of Strathmore's Regiment, a prisoner at Preston in 1716. [CS.V.162] [NRS.GD1.53.72]

SCRYMGEOUR, JOHN, of Bowhill, Auchterderran, Fife, estate forfeited, 1715. [NRS.E618][NRAS.3503]

SEATON, DANIEL, was transported via Liverpool aboard the Scipio bound for Antigua on 30 March 1716. [SPC.1716.310][CTB.31.204]

SELLER, WILLIAM, a writer in Edinburgh, a prisoner at Preston, 1715. [NRS.GD1.53.72]

SETON, ARCHIBALD, of Touch, a letter, 1716. [HMC.II.94]

SETON, DAVID, of Lafreish, a prisoner at Carlisle in December 1716. [SUL.Cheap.5.537]

SETON, GEORGE, born 1678, Earl of Winton, captured at Preston in 1715, estate forfeited, 1715, was imprisoned in the Tower of London, escaped to Rome and died there on 19 December 1749. [JCR.45][SM.10.54][SI.366][SP.VII.504][NRS.GD1.53.72.1; E661]

SEATON, GEORGE, of Garleton, a Jacobite in 1715, a prisoner at Preston and in London. [CS.V.161/186] [NRS.GD1.53.72]

SETON, GEORGE, of Barnes, son of Sir John Seton and his wife Margaret Hay, fought at Preston in 1715, imprisoned in Newgate, London, discharged. [JAB.181][CS.V.160/186] [NRS.GD1.53.72]

SETON, JAMES, Lord Kingston, born 29 January 1667 in the parish of Whittinghame, East Lothian, estate forfeited in 1715, died in 1726. [NRS.E680][SP.V.197]

SETON, PATRICK, of Lathrisk, parish of Kettle, Fife, estate forfeited in 1715. [NRS.E681]

SETON, ROBERT, of Lafreish, a prisoner at Carlisle in December 1716. [SUL.Cheap.5.537]

SELLER, WILLIAM, a writer in Edinburgh, a Jacobite in 1715, a prisoner at Preston. [CS.V.161]

SEMPILL, ROBERT, born in 1672, son of Archibald Sempill, a French Army officer sent to aid the Jacobites, sailed from Calais to Aberdeen in 1715, died in Paris in 1737. [JAB.179][JP.164] [TNA.SP54.11.181]

SHAND, THOMAS, son of Thomas Shand of Craig and his wife Anna Duncan, a Jacobite in 1715, a merchant in Aberdeen, died 1748. [JAB.182]

SHAND, WILLIAM, servant to John Abernethy of Mayen, captured at Sheriffmuir, imprisoned at Stirling. [JAB.10]

SHARP, WILLIAM, a baker in Perth, a Jacobite in 1715, carried arms, a prisoner. [NRS.B59.30.36]

SHAW, ALEXANDER, was transported via Liverpool aboard the Wakefield bound for South Carolina on 21 April 1716. [SPC.1716.309][CTB.31.206]

SHAW, ANGUS, a Subaltern in McIntosh's Regiment, a prisoner at Preston in 1715, was transported via Liverpool aboard the Elizabeth and Anne bound for Jamaica or Virginia on 29 June 1716, landed at York, Virginia. [SPC.1716.310][CTB.31.208] [VSP.I.185]

SHAW, DANIEL, an Ensign of McIntosh's Regiment, a prisoner at Preston. [CS.V.162] [NRS.GD1.53.72]

SHAW, DONALD, was transported via Liverpool aboard the Elizabeth and Anne bound for Jamaica or Virginia on 29 June 1716, landed at York, Virginia. [SPC.1716.310][CTB.31.208][VSP.I.185]

SHAW, DONALD, was transported via Liverpool aboard the Susannah bound for South Carolina on 7 May 1716. [SPC.1716.309][CTB.31.206]

SHAW, EWAN, was transported via Liverpool aboard the Susannah bound for South Carolina on 7 May 1716. [SPC.1716.309][CTB.31.206]

SHAW, FERGUS, a Subaltern of Macintosh's Regiment, a prisoner at Preston, 1715. [NRS.GD1.53.72]

SHAW, JAMES, of Dalquhairn, a prisoner at Preston in 1715. [CS.V.161] [NRS.GD1.53.72]

SHAW, JAMES, was transported via Liverpool aboard the Friendship bound for Virginia on 24 May 1716, landed in Maryland in August 1716. [SPC.1716.311][CTB.31.206]

SHAW, JAMES, was transported via Liverpool aboard the Goodspeed bound for Virginia on 28 July 1716, landed in Maryland in October 1716. [SPC.1716.310][CTB.31.209][HM.389]

SHAW, JOHN, was transported via Liverpool aboard the Elizabeth and Anne bound for Jamaica or Virginia on 29 June 1716, landed at York, Virginia. [SPC.1716.310][CTB.31.208][VSP.I.1856]

SHAW, JOHN, was transported via Liverpool aboard the Scipio bound for Antigua on 30 March 1716. [SPC.1716.310][CTB.31.204]

SHAW, JOHN, was transported via Liverpool aboard the Wakefield bound for South Carolina on 21 April 1716. [SPC.1716.309][CTB.31.205]

SHAW, JOHN, was transported via Liverpool aboard the Susannah bound for South Carolina on 7 May 1716. [SPC.1716.309][CTB.31.206]

SHAW, PATRICK, a servant of John Abernethy of Mayen, possibly captured at Sheriffmuir, imprisoned in Stirling in 1715. [JAB.10]

SHAW, PETER, was transported via Liverpool aboard the Susannah bound for South Carolina on 7 May 1716. [SPC.1716.309][CTB.31.206]

SHAW, RICHARD, a Captain of McIntosh's Regiment, a prisoner at Preston. [CS.V.162] [NRS.GD1.53.72]

SHAW, THOMAS, a laborer, a prisoner at Preston, condemned on 23 January 1716, [CS.V.192], possibly was transported via Liverpool aboard the Goodspeed bound for Virginia on 28 July

1716, landed in Maryland in October 1716.
[SPC.1716.310][CTB.31.209][HM.388]

SHAW, WILLIAM, quartermaster of the McIntosh Regiment, a prisoner at Preston. [CS.V.162] [NRS.GD1.53.72]

SHAW, WILLIAM, was transported via Liverpool aboard the Susannah bound for South Carolina on 7 May 1716. [SPC.1716.309][CTB.31.206]

SHAW, WILLIAM, was transported via Liverpool aboard the Goodspeed bound for Virginia on 28 July 1716, landed in Maryland in October 1716. [SPC.1716.310][CTB.31.209][HM.389]

SHEPHERD, ALEXANDER, beadle of the parish of Arbroath, Angus, deposed in 1716. [NRS.CH2.15.3]

SHIELDS, JOHN, was transported via Liverpool aboard the Scipio bound for Antigua on 30 March 1716. [SPC.1716.310][CTB.31.204]

SHIRREFFS, ALEXANDER, a farmer at Drimnagour, Kildrummy, Aberdeenshire, son of James Shirreffs and his wife Christian Blair, fought at Sheriffmuir, a prisoner in Carlisle, released. [JAB.182]

SHONGER, ALEXANDER, was transported via Liverpool aboard the Friendship bound for Virginia on 24 May 1716, landed in Maryland in August 1716. [SPC.1716.311][HM.387]

SHORTER, DUNCAN, was transported via Liverpool aboard the Two Brothers bound for Jamaica on 26 April 1716, landed on Montserrat in June 1716. [SPC.1716.313][CTB.31.206][CTP.CC.43]

SIBBALD, JAMES, an Episcopalian preacher in Keith, Banffshire, a Jacobite in 1715. [JAB.243]

SIMMS, ANDREW, footman from 1695 to 1739, a Jacobite in 1715. [SI.361]

SIMM, WILLIAM, was transported via Liverpool aboard the Friendship bound for Virginia on 24 May 1716, landed in Maryland in August 1716. [SPC.1716.311][HM.386]

SIMPSON, COLIN, of Whitehill, a Jacobite, a letter, 1715. [NRS.GD1.616.12]

SIMPSON, JAMES, a maltman and a burgess of Perth, a Jacobite in 1715, carried arms, a prisoner. [NRS.B59.30.36/37/40]

SIMPSON, JAMES, was transported via Liverpool aboard the Susannah bound for South Carolina on 7 May 1716. [SPC.1716.309][CTB.31.206]

SIMPSON, WILLIAM, an Episcopalian preacher in Dun, Angus, deposed in 1716. [NRS.CH2.575.1]

SIMPSON, WILLIAM, a bailie and burgess of Aberdeen, a acobite in 1715. [JAB.182]

SIMPSON, WILLIAM, was transported via Liverpool aboard the Goodspeed bound for Virginia on 28 July 1716, landed in Maryland in October 1716. [SPC.1716.310][CTB.31.209][HM.388]

SINCLAIR, GEORGE, a merchant in Aberdeen, a Jacobite tax collector in 1715. [JAB.209]

SINCLAIR, JAMES, was transported via Liverpool aboard the Goodspeed bound for Virginia on 28 July 1716, landed in Maryland in October 1716. [SPC.1716.310][CTB.31.209][HM.388] [Md.Arch.34.164]

SINCLAIR, JOHN, son of Lord Henry Sinclair, fought at Sheriffmuir in 1715, died in Dysart, Fife, on 2 November 1750. [SP.VII.587]

SINCLAIR, PATRICK, was transported via Liverpool aboard the
Wakefield bound for South Carolina on 21 April 1716.
[SPC.1716.309][CTB.31.205]

SINCLAIR, WILLIAM, was transported via Liverpool aboard the
Anne bound for Virginia on 31 July 1716.
[SPC.1716.310][CTB.31.209]

SINCLAIR, ..., 1716, a Jacobite in 1715. [NRS.GD1.616.28]

SIVEWRIGHT, JAMES, in Westerton, Huntly, Aberdeenshire, a
Jacobite in 1715, surrendered on 13 March 1716. [JAB.121/183]

SKENE, JAMES, son of John Skene of Halyards, Fife, a Captain at
Preston, a prisoner, pardoned, died in 1736. [JAB.183]

SKINNER, GEORGE, a merchant in Edinburgh, a Jacobite in 1715,
imprisoned at Preston and in London. [CS.V.161/186]
[NRS.GD1.53.72]

SKINNER, JOHN, an Episcopalian minister at Fetteresso,
Kincardineshire, in 1715. [F.V.465]

SKINNER, JOHN, born 1649, minister at Bothkennar, Stirlingshire,
from 1676, deposed in 1717. [F.IV.300]

SMALL, JAMES, was transported via Liverpool aboard the
Friendship bound for Virginia on 24 May 1716, landed in
Maryland in August 1716. [SPC.1716.311][HM.387]

SMITH, ALEXANDER, from Dunlichty, Inverness-shire, died in
Lancaster Prison on 3 May 1716. [LBR]

SMITH, ALEXANDER, from Moy, Inverness-shire, died in Lancaster
Prison on 11 May 1716. [LBR]

SMITH, ALEXANDER, a prisoner at Carlisle in December 1716.
[SUL.Cheap.5.537]

SMITH, ALEXANDER, was transported via Liverpool aboard the Two Brothers bound for Jamaica on 26 April 1716, landed on Montserrat in June 1716.
[SPC.1716.313][CTB.31.205][CTP.CC.43]

SMITH, ALEXANDER, a merchant, a Jacobite in 1716. [JAB.217]

SMITH, ALEXANDER, was transported via Liverpool aboard the Friendship bound for Virginia on 24 May 1716, landed in Maryland in August 1716. [SPC.1716.311][HM.386]

SMITH, ALEXANDER, an Episcopalian preacher in Bellie, Banffshire, a Jacobite in 1715. [JAB.244]

SMITH, ANDREW, from Doon, Inverness-shire, died in Lancaster Prison on 15 February 1716. [LBR]

SMITH, ANDREW, from Edinburgh, a prisoner at Preston in 1715. [CS.V.161] [NRS.GD1.53.72]

SMITH, CHARLES, was transported via Liverpool aboard the Elizabeth and Anne bound for Jamaica or Virginia on 29 June 1716. [SPC.1716.310][CTB.31.208]

SMITH, DANIEL, was transported via Liverpool aboard the Two Brothers bound for Jamaica on 26 April 1716, landed on Montserrat in June 1716.
[SPC.1716.313][CTB.31.205][CTP.CC.43]

SMITH, DAVID, was transported via Liverpool aboard the Susannah bound for South Carolina on 7 May 1716.
[SPC.1716.309][CTB.31.206]

SMITH, DONALD, a husbandman, a prisoner at Preston, condemned on 25 January 1716. [CS.V.193]

SMITH, DONALD, was transported via Liverpool aboard the Wakefield bound for South Carolina on 21 April 1716. [SPC.1716.309][CTB.31.205]

SMITH, DONALD, was transported via Liverpool aboard the Susannah bound for South Carolina on 7 May 1716. [SPC.1716.309][CTB.31.206]

SMITH, FARQUHAR, from Dunlichtie, Inverness-shire, died in Lancaster Prison on 1 January 1716. [LBR]

SMITH, JAMES, from Alvie, Inverness-shire, died in Lancaster Prison on 2 July 1716. [LBR]

SMITH, JAMES, a former bailie of Perth, a Jacobite in 1715. [NRS.B59.30.36]

SMITH, JORAM, a barber in Aberdeen, a Jacobite in 1715. [JAB.213]

SMITH, PATRICK, son of John Smith of Inveramsay, Procurator Fiscal of Aberdeenshire, a Jacobite in 1715, died 1743. [JAB.183]

SMITH, PATRICK, a blacksmith, a prisoner at Preston condemned on 25 January 1716. [CS.V.193]

SMITH, PATRICK, was transported via Liverpool aboard the Susannah bound for South Carolina on 7 May 1716. [SPC.1716.309][CTB.31.206]

SMITH, PATRICK, was transported via Liverpool aboard the Goodspeed bound for Virginia on 28 July 1716, landed in Maryland in October 1716. [SPC.1716.310][HM.388]

SMITH, ROBERT, a Jacobite in 1715. [JAB.217]

SMITH, ROBERT, was transported via Liverpool aboard the Elizabeth and Anne bound for Jamaica or Virginia on 29 June

1716, landed at York, Virginia.
[SPC.1716.310][CTB.31.208][VSP.I.185]

SMITH, THOMAS, was transported via Liverpool aboard the
Friendship bound for Virginia on 24 May 1716, landed in
Maryland in August 1716. [SPC.1716.311][HM.387]

SMITH, THOMAS, died in Lancaster Prison on 2 January 1716.
[LBR]

SMITH, WILLIAM, Regent of Marischal College, Aberdeen, a
Jacobite in 1715. [TNA.SP54.11.181][JAB.184]

SMITH, WILLIAM, a weaver and a burgess of Perth, a Jacobite in
1715, a soldier of the Perth company, a prisoner.
[NRS.B9.30.17.40]

SMITH, WILLIAM, a merchant in Aberdeen, a Jacobite tax
collector in 1715. [JAB.209]

SMITH, WILLIAM, a hammerman in Perth, a Jacobite in 1715.
[NRS.B59.30.37]

SMYTHE, DAVID, of Methven, Perthshire, fought at Sheriffmuir in
1715; a prisoner in Edinburgh Castle, 1717.
[MHP.293][NRS.GD220.5.721.2]

SMYTH, JOHN, the elder, a hammerman and a burgess of Perth, a
Jacobite in 1715, carried arms, a prisoner. [NRS.B59.30.36/37/40]

SMYTH, JOHN, the younger, a hammerman and a burgess of
Perth, a Jacobite in 1715, carried arms, a prisoner.
[NRS.B59.30.36/37/40]

SMITH, ..., brother of Smith of Methven, Perthshire, a Jacobite
at Sheriffmuir, 1715. [NRS.RH2.4.308/170];

SOMERVILLE, JAMES, born 1693, son of James Somerville of Kennox, Ayrshire, a physician, was transported via Liverpool aboard the Goodspeed bound for Virginia on 28 July 1716, landed in Maryland in October 1716, died15 February 1751, in Chester County, Maryland. [SPC.1716.310][HM.389][CTB.31.209] [SG.37.111][CF.2.6691][NRS.208.430][MdArch.25.347-349]

SOUPER, WILLIAM, of Gilcomston, born 1661, son of John Souper, a merchant in Aberdeen, a Jacobite in 1715, died on 20 September 1724. [JAB.185]

SPALDING, ALEXANDER, was transported via Liverpool aboard the Friendship bound for Virginia on 24 May 1716, landed in Maryland in August 1716. [SPC.1716.311][HM.386]

SPEEDIMAN, DAVID, a glover in Aberdeen, a Jacobite in 1715. [JAB.189]

SPENCE, ANDREW, a maltman and a burgess of Perth, a Jacobite in 1715, carried arms, surrendered. [NRS.B59.30.36/40]

SPENCE, WILLIAM, a hook-maker in Aberdeen, a Jacobite in 1715. [JAB.213]

SPENCE, ..., a bailie, a Jacobite in 1715, a prisoner at Carlisle in December 1716. [SUL.Cheap.5.537]

STALKER, DAVID, a baker and a burgess of Perth, a Jacobite in 1715, carried arms, a prisoner. [NRS.B59.30.36/37/40]

STEEL, GEORGE, a Jacobite in 1715, a soldier of the Perth company. [NRS.B59.30.17]

STEUART, JOHN, of Dalguise, Perthshire, fought at Sheriffmuir in 1715. [MHP.294]

STEWART, ALEXANDER, a Subaltern of Nairne's Regiment, fought at Preston, a prisoner. [CAT.210][CS.V.161] [NRS.GD1.53.72]

STEWART, ALEXANDER, a Subaltern of Charles Murray's Regiment, in 1715, a prisoner in Preston, tried on 27 January 1716, sentenced to death. [MHP.303][CAT.II.211][CS.V.161] [NRS.GD1.53.72]

STEWART, ALEXANDER, of Tullibardine's Regiment, a prisoner at Sheriffmuir in 1715. [CAT.II.206]

STEWART, ALEXANDER, of Innerslanie, Blair Atholl, Perthshire, Forester to the Duke of Atholl, a prisoner at Sheriffmuir in 1715, was marched from prison in Blackness and in Stirling to Carlisle in September 1716. [CAT.II.206/239]

STEWART, ALEXANDER, a gentleman, a prisoner at Preston, condemned on 27 January 1716. [CS.V.193]

STEWART, ALEXANDER, was transported via Liverpool aboard the Elizabeth and Anne bound for Jamaica or Virginia on 29 June 1716, landed at York, Virginia.
[SPC.1716.310][CTB.31.208][VSP.I.185]

STEWART, ALEXANDER, was transported via Liverpool aboard the Scipio bound for Antigua on 30 March 1716.
[SPC.1716.309][CTB.31.206]

STEWART, ALEXANDER, was transported via Liverpool aboard the Susannah bound for South Carolina on 7 May 1716.
[SPC.1716.309][CTB.31.206]

STEWART, ALEXANDER, son of Allan Stewart, a Jaacobite in 1715, at Suadadilmore, Ardnamurchan, in 1716. [NRS.SC54.22.17.1]

STEWART, ANDREW, of Auchlunkart, son of Patrick Stewart and his wife Anna Gordon, a Jacobite in 1715, surrendered at Banff in1716, died on 17 September 1719. [JAB.189]

STEWART, ANGUS, of Tullibardine's Regiment, a prisoner at Sheriffmuir in 1715. [CAT.II.206]

STEWART, ARCHIBALD, a Jacobite in 1715, in Laga, Ardnamurchan, 1716. [NRS.SC54.22.17.1]

STEWART, CHARLES, was transported via Liverpool aboard the Scipio bound for Antigua on 30 March 1716. [SPC.1716.310][CTB.31.204]

STEWART, DANIEL, was transported via Liverpool aboard the Scipio bound for Antigua on 30 March 1716. [SPC.1716.310][CTB.31.204]

STEWART, DANIEL, was transported via Liverpool aboard the Goodspeed bound for Virginia on 28 July 1716, landed in Maryland in October 1716. [SPC.1716.310][CTB.31.209][HM.388]

STEWART, DAVID, a Subaltern in McIntosh's Regiment, a prisoner at Preston, petitioned for transportation in 1716, was transported via Liverpool aboard the Friendship bound for Virginia on 24 May 1716, landed in Maryland in August 1716. [SPC.1716.311][HM.386][CAT.II.240] [NRS.GD1.53.72]

STEWART, DONALD, was transported via Liverpool aboard the Wakefield bound for South Carolina on 21 April 1716. [SPC.1716.309][CTB.31.205]

STEWART, DONALD, was transported via Liverpool aboard the Elizabeth and Anne bound for Jamaica or Virginia on 29 June 1716, landed at York, Virginia. [SPC.1716.310][CTB.31.208][VSP.I.185]

STEWART, DUNCAN, born 1660, son of Donald Stewart of Invernahyle, minister of Blair Atholl, Perthshire, from 1709 to 1718, a Jacobite in 1715, died around 1728. [F.4.144]

STEWART, DUNCAN, was transported via Liverpool aboard the Susannah bound for South Carolina on 7 May 1716. [SPC.1716.309][CTB.31.206]

STEWART, DUNCAN, was transported via Liverpool aboard the Two Brothers bound for Jamaica on 26 April 1716, landed on Montserrat in June 1716. [SPC.1716.313][CTB.31.206][CTP.CC.43]

STEWART, GEORGE, son of Patrick Stewart of Tanachie, a Jacobite in 1715, died in December 1748. [JAB.191]

STEWART, HUGH, was transported via Liverpool aboard the Susannah bound for South Carolina on 7 May 1716. [SPC.1716.309][CTB.31.206]

STEWART, JAMES, a prisoner at Carlisle in December 1716. [SUL.Cheap.5.537]

STEWART, JAMES, was transported via Liverpool aboard the Elizabeth and Anne bound for Jamaica or Virginia on 29 June 1716, landed at York, Virginia. [SPC.1716.310][CTB.31.208][VSP.I.186]

STEWART, JAMES, Lieutenant of Tullibardine's Regiment, a prisoner at Sheriffmuir in 1715. [CAT.II.206]

STEWART, JAMES, of Tullypowrie, a Subaltern of Murray's Regiment in 1715, a prisoner at Preston. [CAT.II.211][CS.V.161]

STEWART, JAMES, a Captain of Lord Nairne's Regiment, a prisoner at Preston, died in London in 1716. [CAT.II.210][CS.V.161] [NRS.GD1.53.72]

STEWART, JAMES, a subaltern in Murray's Regiment, a prisoner at Preston, 1715. [NRS.GD1.53.72]

STEWART, JAMES, Major of Lord Charles Murray's Regiment in a1715, a prisoner at Preston. [CAT.II.211][CS.V.161] [NRS.GD1.53.72]

STEWART, JAMES, of the Lands of Boyne, fought at Sheriffmuir, a prisoner in Blackness in 1715. [JAB.190]

STEWART, Colonel JOHN, of Innernytie, Perthshire, of Lord Nairn's Regiment, fought at Sheriffmuir in 1715. [MHP.294/303]; estate forfeited in 1715, [NRS.E635], at the Jacobite Court at Urbino, Italy, in 1717. [JU] [NRS.GD1.53.72]

STEWART, JOHN, of Kynachan, Lieutenant Colonel of Lord Nairne's Regiment, at Preston in 1715, a prisoner. [MHP.303][CAT.II.210][CS.V.161]

STEWART, JOHN, was transported via Liverpool aboard the Susannah bound for South Carolina on 7 May 1716. [CTB.31.206]

STEWART, JOHN, of Foss, an officer of the Atholl Regiment, was captured crossing the Forth in October 1715, a prisoner in Edinburgh Castle, marched via Blackness, and Stirling prisons to Carlisle, tried – pled not guilty and was liberated on bail. [CAT.II.197/215/239][SUL.Cheap.5.537]

STEWART, JOHN, of Glenbuckie, Balquhidder, an officer of the Atholl Regiment, was captured crossing the Forth in October 1715, a prisoner in Edinburgh Castle, was marched via Blackness and Stirling prisons to Carlisle, tried – pled not guilty and was released on bail. [CAT.II.197/215/239][SUL.Cheap.5.537]

STEWART, JOHN, a Subaltern in Nairne's Regiment, a prisoner at Preston. [CAT.II.210] [CS.V.161] [NRS.GD1.53.72]

STEWART, JOHN, a Subaltern in Murray's Regiment, a prisoner at Preston in 1715. [CAT.II.211][CS.V.161] [NRS.GD1.53.72]

STEWART, JOHN, was transported via Liverpool aboard the Goodspeed bound for Virginia on 28 July 1716, landed in Maryland in October 1716. [SPC.1716.310][CTB.31.209][HM.388]

STEWART, JOHN, a Captain of Nairne's Regiment, fought at Preston, a prisoner. [CAT.II.210][CS.V.161] [NRS.GD1.53.72]

STEWART, JOHN, of Dalguise, a cavalry officer, fought at Sheriffmuir. [CAT.II.240]

STEWART, JOHN, brother of Alexander Stewart of Easter Kinnaird, a Subaltern of Murray's Regiment, a prisoner at Preston in 1715. [CAT.II.211][CS.V.161]

STEWART, JOHN, was transported via Liverpool aboard the Elizabeth and Anne bound for Jamaica or Virginia on 29 June 1716, landed at York, Virginia.
[SPC.1716.310][CTB.31.208][VSP.I.186]

STEWART, JOHN, a Jacobite in 1715, a soldier of the Perth company. [NRS.B59.30.17]

STEWART, JOHN, a gentleman, a prisoner at Preston, condemned on 30 January 1716. [CS.V.194]

STEWART, JOHN, of Drumin, a Jacobite in 1715, surrendered at Banff on 16 March 1716. [JAB.191]

STEWART, JOHN, was transported via Liverpool aboard the Two Brothers bound for Jamaica on 26 April 1716, landed on Montserrat in June 1716.
[SPC.1716.313][CTB.31.206][CTP.CC.43]

STEWART, JOHN, in Ballaterach, a Jacobite in 1715. [JAB.191]

STEWART, JOHN, of Boggs, Banffshire, a Jacobite in 1715. [JAB.192]

STEWART, JOHN, was transported via Liverpool aboard the Scipio bound for Antigua on 30 March 1716. [SPC.1716.310]

STEWART, JOHN, of Dens and Crichie, born 1659, an army officer, a Jacobite in 1715, died 1729. [JAB.193]

STEWART, MALCOLM, of Achmerkbeag, Atholl, Perthshire, a Subaltern of Nairne's Regiment, 1715, captured at Preston, tried 27 January 1716, sentenced to death, changed to transportation; a prisoner in Liverpool, a letter, 1716; was transported via Liverpool aboard the Elizabeth and Anne bound for Jamaica or Virginia on 29 June 1716, landed at York, Virginia; in Virginia 1731. [NRS.GD132.805] [MHP.303][CAT.II.210][VSP.1.186] [NRS.GD132/805/1-2][SPC.1716.310][CTB.31.208] [CS.V.161/193] [NRS.GD1.53.72]

STEWART, NEIL, was transported via Liverpool aboard the Susannah bound for South Carolina on 7 May 1716. [CTB.31.206][SPC.1716.309]

STEWART, PATRICK, was transported via Liverpool aboard the Susannah bound for South Carolina on 7 May 1716. [CTB.31.206][SPC.1716.309]

STEWART, PATRICK, was transported via Liverpool aboard the Elizabeth and Anne bound for Jamaica or Virginia on 29 June 1716, landed at York, Virginia. [SPC.1716.310][CTB.31.208][VSP.1.186]

STEWART, PETER, a Lieutenant of Tullibardine's Regiment, fought at Sheriffmuir, a prisoner in Carlisle in December 1716. [CAT.II.206][SUL.Cheap.5.537]

STEWART, ROBERT, of Glenbeich, Comrie, Perthshire, estate forfeited in 1715. [NRS.E673]

STEWART, ROBERT, a Subaltern of Nairne's Regiment, a prisoner at Preston in 1715, tried and found guilty on 1 February 1716. [MHP.303] [CAT.II.210] [NRS.GD1.53.72]

STEWART, ROBERT, of Appin, Argyll, fought at Killiecrankie in 1689, also at Sheriffmuir in 1715, his estate was forfeited in 1715. [NRS.E663]; a Jacobite at Sheriffmuir, 1715. [NRS.RH2.4.308/170];

STEWART, ROBERT, possibly from Perthshire, a Jacobite prisoner, petitioned for transportation in 1716, was transported via Liverpool aboard the Elizabeth and Anne bound for Jamaica or Virginia on 29 June 1716, landed at York, Virginia; indentured as a servant in the service of Captain Edward Trafford for seven years, at Williamsburg 17 October 1716. [NRS.GD1.53.73] [SPC.1716.310][CTB.31.208][VSP.1.186] [CAT.II.240]

STEWART, WALTER, was transported via Liverpool aboard the Hockenhill bound for St Kitts on 21 April 1716, mutinied and landed on Sint Maartens in September 1716. [CTB.31.207][JAB.21][SPC.1716.312][JAB.21]

STEWART, WILLIAM, of Aucholzie, Glen Muick, Aberdeenshire, a Jacobite in 1715, a prisoner at Carlisle, died 1727. [CRA.64][JAB.194][SUL.Cheap.5.437]

STEWART, WILLIAM, of Tullibardine's Regiment, a prisoner at Sheriffmuir in 1715, possibly transported via Liverpool aboard the Scipio bound for Antigua on 30 March 1716. [CAT.II.206][SPC.1716.310][CTB.31.204]

STIRLING, CHARLES, of Kippendavie, an officer of the Perthshire Horse, fought at Sheriffmuir in 1715. [MHP.294]

STIRLING, GEORGE, an apothecary, councillor and a burgess of Perth, a Lieutenant of the Perth company in 1715, surrendered. [NRS.B59.30.17/37/40]

STIRLING, Sir HENRY, of Ardoch, Perthshire, settled in Russia in 1716, he married Ann daughter of Admiral Thomas Gordon in St Petersburg in 1726, in St Petersburg in 1729, returned to Scotland. [NRS.GD24.1.464.L2]

STIRLING. JAMES, of Keir, Stirlingshire, fought at Sheriffmuir in 1715, estate forfeited in 1715. [MHP.294/303][NRS.E637]

STRACHAN, ALEXANDER, a merchant in Aberdeen, a Jacobite in 1715. [JAB.195]

STRACHAN, CHARLES, was transported via Liverpool aboard the Wakefield bound for South Carolina on 21 April 1716. [SPC.1716.309][CTB.31.205]

STRACHAN, JAMES, son of Sir James Strachan of Thornton, Kincardineshire, a Jacobite in 1715. [JAB.245]

STRACHAN, THOMAS, a bailie of Aberdeen, a Jacobite in 1715. [JAB.195]

STRACHAN, WILLIAM, a merchant in Aberdeen, a Jacobite in 1715. [JAB.195]

STRAITON, ALEXANDER, a Jacobite in 1715, a prisoner at Preston and in London. [CS.V.160/186] [NRS.GD1.53.72]

STRATON, JOHN, an Episcopalian preacher in Arbirlot, Angus, and schoolmaster of Arbroath, Angus, a Jacobite in 1715, deposed in 1716. [HHA.170/171]

STROAK, WILLIAM, was transported via Liverpool aboard the Elizabeth and Anne bound for Jamaica or Virginia on 29 June 1716, landed at York, Virginia. [SPC.1716.310][CTB.31.208][VSP.1.186]

STROCK, JAMES, was transported via Liverpool aboard the Scipio bound for Antigua on 30 March 1716. [SPC.1716.310][CTB.31.204]

STRONACH, GEORGE, of Tulloch, Captain of baggage of the Jacobite troops of the Marquis of Huntly in 1715 [NRS.GD44.51.500.8]

STUART, CHARLES, in Gairth, 1715. [NRS.GD1.53.70]

STUART, FRANCIS, brother of the Earl of Moray, Jacobite treasurer in 1715. [MHP.293]

STUART, ROBERT, was transported via Liverpool aboard the Elizabeth and Anne bound for Jamaica or Virginia on 29 June 1716, landed at York, Virginia; assigned to William Gordon there, later sent to Scotland on business, certificate, 3 May 1717. [SPC.1716.310][VSP.1.186][NRS.GD1.53.74]

SUTHERLAND, JOHN, was transported via Liverpool aboard the Scipio bound for Antigua on 30 March 1716. [SPC.1716.310][CTB.31.204]

SUTHERLAND, KENNETH, Lord Duffus, son of James Duffus and his wife Margaret McKenzie, a Jacobite in 1715, fought at Sheriffmuir, fled to Sweden in 1716, returned and imprisoned in the Tower of London, released in 1717, estate forfeited, to Russia in 1722, an Admiral of the Russian Navy, died 30 March 1734. [SP.II.212][Scottish National Portrait Gallery] [NRS.RH2.4,308/170]

SUTHERLAND, WILLIAM, of Roscommon, son of James Duffus and his wife Margaret McKenzie, a Jacobite in 1715, fled abroad in 1716. [SP.II.213]

SWAN, WILLIAM, born 1658, son of Reverend Alexander Swan and his wife Margaret Leslie, minister of Pitsligo, Aberdeenshire, deposed in 1716, died in 1742. [JAB.245][F.VI.234]

SWELL, JAMES, a barber and a bailie of Perth, a Jacobite in 1715. [NRS.B59.30.10/37/40]

SWORD, HUMPHREY, at the Bridge of Linlithgow, West Lothian, a prisoner at Preston, was transported via Liverpool aboard the

Goodspeed bound for Virginia on 28 July 1716, landed in Maryland in October 1716. [NRS.GD1.53.72] [SPC.1716.310][CTB.31.312][HM.389][CS.V.161]

SYMON, JAMES, a Jacobite in 1715, Corporal of the Perth company. [NRS.B59.30.30.17]

TAIT, THOMAS, was transported via Liverpool aboard the Scipio bound for Antigua on 30 March 1716. [SPC.1716.310][CTB.31.204]

TALLINES, COLIN, an Ensign of McIntosh's Regiment, a prisoner at Preston. [CS.V.162] [NRS.GD1.53.72]

TAUS, ANGUS, a Jacobite from Blair Atholl, Perthshire, a prisoner marched via prison in Blackness and in Stirling to Carlisle in1716. [CAT.II.239]

TAUS, CHARLES, a tenant of the Earl of Aboyne, a Jacobite in 1715. [JAB.207]

TAYLOR, GEORGE, a writer in Edinburgh, fought at Sheriffmuir, 1715., imprisoned in Carlisle in December 1716. [CAT.II.205] [SUL.Cheap.5.37]

TAYLOR, JAMES, was transported via Liverpool aboard the Scipio bound for Antigua on 30 March 1716. [SPC.1716.310][CTB.31.204]

TAYLOR, JOHN, a Jacobite in 1715. [JAB.217]

TAYLOR, JOSEPH, Deacon of the Cordiners of Perth, a burgess of Perth, a Jacobite in 1715, Ensign and later Captain of the Perth company. [NRS.B59.30.11/37/40]

TAYLOR, ROBERT, in Kirkden parish, Angus, a Jacobite in 1715. [HHA.170]

TAYLOR, THOMAS, a baker and a burgess of Perth, a Jacobite in 1715, carried arms, a prisoner. [NRS.B59.36/37/40]

THOMSON, ANDREW, a Jacobite tax collector in Aberdeen, 1715. [JAB.209]

THOMSON, CHARLES, an Episcopalian preacher in Kinnell, Angus, a Jacobite in 1715. [HHA.170]

THOMSON, DANIEL, was transported via Liverpool aboard the Elizabeth and Anne bound for Jamaica or Virginia on 29 June 1716, landed at York, Virginia. [SPC.1716.310][VSP.1.185][CTB.31.208]

THOMSON, GEORGE, was transported via Liverpool aboard the Friendship bound for Virginia on 24 May 1716, landed in Maryland in August 1716. [SPC.1716.311][HM.387][MdArch.34.164]

THOMSON, JOHN, a Jacobite in 1715. [JAB.217]

THOMSON, PATRICK, master of Aberdeen Grammar School, a Jacobite in 1715. [JAB.196]

THOMSON, ROBERT, son of George Thomson a merchant in Aberdeen, minister at Lethnot and Navar, Angus, deposed in 1716. [F.V.399]

THOMSON, WILLIAM, the Jacobite Cess Collector of Cullen, Banffshire, 1715. [JAB.196][TNA.SP54.12.353]

THREIPLAND, Sir DAVID, of Fingask, Perthshire, fought at Sheriffmuir in 1715, estate forfeited in 1715, exiled to France. [MHP.294] [NRS.E630][NRS.RH.2.4.310.156]

THREIPLAND, DAVID, son of Sir David Threipland, fought at Sheriffmuir in 1715, was captured and imprisoned in Edinburgh, escaped, was killed at Prestonpans in 1745. [MHP.294/296]

THREIPLAND, GEORGE, a merchant, burgess and councillor of Perth a Jacobite in 1715, carried arms. [NRS.B59.30.36/37/40]

TODD, ARCHIBALD, portioner of Drumcrief, a prisoner at Preston. [CS.V.160] [NRS.GD1.53.72]

TODD, JAMES, a Jacobite in 1715, a soldier of the Perth company. [NRS.B59.30.17]

TODD, JOHN, was transported via Liverpool aboard the Scipio bound for Antigua on 30 March 1716. [SPC.1716.310]

TOSSACH, ROBERT, a slater and a burgess of Perth, a Jacobite in 1715, a soldier of the Perth company. [NRS.B59.30.17.40]

TULLOCH, DAVID, born 1689, son of Alexander Tulloch and his wife Margaret Simpson, a Jacobite in 1715. [JAB.196]

TULLOCH, THOMAS, of Sannoch, a prisoner at Carlisle in December 1716. [SUL.Cheap.5.537]

TURNER, JOHN, born 1694, son of Robert Turner of Turnerhall and his wife Margaret Rose, Logie Buchan, Aberdeenshire, a Jacobite in 1715, died 1730. [CRA.187][JAB.197]

TURNER, ROBERT, of Turnerhall, Logie Buchan, son of Andrew Turner of Kinminity, a Jacobite in 1715, died 21 January 1741. [JAB.197][CRA.187]

TURNER, WILLIAM, was transported via Liverpool aboard the Elizabeth and Anne bound for Jamaica or Virginia on 29 June 1716, landed at York, Virginia. [SPC.1716.310][VSP.1.185][CTB.31.208]

TYRIE, DAVID, of Dunnydeer, son of John Tyrie and his wife Margaret Tulloch, a Jacobite in 1715, died in 1750. [JAB.198]

URQUHART, ADAM, a Lieutenant of the Earl of Panmure's Regiment in 1715. [NRS.GD45.17.933; GD45.1.201]; entered Russian service in 1717, was killed in 1718. [CC.116]

URQUHART, ALEXANDER, of Newhall, a Jacobite in 1715. [NRS.GD220.5.662]

URQUHART, JAMES, was transported via Liverpool aboard the Elizabeth and Anne bound for Jamaica or Virginia on 29 June 1716, landed at York, Virginia.
[SPC.1716.310][VSP.1.186][CTB.31.208]

URQUHART, JAMES, son of Jonathan Urquhart of Cromarty and his wife Jean Graham, a Jacobite in 1715, a Colonel, a prisoner at Carlisle, discharged, died in 1741. [JAB.199][TNA.SP54.12.130]

URQUHART, Dr JAMES, son of Dr Patrick Urquhart, Regent of King's College, Aberdeen, a Jacobite in 1715. [JAB.200]

URQUHART, JOHN, son of James Urquhart of Knockleith and his wife Margaret Fraser, a shipmaster, a Jacobite in 1715, died in Banff on 19 June 1756. [JAB.202]

URQUHART, Dr PATRICK, born 1641, son of Patrick Urquhart of Meldrum and his wife Margaret Ogilvy, Professor of Medicine in King's College, Aberdeen, a Jacobite in 1715. [JAB.200]

URQUHART, WILLIAM, a merchant in Fraserburgh, Aberdeenshire, a Jacobite in 1715. [JAB.202]

VCALESTER, JOHN MCDHOIL CAMERON, in Achalinan, in Morvern, Inverness-shire, a Jacobite in 1715. [NRS.SC54.22.17.1-2]

VCMARTINE, JON DHU MCEAN, in Tenguilla, in Ferinish and Carnacailliche, a Jacobite in 1715, in McLean's Regiment. [NRS.SC54.22.17.1-2]

WALKER, ANDREW, a baker and councillor of Perth, a Jacobite in 1715, carried arms, surrendered. [NRS.B59.30.36]

WALKER, JAMES, a carter and a burgess of Perth, a Jacobite in 1715. [NRS.B59.30.37/40]

WALKER, JAMES, an apothecary in Perth, a Jacobite in 1715, carried arms, a prisoner, [NRS.B59.30.15]

WALKER, PATRICK, in Perth, a Jacobite in 1715, carried arms, a prisoner. [NRS.B59.30.36]

WALKER, WILLIAM, a drummer in Old Aberdeen, a Jacobite in 1715. [JAB.212]

WALKINSHAW, JOHN, of Scotstoun, Renfrewshire, estate forfeited in 1715. [NRS.E686]

WALKINSHAW, ..., of Barrowfield, Lieutenant Colonel of Lord Strathmore's Regiment, a prisoner at Sheriffmuir in 1715. [CAT.II.205]

WALLACE, ROBERT, was transported via Liverpool aboard the Two Brothers bound for Jamaica on 26 April 1716, landed on Montserrat in June 1716.
[SPC.1716.313][CTB.31.206][CTP.CC.43]

WARRANDER, WILLIAM, the bursar of King's College, Aberdeen, a Jacobite in 1715. [JAB.212]

WATSON, ALEXANDER, a magistrate of Dundee, a Jacobite in 1715. [NRS.RH2.4.308/170]; an Episcopalian and councillor of Dundee, a Jacobite in 1714. [NRS.GD220.5.357.4]

WATSON, DAVID, an Episcopalian preacher in Fearn, Angus, deposed in 1716. [NRS.CH2.575.1]

WATSON, DAVID, a mason in Perth, a Jacobite in 1715, carried arms, a prisoner. [NRS.B59.30.10.37]

WATSON, JAMES, an Episcopalian preacher in Kinnell, Angus, in 1715. [HHA.170]

WATSON, JAMES, was transported via Liverpool aboard the Elizabeth and Anne bound for Jamaica or Virginia on 29 June 1716, landed at York, Virginia.
[SPC.1716.310][VSP.1.186][CTB.31.208]

WATSON, PETER, was transported via Liverpool aboard the Scipio bound for Antigua on 30 March 1716.
[SPC.1716.310][CTB.31.204]

WATSON, ROBERT, a gentleman at the Jacobite court, 1718-1729. [SI.366]

WATSON, ROBERT, a cook at the Jacobite Court in Urbino, Italy, 1717. [JU]

WATSON, WILLIAM, was transported via Liverpool aboard the Scipio bound for Antigua on 30 March 1716.
[SPC.1716.310][CTB.31.204]

WATSON, ..., 1716., a Jacobite in 1715. [NRS.GD1.616.28]

WATT, ALEXANDER, was transported via Liverpool aboard the Elizabeth and Anne bound for Jamaica or Virginia on 29 June 1716, landed at York, Virginia.
[SPC.1716.310][VSP.1.185][CTB.31.208]

WEBSTER, JAMES, was transported via Liverpool aboard the Friendship bound for Virginia on 24 May 1716, landed in Maryland in August 1716. [SPC.1716.311][HM.386]

WEDDERBURN, ALEXANDER, town clerk of Dundee, deprived of his office in 1716. [DCA.TC.CC.1/132]

WETHERSPOON, JOHN, a Jacobite in 1715, a soldier of the Perth company. [NRS.B59.30.17]

WHITE, ALEXANDER, was transported via Liverpool aboard the Elizabeth and Anne bound for Jamaica or Virginia on 29 June 1716, landed at York, Virginia.
[SPC.1716.310][VSP.1.185][CTB.31.208]

WHYTE, ANDREW, a merchant in Aberdeen, a Jacobite tax collector. [JAB.209]

WHITE, GEORGE, minister of Maryculter, Aberdeenshire, deposed in 1718, died in 1724. [F.VI.61][JAB.245]

WHITE, HECTOR, was transported via Liverpool aboard the Goodspeed bound for Virginia on 28 July 1716, landed in Maryland in October 1716. [SPC.1716.310][CTB.31.209][HM.388]

WHITE, JAMES, the elder, a Jacobite in 1715. [JAB.217]

WHITE, JAMES, was transported via Liverpool aboard the Friendship bound for Virginia on 24 May 1716, landed in Maryland in August 1716. [SPC.1716.311][HM.387]

WHYTE, JOHN, a merchant in Perth, a Jacobite in 1715, carried arms, a prisoner. [NRS.B59.30.36/37]

WHYTE, JOHN, was transported via Liverpool aboard the Elizabeth and Anne bound for Jamaica or Virginia on 29 June 1716, landed at York, Virginia.
[SPC.1716.310][VSP.1.185][CTB.31.208]

WHYTE, ROBERT, a merchant in Perth, a Jacobite in 1715, carried arms, a prisoner. [NRS.B59.30.36]

WILLIAMSON, THOMAS, a messenger in Dunkeld, Perthshire, a Jacobite in 1715. [NRS.B59.20.1]

WILSON, ALEXANDER, an Episcopalian and councillor of Dundee, a Jacobite in 1714. [NRS.GD220.5.357.4]

WILSON, DAVID, a mason and a burgess of Perth, a Jacobite in 1715. [NRS.B59.30.40]

WILSON, GEORGE, of Finzeach, son of George Wilson and his wife Christian Robertson, a burgess of Aberdeen, a Jacobite in 1715, died on 4 June 1725. [JAB.204][CRA.109]

WILSON, GEORGE, a wright and a burgess of Perth, a Jacobite in 1715, an Ensign, later Captain, of the Perth company. [NRS.B59.10/11/36/37/40]

WILSON, HENRY, was transported via Liverpool aboard the Friendship bound for Virginia on 24 May 1716, landed in Maryland in August 1716. [SPC.1716.311][HM.386]

WILSON, JAMES, was transported via Liverpool aboard the Wakefield bound for South Carolina on 21 April 1716. [SPC.1716.309][CTB.31.205]

WILSON, MATTHEW, in Perth, a Jacobite in 1715. [NRS.B59.30.10]

WILSON, PATRICK, a burgess of Perth, servant to Mark Wood, a Jacobite in 1715, surrendered. [NRS.B59.30.17/37/40]

WILSON, THOMAS, a magistrate of Dundee, a Jacobite in 1715. [RH2.4.308/170]

WILSON, WILLIAM, a baker and a burgess of Perth, a Jacobite in 1715, a soldier of the Perth company, surrendered. [NRS.B59.30.17/37/40]

WINRAHAM, JOHN, from Eyemouth, Berwickshire, a Jacobite in 1715, a prisoner at Preston. [CS.V.160] [NRS.GD1.53.72]

WILHOME, HENRY, a prisoner at Preston, 1715. [NRS.GD1.53.72]

WOOD, JOHN, a maltman and a burgess of Perth, a Jacobite in 1715, a soldier of the Perth company, surrendered. [NRS.B59.17/37/40]

WOOD, MARK, a merchant in Perth, Dean of Guild, a Jacobite in 1715. [NRS.B59.30.36]

WRIGHT, JOHN, a gentleman, a prisoner at Preston. [CS.V.160] [NRS.GD1.53.72]

WRIGHT, WILLIAM, was transported via Liverpool aboard the Elizabeth and Anne bound for Jamaica or Virginia on 29 June 1716, landed at York, Virginia. [SPC.1716.310][VSP.1.185][CTB.31.208]

WYLD, JOHN, servant to Patrick McLaren, a wright in Perth, a Jacobite in 1715. [NRS.B59.30.40]

WYLD, ..., in Perth, a Jacobite in 1715. [NRS.B59.30/37/40]

YOUNG, JOHN, a merchant and a burgess of Perth, a Jacobite in 1715. [NRS.B59.30/37/40]

YOUNG, ROBERT, was transported via Liverpool aboard the Wakefield bound for South Carolina on 21 April 1716. [SPC.1716.309][CTB.31.205]

YOUNG, WILLIAM, was transported via Liverpool aboard the Scipio bound for Antigua on 30 March 1716. [SPC.1716.310][CTB.31.204]

www.ingramcontent.com/pod-product-compliance
Lightning Source LLC
Chambersburg PA
CBHW050710280326
41926CB00088B/2911